Gender, Religion and Domesticity in the Novels of Rosa Nouchette Carey

From *Notable Women Authors of the Day* (1906), opposite p. 145

Gender, Religion and Domesticity in the Novels of Rosa Nouchette Carey

Elaine Hartnell

Routledge
Taylor & Francis Group
LONDON AND NEW YORK

First published 2000 by Ashgate Publishing

Reissued 2018 by Routledge
2 Park Square, Milton Park, Abingdon, Oxon OX14 4RN
711 Third Avenue, New York, NY 10017, USA

Routledge is an imprint of the Taylor & Francis Group, an informa business

A Library of Congress record exists under LC control number: 2001266049

ISBN 13: 978-1-138-72856-1 (hbk)
ISBN 13: 978-1-138-72854-7 (pbk)
ISBN 13: 978-1-315-19047-1 (ebk)

Contents

List of Figures

Acknowledgements

I wish to record my grateful thanks to all those individuals and organizations who made it possible for me to complete this book. On the home front, I would especially like to mention William Hughes and Rita Hartnell (Mama), my three 'sisters', Alita Thorpe, Suzanne Forbes and Diane Mason, Peggy and Bill Burns and Anna and Martin Wrigley.

Amongst my academic friends and colleagues, I must name Professor Clare Hanson, who introduced me to the highways and byways of critical theory and listened to my pet theories on poetry and psychoanalysis. I would also like to record my thanks to Professor Vince Newey for his constant support and encouragement throughout my time at Leicester University. My thanks to Professor Ben Fisher at the University of Mississippi for obtaining for me a number of reviews of Carey's work but even more so for being a good friend. Thanks also to three people who have helped me to shape my ideas about Rosa Carey the woman: Dr Jane Crisp, Wendy Forrester and the late Regina Glick. I would like thank Professor Roger Sales and Dr Victor Sage of the University of East Anglia for their moral support and helpful suggestions on a number of research-related matters. Other supportive colleagues deserving a mention include those I met at HMSO, especially Kevin Gibbons, and also Barry Adamson and Dr Guy Stephens.

My debts to organizations are innumerable but I would especially like to acknowledge the St Etheldreda's Educational fund for two grants in the early stages of my research, and the Arts Budget Centre Research Committee at the University of Leicester for the research award which enabled me to undertake archive work at the University of London. Finally, many thanks to the wonderful librarians at Cambridge University Library and at SOAS.

For Mama, who has always believed in me

For Jane Crisp and for Bill Hughes

and

In Memoriam

My father, Brian Thomas Hartnell

and

Regina Glick, who so enjoyed Rosa Carey's novels

Figure 1: Frontispiece to Carey's last novel, *The Key of the Unknown* (1909)

Introduction

The Problem of History

According to Elaine Showalter, Rosa Nouchette Carey was 'a popular sentimental novelist around the turn of the [twentieth] century'.[1] But what does this mean? At this stage, the accuracy of the statement is not in question.[2] The major question is that of how a twenty-first-century subject can relate to this primarily nineteenth-century subject and her culture in any meaningful way. More specifically, the reader of Showalter's 'historical' statement may question both the extent to which it is possible to access the past within its own cultural context and the extent to which it is possible to eliminate, or rather minimize, the biasing effect of present-day methodology.

Of course, it is impossible to opt out of the twenty-first-century context altogether. Unique and unconnected historical events do not, in themselves, constitute history. Rather, the unrelated texts which testify to the existence of historical events must be read, structured and interpreted by posterity.[3] This very act of interpretation is different in different historical periods and each act of interpretation may fulfil some purpose within the culture of the perceiving subject beyond that of a neutral wish to know 'how it was'. As Paul Hamilton notes:

---

1 Elaine Showalter, *A Literature of Their Own* (London: Virago, 1988), p. 56.

2 Carey's first novel was published in 1868; her last in 1909. She remained in print until at least 1924.

3 Paul Hamilton sets out the problem inherent in balancing the necessity for accuracy with the necessity for meaning by reference to Aristotle's *Poetics*:

> If the historian tells a coherent tale, one that has a point and a purpose, its probability may undermine its possibility and leave the author justified as a philosopher and discredited as an historian ... If, instead, the history ... records a host of improbabilities, however possible, faithfulness to what happened or could have happened will produce a discourse without point and purpose, philosophically negligible, random in its accuracy and literal in its confusion.

See Paul Hamilton, *Historicism*, The New Critical Idiom (London: Routledge, 1996), p. 9 (Hereafter, Hamilton 1996). In keeping with his view that historical events are unique rather than scientifically reproducible, Hamilton chooses to examine the nature of history according to the texts of a specific historical moment rather than to state a universal principle. It is acknowledged that this Introduction somewhat artificially abstracts a universal principle from his work in order to discuss the problems of historicizing the work of Rosa Carey.

> Our interpretative decisions ... will be based on a judgement between different possibilities of the time; and the history of interpretations shows such adjudications to be abundantly and primarily expressive of their own periods of utterance. Historicism is the name given to this apparent relativizing of the past by getting to know the different interpretations to which it is open and deciding between them on grounds expressing our own contemporary preoccupations. (Hamilton 1996, p. 19)

However, more than the 'contemporary preoccupations' inherent in the project of investigating the relationship between past and present have changed over time. The very term used to describe the project, historicism, has also been glossed in different ways. The *Shorter Oxford English Dictionary* includes amongst its definitions of 'historicism' the following:

> The theory that all social and cultural phenomena are relative and historically determined, and are hence only to be understood in their historical context. (1902) ... a tendency in philosophy to see historical development as the most fundamental aspect of human existence. (1939)[4]

Both of these glosses are at best unfashionable and at worst unhelpful to the literary critic of today. The first denies that the past can be of any relevance to the present; the second, by referring to an 'historical development', which hints at 'progress', implicitly appeals for its verification to a disestablished former absolute such as revealed religion or humanism. Both definitions also omit the contribution of the perceiving critic.

By comparison, most current historico-literary criticism attempts to divest itself of direct appeals to metanarratives and anchors its concerns predominantly in the 'here and now'.[5] Yet in spite of its disjunction with the notion of progress, literary criticism has much invested in the historicist project. After all, to read a text without reference to the conditions of its creation is to miss out on many of the resonances that make it a work of art rather than an object of scientific investigation; to exclude historicism from critical methodology steers literary criticism towards a potentially stultifying formalism.[6] The latter type of methodology is not structured to take into

4 *The Shorter Oxford English Dictionary*, 2 vols (Oxford: Clarendon Press, 1991), p. 2635 (hereafter, *Shorter OED* 1991). Notably, 'historicism' is listed amongst the Addenda to the *Shorter OED* and is only deemed to have been in currency since 1901.

5 However, it is difficult to go beyond the notion of progress. Present-day historicism is laden with ethical considerations and even Hamilton's belief that 'the present can be significantly altered for the better,' though '[t]he result might not be progress' sounds very little different from it (Hamilton 1996, pp. 5–6).

6 Cf. Hamilton 1996, p. 151.

account vanished contexts, cultural diversity, silenced voices or ethical issues of any kind.[7]

The present generation of critics taking a close interest in the historicity of literature style themselves New Historicists, one of the best known being Stephen Greenblatt. Greenblatt carefully distinguishes the tentative nature of New Historicist research from the supreme confidence expressed by the formalists. Accordingly, he claims that New Historicists 'have turned from a celebration of achieved aesthetic order to an exploration of ideological and material bases for the production of this order'.[8] Greenblatt further distances himself from the formalists by both acknowledging 'the impossibility of fully reconstructing and reentering the culture of the sixteenth century, of leaving behind one's own situation'.[9]

Greenblatt bases his methodology for any possible bridging of the gap between past and present largely upon the social anthropology of Clifford Geertz.[10] According to Hamilton, Geertz's contribution to Greenblatt's thought may be seen as that of providing a theory of 'being here' whilst writing about 'being there'. In practice, this means that Geertz advocates, and Greenblatt endorses, extensive readings of appropriate cultural contexts:

> We get over the paradox of inevitably 'being here' whilst writing about 'being there' by fashioning a 'conversation' across the divide. To do this, we do not create 'a universal, Esperanto-like culture' in which we all share, but try to learn and to speak the different languages already in existence ... In Geertz's ethnology, everything is the context for something else; nothing is the privileged repository of significance. The point is not to devise with hindsight a better explication of past events, but to enhance the way in which they are already 'scientifically eloquent' in their own. (Hamilton 1996, p. 153–4).

Thus, two aspects of Greenblatt's methodology appear to be particularly relevant to a discussion of Rosa Carey and her world. The first of these is the notion that any point in the past should be perceived as a unique matrix of cultural artifacts and cultural significations; as a matrix of 'languages' to be learnt. To quote Greenblatt (who is himself quoting Geertz): '[t]here is no such thing as a human nature independent of culture' (Greenblatt 1984, p. 3). The

---

7 However Hamilton notes that, in practice, much current criticism is a hybrid of both historicism and critical formalism (Hamilton 1996, p. 151). This book also utilizes both methodologies.

8 Stephen Greenblatt, *Learning to Curse* (London: Routledge, 1992), p. 168 (hereafter, Greenblatt 1992).

9 Stephen Greenblatt, *Renaissance Self-Fashioning* (Chicago: Chicago Press, 1984), p. 5.

10 However, his indebtedness to Marxist theorists such as Williams and Foucault is explicitly stated in the introduction to *Learning to Curse*.

second is his belief that the critic should establish some kind of empathy with the past; should initiate 'a "conversation" across the divide,' this entailing points of contact or analogy. Parts of Greenblatt's writing are anecdotal, almost confessional, but this insistence upon empathy with the past is far from merely emotive. For Greenblatt, empathy generates meaning and relevance rather than subjectivity. In *Learning to Curse*, he explains that his own critical practice was shaped by the horrors of the Vietnam War:

> Writing that was not engaged, that withheld judgements, that failed to connect the present with the past seemed worthless ... To study [Renaissance culture] ... did not present itself as an escape from the turmoil of the present; it seemed rather as an intervention, a mode of relation ... it seemed to be powerfully linked to the present both analogically and causally. (Greenblatt 1992, p. 167)

However, elsewhere, this personal encounter with history is translated into more objective terms and presented as a theoretical position which may be espoused by anyone, regardless of her or his life experience:

> We do not have direct access to these [Renaissance] figures or their shared culture, but the operative condition of all human understanding – of the speech of our contemporaries as well as of the writings of the dead – is that we have indirect access or at least that we experience our constructions as the lived equivalent of such access. (Greenblatt 1984, p. 7)

Thus Greenblatt further enhances the 'conversation' between sixteenth-century England and a troubled late twentieth-century America by drawing on a common 'human understanding.'[11] However, it is equally possible to use his methodology to forge a 'conversation' between the England of the nineteenth and early twentieth centuries and the critic of today. By recourse to extensive cultural observation and human empathy, it is possible to know something of

11 This appeal to a universal 'human understanding' is obviously problematic. However, the notion of 'the human' and hence of human understanding is helpfully glossed by Lyotard. To Lyotard, 'human-ness' (my term) is a dialectic. Lyotard therefore poses a question rather than making a definitive statement.

> What shall we call human in humans, the initial misery of their childhood, or their capacity to acquire a 'second' nature which, thanks to language, makes them fit to share in communal life, adult consciousness and reason? That the second depends on and presupposes the first is agreed by everyone.

See J.-F. Lyotard, *The Inhuman* (Cambridge: Polity Press, 1993), p. 3 (hereafter, Lyotard 1993). This definition of 'human-ness' as the struggle to accommodate self to society for the purpose of communication, if not truly universal, is open enough to admit both historical and cross-cultural usage and specific enough, particularly in its attention to misery, to permit the establishment of empathies.

the historical Rosa Carey, the books that she wrote and the England that she knew. At the very least, the New Historicist methodology serves to remind the critic of the twenty-first century that her or his present-day engagement with the nineteenth and early twentieth centuries should be subsumed within an attempt to understand the historical project and not constructed into a set of hierarchical relations with it. With the twenty-first-century subject thus positioned in relation to history, it is possible to move on and engage with questions relating to the specific material of this study: an author, her readership and their cultural context.

The Author and the Reader as Subjects

The matter of authorship has been much debated in recent years, with dominant academic thought resting in the assumption that an author simply delimits the edge of the text rather than being the unified subject who can claim the text as the product of her or his own creativity.[12] This belief is sustained from two theoretical concepts which merge into a world-view that is difficult to refute. They are intertextuality and the notion of the wholly-constructed subject.[13] The former is predicated upon the notion that no text is unique or new because it always consists of fragments of previous texts; the latter challenges the critic to objectively demonstrate the presence of a subject who is more than the sum of her or his biology and conditioning. By this reasoning, 'no-one' is writing 'what has already been written'. Barthes therefore announces 'the death of the author'; whilst Foucault proclaims that

> a change in the order of discourse does not presuppose 'new ideas,' a little invention and creativity, a different mentality, but transformations of practice, perhaps also in neighbouring practices, and in their common articulation. I have not denied ... the possibility of changing discourse: I have deprived the ... subject of the exclusive and instantaneous right to do it.[14]

Some critics have also aligned Lyotard with this ontology of the wholly-constructed subject.[15] However, if this is the case, his subject betrays an

---

12 See, for example, Michel Foucault, 'What is an Author?' in Paul Rabinow (ed.) *The Foucault Reader* (London: Penguin, 1986), p. 107.

13 On the subject of intertextuality see, for example, Michel Foucault, *The Archaeology of Knowledge* (New York: Pantheon Books, 1972), p. 23.

14 Roland Barthes, 'The Death of the Author' in Stephen Heath (ed., trans.), *Image Music Text* (London: Fontana, 1987), pp. 142–8; Michel Foucault, *The Archaeology of Knowledge and The Discourse on Language* (New York: Pantheon Books, 1972), p. 209.

15 See, for example, David Hawkes, *Ideology*, The New Critical Idiom (London: Routledge, 1996), p. 171.

embarrassing autonomy. This is one reason why his writings, and in particular *The Inhuman* and *The Postmodern Condition: A Report on Knowledge*, are so pertinent to the present moment in literary criticism.[16] The discipline is heading towards, as it were, a post-Postmodernism in which there appears to be, for what ever reason, a movement towards a rehabilitation of the subject. This issue is an important one: the composition of the subject will determine what it is possible for a subject to achieve; and an author (however conceived) is, in this respect at least, a subject like any other. If it is conceded that environmental factors affect the composition of the subject then it may be said that the subject is at least partially constructed. In this case, there must be, within the subject, a number of contradictions. (As society is plural and antagonistic, so must the subject reflect these qualities.) However, if there is any sense in which the subject is *un*constructed then the number of contradictions necessarily increases. The constructed individual will be at war within her or himself; the partially *un*constructed individual will additionally be at odds with society.

In *The Inhuman*, Lyotard certainly acknowledges that a portion of the subject, as constituted at birth, is resistant to subsequent construction (education). Positing that human beings have two natures – 'the initial misery of ... childhood' and the '"second" nature' which, 'thanks to language, makes them fit to share in communal life, adult consciousness and reason' – he briefly discusses the relationship between them:

> That the second depends on and presupposes the first is agreed by everyone. The question is only that of knowing whether this dialectic, whatever name we grace it with, leaves no remainder.
>
> If this were the case, it would be inexplicable for the adult himself or herself not only that s/he has to struggle constantly to assure his or her conformity to institutions and even to arrange them with a view to a better living-together, but that the power of criticizing them, the pain of supporting them and the temptation to escape them persist in some of his or her activities. I do not mean only symptoms and particular deviancies, but what, in our civilization at least, passes as institutional: literature, the arts, philosophy. There too, it is a matter of traces of an indetermination, a childhood, persisting up to the age of adulthood. (Lyotard 1993, p. 3)

Thus, it would seem that the civilized '"second" nature' is tailored to the precise requirements of society but that the untutored, residual, 'child' nature operates under no such imperative. According to Lyotard, then, this residual nature permits not only the critique of society but also the possibility of

16 J.-F. Lyotard, *The Postmodern Condition, A Report on Knowledge* (Manchester: Manchester University Press, 1987) (hereafter, Lyotard 1987).

individualized creative expression.[17] However, Lyotard had already prefigured this limited autonomy for the subject in *The Postmodern Condition*. Contending that communication within society comprises a series of 'language games', *The Postmodern Condition* posits that society manifests itself as a network of communications in which every subject participates:[18]

> no self is an island; each exists in a fabric of relations that is now more complex and mobile than ever before. Young or old, man or woman, rich or poor, a person is always located at 'nodal points' of specific communication circuits, however tiny these may be. Or better: one is always located at a post through which various kinds of message pass. No one, not even the least privileged among us, is entirely powerless over the messages that traverse and position [them] at the post of sender, addressee or referent. (Lyotard 1987, p. 15)

If, as Lyotard claims, 'no one … is entirely powerless over the messages that traverse and position [them],' and if individuals are indeed included in 'communication circuits', then the subject is capable of both originating and circulating utterances. Here, too, the existence of an autonomous subject in turn yields the possibility of an autonomous author.

It is worth pausing here to 'unpack' the terminology used in this passage, for the terms 'sender', 'addressee' and 'referent' provide the key to Lyotard's understanding of the dynamics of society. They are initially glossed very simply: 'sender (the person who utters the statement) ... addressee (the person who receives it), and … referent (what the statement deals with)'.[19] However, the three concrete terms are made more complex as Lyotard converts them from apparently fixed entities into fluid energies which are activated by, or at least activated within, the subject at various times. The subject is, from the first, constructed as a referent:

---

17 The existence of a Lyotardian, partially unconstructed subject is posited here on two grounds: in order to accommodate the presence of otherwise perverse behaviour and in order to locate creativity within the individual. If totally constructed by society, the subject would be entirely tailored to the requirements of society. However, in a ('first') world where capitalism demands consumption for its continuance, people who are anti-capitalist or anti-consumerism at least appear to be making autonomous choices. Moreover, where similarly constructed subjects might be expected to display similar levels of creativity, this does not happen. An ontology which posits the presence of a wholly constructed subject neither exhibits consistency nor accounts for difference.

18 '[L]anguage games are the minimum relation required for society to exist' (Lyotard 1987, p. 15.)

19 Lyotard 1987, p. 9. The word 'referent' appears, certainly at this stage, to carry little of the baggage associated with Saussure's use of the term. Similarly, the word 'statement' carries little of the technical exactness with which Foucault defines it.

> even before [birth], if only by virtue of the name ... given, the human child is ... positioned as the referent in the story recounted by those around [them], in relation to which [they] will inevitably chart [their] course. (Lyotard 1987, p. 15)

The new subject-referent is thus delivered into an ongoing process of definition. Meanwhile, senders and addressees (who are, in different contexts, referents in their own right) perpetually exchange roles with each other in order for communication to be a two-way process. However, the language games played by senders and addressees have consequences which go beyond these routine transitions. The protagonists are

> placed at the crossroads of pragmatic relationships, but they are also displaced by the messages that traverse them, in perpetual motion. Each language partner, when a move pertaining to [them] is made, undergoes a 'displacement', an alteration of some kind that not only affects [them] in [their] capacity as addressee and referent but also as sender. These 'moves' necessarily provoke 'countermoves ... ' (Ibid., p. 16).

In other words, the recipient of a statement is altered by its articulation and her or his own future utterances are modified. This is to attribute powerful effects to the transformational nature of language at all levels of communication. It is also to bring into question the nature of the aesthetic text. Where the subject flows effortlessly from one role into another; where two or more roles are enacted by the subject simultaneously, it seems unlikely that there can be any meaningful distinctions between author and reader or between text and author. However, this is to needlessly reduce communications to their lowest common denominators. In practice, some texts are privileged over others and some senders are privileged over others. The mechanisms which are largely responsible for maintaining the privileged status of certain texts and senders – institutions – are discussed below.

To summarize, the Lyotardian subject is partially unconstructed and resistant to construction, and partially constructed by the circumstances into which she or he is born. Subsequently, she or he experiences constant (though only partial) re-construction by society at large. Hence, although such a subject may have 'some power over the utterances that traverse and position [her/him],' in practice, any autonomous thoughts and utterances are largely contained by the circumstances into which she or he is born as a 'referent' and by the messages subsequently received by her or him as an 'addressee'. This is the version of the subject envisaged throughout this book. Its central subject, Rosa Carey, may be viewed as one who made her debut, as a 'referent', into a 'story' constructed by bourgeois others, who was shaped by the attitudes of the social class into which she was born, and whose initial interpellation did not remain unchallenged. For Carey subsequently became an addressee, a recipient of diverse referents which had the power to modify her initial bourgeois construction, or at least to render it problematic. As a consequence she was obliged to deal with these non-homogenous messages in some way – to accept and assimilate them, to reject them, or to adapt them. The resultant 'displacements' correspondingly modified or problematized another of her subsequent roles, that of 'sender'. An ordered, though not necessarily well-ordered, version of these re-presented messages is available through the texts of Carey's novels, the publication of the texts being what, in conventional terms, transforms her from a sender into an author. At the same time, the presence of the written text transforms Carey's addressee into what is conventionally understood as a reader.[20]

The adoption of Lyotard's version of the subject permits a text to be viewed from both the author's and the reader's perspective without totally investing the agency of meaning in one party or the other. The author is not dead and the reader is neither simply a 'virtual site' where 'various codes can be located', nor a unified and passive consumer.[21] Writer and reader are identical in construction as both are positioned at various times in the roles of sender, addressee and referent. Each attempts to extract meaning from the 'messages that traverse and position them' and is 'displaced' during the activity; and each, as a multiple and contradictory subject, has the task of trying reconcile the fundamentally irreconcilable. In other words, an author is bound to write a multifaceted text and a reader is bound to see within it a multiplicity of possible meanings. By looking at Carey's fictional negotiation of the conflicting and unresolved referents which interpellated her within Victorian/Edwardian society, it is possible to suggest, in general terms, why a nineteenth-century subject might have gained pleasure from reading the novels.

For example, there was a particular disjunction between messages that asserted Carey's subordination on grounds of sex and those which asserted her access to power on account of middle-class affiliation. Carey's response to these messages, of whatever kind, would have been of interest to women readers, if only on the narcissistic grounds that they could read about their own, similar, experience of being women. However, Carey did not simply replicate any gender-based oppression. For class status could, to a limited extent, override gender. She was thus in the position to articulate some kind of protest.

20 Lyotard's work on the status of reading as an activity discrete from theory or interpretation is acknowledged. For a summary of this work see Bill Readings, *Introducing Lyotard: Art and Politics* (London: Routledge, 1992), p. xix. However, in this context, the verb 'to read' is used in the conventional sense of 'to apprehend mentally the meaning of written or other characters; to be engaged in doing this' (*The Shorter Oxford English Dictionary*, p. 1754).

21 Cited by Sara Mills (ed.) in *Gendering the Reader* (Hemel Hempstead: Harvester Wheatsheaf, 1994), p. 12.

The result in Carey's writing is that she appears to both support the dominant and subvert it within the same novel.

This contradiction arose because Carey was, as a woman, relatively powerless. Desiring the publication of her work, she was obliged, in her writing, to uphold the (inherently patriarchal) dominant. However, by indirect methods the dominant could be subverted. Thus, the novels contain passages in which characters of both genders support the dominant discourse of male supremacy through direct speech, whilst simultaneously an extradiegetic and apparently impartial narrator dramatizes the psychological cost to women of conforming to societal expectation. Elsewhere, Carey utilizes humour to make male characters appear at a disadvantage, though, once again, she does not directly undermine the institution of patriarchy. The presence of such implicitly critical passages suggests a form of collusion with a readership known to be primarily female. From this perspective, Carey appears to be pro-woman and thus a writer of texts which would be attractive to a great variety of female readers.

However, she had much to gain by not disputing everything that the dominant stood for. It was by upholding the social mores of her class that she was permitted the limited and conditional power available to the bourgeois women of her day; and it was by ostensibly 'knowing her place' as a woman and a lady that she was permitted to make public statements of a contestatory nature via her writing. She may be seen to have colonized a permitted space: the realm of the domestic as defined by the dominant. That is, her novels were published within the public domain but they were almost exclusively about, and almost exclusively read by women within, the private domain of the home. Thus, the novels are not overtly novels of protest even though they are effectively novels of subversion. Nor are they novels which privilege gender concerns over those of class. Rather, matters of gender and class sit uneasily together and are hierarchicalized according to context, if not simply according to the whim of the author at any given point. It is not even possible to posit subversive intention on Carey's part, though apparently subversive practices may be identified.

It is more profitable to attest to the availability of a number of conflicting readings in her texts, these giving rise to more than one position for even the 'implied reader'.[22] For example, the subversive separation of direct speech and narratorial description, as outlined above, does not position the reader unequivocally within one reading or the other. Solely within the parameters of class-based power and sex-based subordination, the nineteenth-century reader

22 Wolfgang Iser's concept of the 'implied reader' may be glossed as 'the reader whom the text creates for itself', this 'amount[ing] to "a network of response-inviting structures" which predispose us to read in certain ways'. See Raman Selden, *A Reader's Guide To Literary Criticism*, 2nd edn (Hemel Hempstead: Harvester Wheatsheaf, 1989), p. 119.

might position herself as an advocate of women's rights or as an adherent of the dominant; as someone aspiring to membership of the middle classes or as an impartial observer who is reading about 'others' whom she has no wish to emulate. Yet this is not to suggest that an infinite number of readings is available. For, as Sara Mills suggests,

> texts must structure the reader's response to some extent through certain clues and frames which signal to the reader the range of readings which are possible. (Mills 1994, p. 9)

And, in practice, there is a further constraint on the generation of meaning. Besides being shaped by cumulative individual experience, both literary production and reader response are subject to the impersonal structures in society which, in *The Postmodern Condition*, Lyotard has termed 'institutions'. He cites, amongst other examples of these, philosophy, religion, the army, businesses, the family and bureaucracies. Lyotard describes all dialogue between individuals as 'conversation', this activity requiring a certain amount of consensus (a 'contract') between the parties involved (Lyotard 1987, p. 10; p. 17).[23] However, he notes that

> an institution differs from a conversation in that it always requires supplementary constraints for statements to be declared admissible within its bounds. The constraints function to filter discursive potentials, interrupting possible connections in the communication networks: there are certain things that should not be said. They also privilege certain classes of statements. (Lyotard 1987, p. 17)

Lyotard does not allude to Althusser at this point but his passage on institutions contains more than a slight genuflection towards the latter's notion of 'Ideological State Apparatuses' and, rhetorically, he appears to adopt Althusser's view that institutions function at least 'secondarily by repression'.[24] It is easy to see how Carey's 'discursive potentials' could be inhibited and shaped by such institutions. The very anonymity and magnitude of the institutions is likely to have have made them appear as absolutes; as inherent features of reality rather than as a number of primarily linguistic constructs. Any inhibition of 'discursive potentials' would have been doubly experienced by Carey's reading subject, who would have been both constructed in relation

---

23 From this point, the word 'conversation' should be viewed in a strictly Lyotardian sense and totally divorced from the notion of analogy and empathy to be found in the above discussion about Greenblatt.

24 Louis Althusser, 'Ideology and Ideological State Apparatuses' in *Essays on Ideology* (London: Verso, 1987 [1970]), p. 19.

to institutions in the greater language game of society and re-constructed by Carey's fictional but plausible microcosms.

However, as Lyotard goes on to explain, no institution has a monopoly on meaning or a timeless mandate for its constraints:

> the limits the institution imposes on potential language 'moves' are never established for once and for all ... Rather, the limits are themselves the stakes and provisional results of language strategies, within the institution and without. (Lyotard 1987, p. 17)

This is to restate, using different terms of reference, something which has already been said: that Carey had limited power to originate utterances and that she was potentially able to write into her novels a meaningful resistance to, or affirmation of, the institutional viewpoint. In turn, the nineteenth- and early twentieth-century reader potentially had the power to resist both institutional silencing and Carey's textual closure (if any) with regard to institutions. In linguistic terms, then, resistance to institutions has always been possible. For resistance is simply the result of a process in which the subject makes a personal selection from, or a hierarchicalization of, the referents that are available to her or him, in order to fulfil perceived personal needs.

However, Lyotard's final observation about institutions is the most important: that 'the boundaries [of an institution] only stabilize when they cease to be stakes in the game' (Lyotard 1987, p. 17). Here, he suggests that when an institution becomes well-defined, it ceases to be a vital influence on society; it becomes a form without substance. In short, there is nothing like institutionalizing something to make it go out of fashion. It is easy to envisage a situation in which Victorian institutional voices cried in the wilderness about the pleasures of conservatism and certainty whilst, outside the institutions, or even on an unofficial basis within them, society's true dynamic consisted of perpetual change and development. Institutions could ensure dominance but they could not ensure adherence. This perspective on institutions, applied to the apparent contradictions in Carey's novels, yields the suggestion that she wrote of a society which defined itself through two kinds of 'knowledge' or 'truth' which did not always correspond. Thus, Carey wrote of both the stable boundaries of the institution and of actual changes in society; of idealized behaviours and attitudes and of responses to unique historical situations.

Stable Boundaries and Real Stakes: An Example from Carey's Work

The effect of powerful but not absolute institutions upon this multifaceted but semi-autonomous author may be demonstrated by reference to an episode in her novel *Sir Godfrey's Granddaughters* [1892].[25] In this episode, Pamela, who keeps house for her brother Alick, quarrels with him and then takes her revenge by starving him at dinner time. The bizarre meal she serves up to him is subsequently discussed on three separate occasions. However, each discussion views the episode from a different perspective. The variety of responses to the situation would in itself be interesting. However, the fact that most responses are undermined by a potent though apparently undirected brand of humour completely displaces the implied reader from any position, whether institutional or subversive.

Jessie Brown, whose name is invoked in this first passage, is a good but rather dull friend of the family. The other speaker is Mrs Glyn, the vicar's wife. Pamela begins:

> 'There has been a grand scene of reconciliation, and I am on my best behaviour. I think the meagre diet yesterday had a salutary effect on my high and mighty brother ... '
>
> 'Did they fare so very badly yesterday?' asked Mrs Glyn anxiously; and Pamela's eyes sparkled with naughty fun.
>
> 'Well, it was a cold night, you see, and a leg of mutton on the third day is never very inviting; but there were pickles – plenty of pickles – and with bread and cheese – '
>
> 'Pamela, how could you be so unfeeling! It was really barbarous treatment to those poor tired men,' really waxing a little warm in her sympathy. 'It was carrying a joke too far – it was almost ill-natured.' But Pamela took this outburst with surprising meekness.
>
> 'I think I must call for Jessie Brown,' she observed with a deep sigh, 'or the fruits of repentance will be wanting. What a pity both Mr Glyn and Mr Higginbotham disapprove of auricular confession – it would be such a comfortable ordinance to a sinner like myself.'
>
> 'Pamela!, do not be irreverent!' (*SGG*, pp. 168–9)

In this passage, the focus is upon the perpetrator of the deed. Pamela is 'almost ill-natured' and the suggested remedy (albeit not adopted with any degree of seriousness) is religion. Thus the institutional/dominant position debated is that of femininity (in the form of appropriate behaviour and proper feeling) and its posited *modus operandi* that of personal regulation (in terms of reverence and, where necessary, repentance). When Mrs Glyn later discusses the exchange with her niece Gerda, the parameters are set quite differently:

> 'Aunt Clare,' asked Gerda in a dubious tone, 'do you not think that Pamela treats her brother very badly?'

25 R.N. Carey, *Sir Godfrey's Granddaughters* (London: Macmillan, 1899 [1892]) (hereafter, *SGG*).

> '... I am afraid they are a rather ill-assorted couple to live together ... Things always went smoothly in the old times – [Alick] has told me over and over again. "When [my elder sister,] Hester married, I had no more home comfort," he said once. It is my belief that Pamela is really devoted to her brother, and that in some ways he repels and disappoints her. She is a most exacting little person, and all this flightiness and nonsense is her way of taking her revenge.' (Ibid., p. 169)

In this second passage the focus is primarily upon the man who has supposedly been wronged. The parameters of the debate are the institution of the home (home is a male right; home is 'normally' serviced by a complaisant female), and the expectations of its female inhabitants (familial warmth). This passage more nearly reaches a closure which favours the institutional viewpoint. That is to say, the mode of housekeeping rather than the mode of familial relationships is deemed to be most in need of amendment. Nor is this tentative conclusion disturbed in the initial lines of the final passage on the subject. At first, Hester, the perfect housekeeper, seems poised to close the debate and to firmly position Pamela as the delinquent. However, the force of her criticism is quickly and finally undermined:

> Hester wore her schoolmistress's look ... 'It is no laughing matter, I assure you,' she continued. 'I never saw Alick more put out ... She behaved as badly as possible that night and as [Cook] was in her airs he could get no redress. It was literally a mutton-bone that was placed upon the table; and to make things worse, there were five or six kinds of pickles.' Then, as Gerda laughed, and Mrs Glyn followed her example: 'So it was the most uncomfortable meal possible ... and there was Pam in her ridiculous harlequin dress – that red and pink thing we all hate – smiling and chattering as though nothing were the matter.'
>
> 'I am perfectly ashamed of Pamela,' observed Mrs Glyn, who was quite exhausted with laughing. (Ibid., pp. 173–4)

Although Hester, perfect supplier of home comfort, is theoretically entitled to be outraged, it is she who brings out the full comedy of the situation. Does it really 'make things worse' that there were six kinds of pickle, as opposed to four or seven? And does the fact that Pamela wore a tasteless dress really imply a greater degree of delinquency than would otherwise have been the case? Are Mrs Glyn's final words an effective closure? And if Pamela is so reprehensible, why do Mrs Glyn and Gerda laugh?

Arguably, Rosa Carey elected to present the incident in this comic fashion because it was a way of accommodating, within her writing, the conflicting messages she received with regard to the society in which she lived. Whether or not it was by intent, she wrote of two kinds of truth. In utilizing and upholding traditional attitudes concerning the female role, she was invoking the crystallized boundaries of the institution. In simultaneously representing

Pamela in such a way as to disarm censure, she was acknowledging the real stakes in the game. She was acknowledging that alongside the 'traditional' woman existed 'the girl of the period'; that the modest, dutiful and self-denying 'Angel in the House' might have wanted to be the assertive and autonomous woman who worked outside the home, smoked cigarettes and rode a bicycle.[26] Above all, she was betraying an awareness that the woman of indecision looked upon these disparate paradigms in ambivalent degrees of nostalgia, envy or absolute horror.

Lyotard and Other Theorists

However, the extent to which Lyotard's proffered metanarrative can be utilized to examine the unique events of history is ultimately determined by its ability to mesh with other theories of cultural production. Another gloss on Lyotard's narrative is certainly necessary. For the simplicity and clarity, which aids an understanding of the over-all construction and interpellation of the subject, is less helpful as a method for engaging with the nature of institutions and their work within society.

In *The Postmodern Condition*, Lyotard notes that institutions are as prone to 'displacement' as individual subjects; that the major purpose of an institutional utterance is to articulate the boundaries of the institution from whence it came; and that institutions retain a great and diffused power to make meaningful utterances even whilst they are being challenged or undermined (Lyotard 1987, p. 17; p. 13). However, in keeping with his project of examining society as a series of language games, very little is said about their actual composition. His major comment upon the power or powerlessness of institutions, in relation to the conversations or 'temporary contracts' of individual subjects, forms part of his conclusion to *The Postmodern Condition*. The passage is located specifically in the late 1970s as befits the temporality of the text. However, a more general principle may be abstracted from it:

> the temporary contract is in practice supplanting permanent institutions in the professional, emotional, sexual, cultural, family and international domains, as well as in political affairs. This evolution is of course ambiguous: the temporary contract is favoured by the system due to its

26 The title of Coventry Patmore's sentimental poem, *The Angel in the House* [1854–62], has long been used to represent a woman of domestic tastes and talents, innate piety and a belief in her own inferiority to men. The expression 'the girl of the period' was coined by Eliza Lynn Linton to describe a woman who showed no respect for the traditional values described above. I am not suggesting that Pamela in *Sir Godfrey's Granddaughters* is portrayed as wishing to be a 'girl of the period'. However, she is no household angel and her independence may be viewed as contrary to the dominant version of femininity for the 1890s.

> greater flexibility, lower cost, and ... creative turmoil … In any case, there is no question here of proposing a 'pure' alternative to the system: we all now know, as the 1970s come to a close, that an alternative of that kind would end up resembling the system it was meant to replace. We should be happy that the tendency toward the temporary contract is ambiguous: it is not totally subordinated to the goal of the system, yet the system tolerates it. (Lyotard 1987, p. 66)

Lyotard effectively concedes that, whilst institutional absolutism has long been in a state of decline, the institutional structure as such is unlikely to be totally superseded. The final statement, concerning the system's tolerance of temporary contracts is simply a recapitulation of his earlier statements that '[n]o one ... is entirely powerless over the messages that traverse and position [them]' and that 'the limits the institution imposes on potential language "moves" are never established for once and for all'.

However, in that they retain power even whilst being challenged or undermined, Lyotard's institutions may be sited within Raymond Williams's version of the hegemonic. According to Williams, the hegemonic

> does not just passively exist as a form of dominance. It has continually to be renewed, recreated, defended, and modified. It is also continually resisted, limited, altered, challenged[. S]peak of 'the hegemonic' rather than the 'hegemony', and of 'the dominant' rather than simple domination … [H]egemony ... while by definition ... always dominant ... is never either total or exclusive ... cultural process must then always include the efforts and contributions of those who are in one way or another outside or at the edge of the terms of the specific hegemony … [27]

Yet Williams does more than rhetorically locate institutions within the dominant. He also takes issue with the notion that these organs of the dominant are monolithic ideological and repressive apparatuses. With Althusser explicitly in mind he states that:

> Hegemony is ... not only the articulate upper level of 'ideology', nor are its forms of control ordinarily seen as 'manipulation' or 'indoctrination.' It is a whole body of practices and expectations, over the whole of living: our senses and assignments of energy, our shaping perceptions of ourselves and our world. It is a lived system of meanings and values … It thus constitutes a sense of reality for most people in the society ... beyond which it is very difficult for most members of the society to move, in most areas of their lives. (Williams 1977, p. 110)

27 Raymond Williams, *Marxism and Literature* (Oxford: Oxford University Press, 1977), pp. 110–13 (hereafter, Williams 1977).

This refutation of Althusser has the effect of exploding Lyotard's neatly-packaged institutions into millions of more or less coherent fragments which are then to be found scattered across all levels of society. However, to gloss Lyotard in this way is to study his 'social bond' in greater detail rather than to refute it; it is to provide, for the institution, the treatment that Lyotard has already provided for the individual subject.

Elsewhere, Williams appears to echo Lyotard's institutional 'boundaries' which 'only stabilize when they cease to be stakes in the game'. That is, he provides terminology which makes it possible to historicize the continued existence of the more seriously undermined, as opposed to merely challenged, institution. He supplies the term 'residual' for that which is 'formed in the past, but ... still active in the cultural process' (Williams 1977, p. 122). Then, having explained how the past encroaches upon the present, he completes his theory of cultural production by naming the currently knowable elements of that which is likely to be dominant in the future, the 'emergent' (ibid., p. 123). If we accept the notion that both institution and subject are – and have always been – in a continuous state of mutually-defining flux, then the terms 'dominant', 'residual' and 'emergent' become invaluable tools for focusing upon the functional state of society at any given point in history.

Moreover, such tools permit something of the particular historical moment to be recovered from the specifically literary text.[28] For example, Rosa Carey's novel *Our Bessie*, initially serialized between 1888 and 1889, dramatizes a version of the contemporary societal concern about the changing nature of 'femininity'.[29] The eponymous heroine is 'an old-fashioned little person' who upholds the values of domestic and filial duty (*OB*, p. 102). She might thus be taken to represent the residual. By comparison, a minor character called Florence Atherton is denigrated on the grounds that she is 'a typical girl of the period', who 'talk[s] slang like [her] brothers' (ibid.). She, then, may be viewed as representative of the emergent feminine. However, a third character, Edna, fits into neither category. She neither 'lay[s] aside her dignity and borrow[s] masculine fashions' nor thinks 'disobedience to parents a heinous offence' p. 103; p. 11). She may thus be viewed as representative of the dominant, albeit that her supposed values are described in critical terms.

One final term requires discussion in order to complete the basic theoretical framework of this book, this term being 'discourse'. This widely-used, almost innocuous term is not, however, one concisely glossed by Greenblatt, Williams or Lyotard insofar as they have been quoted here. Therefore, some kind of

---

28 This is not to say that fictional texts simply mirror society. For a discussion of the relationship between fiction and society, see Andrew Blake, *Reading Victorian Fiction* (Basingstoke: Macmillan, 1989), pp. 7–8.

29 All quotations taken from this text are from R.N. Carey, *Our Bessie* (London: Offices of the Girl's Own Paper, 1914) (hereafter, *OB*).

rationale is required for its inclusion. A partial explanation for its use is to be found in Diane Macdonell's description of the concept:

> A 'discourse,' as a particular area of language use, may be identified by the institutions to which it relates and by the position from which it comes and which it marks out for the speaker ... Moreover, any discourse concerns itself with certain objects and puts forward certain concepts at the expense of others.[30]

In other words, a discourse is a group of related referents emanating from within an identifiable group of institutions and acting against similar but oppositional groupings. It would be more convenient if each discourse related to a single, identifiable institution but this is not the case. As Lyotard's subject is positioned by the vast number of messages which traverse them 'in perpetual motion', so institutions, part of the fabric of the dominant, are traversed by messages which 'displace' them into uneasy alliances (inter-institutional 'conversations', perhaps) with one another. The result is a discourse, a group of referents which does not centre on any single institution but which gains a quasi-institutional status of its own. Once again, the adoption of a non-Lyotardian term is not to undermine Lyotard's ontology but rather to emphasize both its plurality and its basis in language games.

It may initially seem that the theories of Lyotard and Williams make an odd juxtaposition. However, they mesh very well. Lyotard's *The Postmodern Condition* provides an ontology for the semi-constructed subject and focuses attention upon 'language games' as the basic means of communication within society, whilst Williams provides a gloss upon Lyotard's apparently Althusserian notion of institutions, highlighting their fragmentary nature and emphasising their assailability. Williams also facilitates the historicization of such institutions (though without any attendant notion of progress) via his theory of dominant, residual and emergent. In turn, the systematic theories of Williams and Lyotard may seem to be of a totally different order to Greenblatt's New Historicist prescription of critical empathy. Yet such empathy is based upon the cultural matrix in all its complexity and plurality; and, above all, it encourages the critic to be self-critical.

30 Diane Macdonell, *Theories of Discourse: An Introduction* (Oxford: Basil Blackwell, 1987), p. 3. In privileging certain concepts, the discourse is similar to the institution. However, the two are distinct.

Figure 2: From *Nellie's Memories* (1922), opposite p. 188

Rosa Carey and the Fiction Market of her Day

Rosa Nouchette Carey [1840–1909] never married and never worked outside the home. Her novels reflect this background, being closely bound up with the concerns of the relatively conservative middle-class Anglican woman of the late nineteenth and early twentieth centuries. Thus, they may be classified as 'domestic' insofar as they tend to deal with the private sphere of the home and family rather than the public sphere of male employments and overtly political activity.[31] Her first novel, *Nellie's Memories* (1868), was published in the decade designated as that of the sensation novel; her last, *The Key of the*

---

31 Many of Carey's female protagonists undertake remunerative employment but they work primarily within the realm of the domestic. They are governesses, companions, teachers and nurses; caring women who often quit paid employment to marry and to undertake similar tasks within their own homes.

The British Library also attributes four pseudonymous novels, published under the name of 'Le Voleur' to Carey. (Full details of these are given in the Bibliography.) However, these are excluded from the total sum of her novels here on the grounds that they do not fit into her attributable *oeuvre* which places her as an author of 'the domestic'. Poorly constructed, predominantly sensational and unlike her other novels in terms of their major subject-matter, the 'Le Voleur' novels do not belong to the entity or construction called Rosa Nouchette Carey, regardless of their authorship.

Unknown (1909), was published two years after Conrad's triumph of Modernism, *The Secret Agent*. In terms of style and genre, her work has seldom been bracketed with the former and never with the latter.[32] Nor, indeed, has she been associated – by her contemporaries or by posterity – with any other literary or cultural innovations. Ouida's creation, the New Woman, is never central to any of Carey's novels and, for all the impression it appeared to make on her works, the *fin de siècle* might well never have happened.[33]

In terms of focus, Carey's novels are similar to those of Margaret Oliphant and Anthony Trollope, many of her male characters being clergymen and the focal point of her fictional societies frequently being the local church. However, Carey's novels are of a more sentimental cast and, indeed, the reviewers blasted her for this perceived fault.[34] It might also be added that, in spite of her ability to clinically dissect character and motivation, her social satire was far gentler than that of her contemporaries. As one reviewer noted, 'the graces and charities of domestic life are treated by her with never-failing sympathy'.[35]

Rather closer comparisons may be made between Carey's novels and those of Charlotte Yonge, Ellen Wood and Annie S. Swan, writers who also have a connexion with Carey in that they were editors of journals who published her work. *Heriot's Choice* was serialized in Yonge's Anglo-Catholic journal, the *Monthly Packet*, between 1877 and 1879, whilst Wood accepted shorter fiction for the *Argosy* during her editorship. Her son Charles, editor after her death,

---

32

> The distinctive features of [the Sensation novel] were its passionate, devious, dangerous and not infrequently deranged heroines, and its complicated, mysterious plots – involving crime, bigamy, adultery, arson and arsenic … [T]hese 'fast' novels ... were all set in the context of the otherwise mundane domestic life of a contemporary middle-class or aristocratic English household …' (Lyn Pykett, *The Improper Feminine* [London: Routledge, 1992], p. 47)

> Eugene Lunn .... offers a general outline of the key characteristics of modernism which would probably command broad assent: aesthetic self-consciousness or self-reflectiveness; simultaneity, juxtaposition, or montage; paradox, ambiguity, and indeterminacy or uncertainty; 'dehumanization', and the disappearance or dispersal of the integrated individual human subject. (Lyn Pykett, *Engendering Fictions: The English Novel of the Early Twentieth Century* [London: Edward Arnold, 1995], p. 10)

33 'The New Woman of the *Fin de Siècle* had a multiple identity. She was, variously, a feminist activist, a social reformer, a popular novelist, a suffragette playwright, a woman poet; she was also often a fictional construct, a discursive response to the activities of the late nineteenth-century women's movement.' Sally Ledger, *The New Woman: Fiction and Feminism at the Fin de Siècle* (Manchester: Manchester University Press, 1997), p. 1 (hereafter, Ledger 1997).

34 See, for example, review of *Sir Godfrey's Granddaughters* in *Graphic*, 25 March 1893, p. 318.

35 Review of *Only the Governess* in *Athenaeum*, 17 March 1888, p. 337.

serialized *The Mistress of Brae Farm* in 1896 and Swan serialized the opening chapters of *Other People's Lives* in the *Woman at Home* in 1897. The location of much of Carey's periodical fiction is certainly an indication of its implied readership and of Carey's own religious and social affiliations. Wood wrote sensation fiction but both her novels and her journal were regarded as morally unexceptionable. Meanwhile, Yonge was a well-known exponent of the Oxford Movement and Swan's religious convictions permeated all the literary projects that passed through her hands. Yet this is not to suggest that Carey's beliefs were entirely congruent with those of Yonge, Wood or Swan. In spite of a close mentorial friendship with Wood which lasted for nearly twenty years, Carey did not so often or so emphatically draw upon the same type of sensational plot as the latter.[36] Similarly, Carey's own writing tended to be neither so resistant to female autonomy as that of Yonge nor so overtly pious as that of Swan.

However, it is likely to have been Carey's close association with the Religious Tract Society rather than her dealings with Wood, Yonge and Swan that most effectively compromised her reputation as a serious writer. For Carey wrote at least seven short novels for the Religious Tract Society's popular journal, the *Girl's Own Paper*, these being serialized between 1883 and 1897 before appearing in volume form under the society's own imprint. She also became a member of the paper's advisory body.[37] These novels were directed at younger readers and were rather more didactic in tone than the rest of her work. Always regarded as conservative, if not thoroughly innocuous, Carey appears to have been regarded more and more consistently as a writer for the young.

Yet in spite of a reputation for writing novels 'without a particle of mystery, wickedness or excitement', Carey's novels were far from devoid of value within their own cultural context and are far from wanting in interest to critics of the present day.[38] Their value to the culture in which they were created is evident in that they were bought and read in fairly large numbers; their value for the present day lies in that they may be made to reveal certain preoccupations of their own era.[39] More specifically, they are interesting for their commitment to women's concerns and for their valorization of female experience. They provide a positive response to the supposed 'spare woman problem', treat housework as real work and depict the woman's caring role as something that can be legitimately and usefully employed in the context of remunerative employment.

---

36 See Helen C. Black, *Notable Women Authors of the Day* (London: Maclaren, 1906), pp. 154–5.

37 Ibid., p. 153.

38 Review of *Dr Luttrell's First Patient* in *Athenaeum*, 6 November 1897, p. 630.

39 Almost 52,000 copies of Carey's first novel, *Nellie's Memories*, and 41,000 copies of her 1884 novel, *Not Like Other Girls*, had been sold by 1908. See Jane Crisp, *Rosa Nouchette Carey: A Bibliography*, Victorian Fiction Research Guides 16 (Queensland: University of Queensland, 1989), p. 2.

Their critical perusal has the power to enlighten the present-day reader about aspects of late nineteenth- and early twentieth-century society eclipsed by the crude division of its fiction into populist Sensationalism, the collision of gender with politics and elitist Modernism. Carey's novels may have been allocated a space labelled 'as harmlessly unexciting as may be imagined' on account of their morality but to read any writer allocated this kind of space is to place into context other literary preoccupations of the day, such as sexual scandal and the early development of metafiction.[40] It is also to make visible other equally valid, equally popular, more widely-distributed movements and tendencies of the nineteenth and early twentieth centuries.

However, in this process of recovering the currently invisible or undervalued aspects of Victorian and Edwardian culture, it is also necessary to examine the assumptions underpinning existing critiques. For any method of classification is based upon expediency rather than inalienable truth, and the 'will to truth' (to use Foucault's phrase) changes over time. Nineteenth-century classifications of Carey's novels as 'domestic', 'unexciting' and so on are based upon the (conditioned) eye of the beholder; are based upon 'a will to knowledge which impose[s] upon the knowing subject – in some ways taking precedence over all experience – a certain position, a certain viewpoint'.[41] Similarly, the academic readers of today have their own agendas and preoccupations; they, too, promote certain types of knowledge to the detriment of others. Writers from both periods frequently deny domestic fiction any kind of critical acclaim, though for different reasons: nineteenth-century patriarchal reviewers because it is not masculine; feminists of the present day because it is not perceived to be empowering to women.

However, to adhere too rigidly to notions of genre and to hierarchies of genre is necessarily limiting; is necessarily to inhibit a conception of all narrative as bricolage. The monolithic genre blocks out significations; disguises the plurality of the text; disables the text as an expression of a disparate culture. It is the current trend in literary theory to show an awareness of a greater level of overlap between categories and to explore the uncertain boundaries between genres. This book therefore works on the a priori assumption that it is possible to reappraise certain genre categories, though without necessarily debunking them completely.

For example, it may be observed that one hostile reviewer of Carey's first novel, *Nellie's Memories*, focused upon the way in which 'the most minute incidents of family life are dwelt upon', completely ignoring both a long episode which reads like a Gothic novel in miniature and some decidedly

---

40 Review of *Sir Godfrey's Granddaughters* in *Graphic*, 25 March 1893, p. 318.

41 See *The Archaeology of Knowledge and The Discourse on Language*, pp. 217–18. For a demonstration of this concept, see below.

sensational elements.[42] These elements do not automatically make *Nellie's Memories* a sensational novel or a Gothic tale. Rather, they complicate its simple classification as nothing more than 'domestic', The chronological date of Carey's novel is beyond reasonable doubt, as is its primary subject-matter. Yet, if it is to be addressed in terms of genre, a single designation is inappropriate. It simultaneously harks back to the eighteenth century and alludes to the sensation novels of more recent peers as well as being a simple chronicle of home life.

As with Carey's novel, so with the century within which most of her novels were written. If it is indeed possible to designate the 1860s as the era of the sensational novel, the writing of the day being typified by the early novels of Ouida, M.E. Braddon, Mrs Henry Wood and Wilkie Collins, it is equally pertinent to point out that there were other writers and other styles worthy of note. The 1860s must also be designated as the era of Charles Dickens and George Eliot, two canonical writers who have by far outlasted their overtly sensational peers. The 1860s also saw Anthony Trollope's later Barsetshire novels (1855–67) and heralded the arrival of Margaret Oliphant's most enduring works, *The Chronicles of Carlingford* (1863–76). Both of these writers are more renowned for their satire on church politics than for the lurid events and uncontrolled sexuality inherent in the fiction usually categorized as Sensational. It is also pertinent to recall that popular though conservative works of primarily domestic fiction were being published by Dinah Mullock Craik in the wake of her best-known novel, *John Halifax, Gentleman* (1856), and by Charlotte Yonge, following the astonishing success of *The Heir of Redclyffe* (1853).[43]

Ultimately, categories such as 'the domestic' and 'the sensational' can have no absolute meaning, whether in terms of content or in terms of their date of production. Such categories may be more profitably viewed as thematics rather than as genres. As Gail Cunningham argues, the domestic in particular was the framework upon which many other kinds of novel were built throughout the nineteenth century:

> The subject matter of fiction ... fell characteristically into a woman's sphere: even in novels whose thematic interests lie primarily elsewhere, the standard plot and setting were almost invariably domestic and family-

42 See the review of *Nellie's Memories* in *Pall Mall Gazette*, 3 December 1868, p. 12. The Gothic section of Carey's novel comprises chapters 18–20, some fifty-three pages. See *Nellie's Memories* (London, Richard Bentley and Son, 1892), pp. 182–235.

43 Craik published *A Noble Life* in 1866; Yonge published *The Clever Woman of the Family* (1865).

orientated, with courtship and marriage providing a major part of the narrative thrust.[44]

Thus, for example, Mrs Henry Wood's best-seller, *East Lynne* (1861), may be described as a sensational novel with strong domestic elements, dealing as it does with a woman who marries to acquire a home, whose attempts to fulfil her domestic duties fail to meet the dominant standard for the day, and who is ultimately replaced by a rational and efficient household manager. The sensational elements, especially that of the unhappy Isabel running away with a base seducer, occupy a comparatively small part of the narrative. Conversely, Rosa Carey's other novel of the 1860s, *Wee Wifie* (1869), is predominantly 'domestic' though it too contains sensational elements: a young woman throws acid at a supposed rival, instead blinding the man she loves; a male protagonist is a drug abuser; and a third character cannot marry in case she has inherited the lunacy which sent her mother to an asylum. The difference between the two novels is merely one of proportion. It is also worth noting at this juncture that the combination of domesticity and sensation was far from rare in Carey's works. However, spectacular wrongdoing, especially on the part of women, is a subject more frequently to be met with during her most prolific period of production, around the turn of the century.[45]

If the 1860s have been labelled the era of sensationalism, the fiction of the 1870s and 1880s has not been so vividly characterized in terms of style or subject matter, whether by contemporaneity or by posterity. However, the beginning of each of these decades may be viewed as the end of an era. For Dickens died in 1870 and Eliot in 1880. Perhaps these decades were (and are) deemed to be periods of interregnum rather than innovation. They were indeed years in which many writers of the 1860s retained their popularity. Yet they also brought changes to the fiction market. These were the decades in which writers of adventure stories, such as G.A. Henty, Rider Haggard and Stevenson, established themselves. Meanwhile, in the early 1880s, Sarah Grand, George Meredith and Olive Schreiner each brought into print at least one work which might be designated a 'New Woman' novel before the commonly-designated decade of the 'New Woman' novel had even begun.[46]

44 Gail Cunningham, 'Society, History and the Reader: the Nineteenth-century Novel' in Andrew Michael Roberts (ed.), *Bloomsbury Guides to English Literature: The Novel* (London: Bloomsbury, 1993), p. 32.

45 In *My Lady Frivol* (1899) a widow, who was possibly an unfaithful wife, gives up the child she has always neglected, in return for a handsome allowance, and becomes an actress. Meanwhile, the child's uncle worries (with cause) that the daughter might take after her unsatisfactory mother. In *The Household Of Peter* (1905), a father who has, in the past, only just prevented his wife from leaving him for a lover, discovers that his daughter has entered into a clandestine marriage.

46 The expression 'New Woman' may be precisely dated to 1894 but the type of fiction which came to be associated with this epithet clearly predates it. For a critic who views the New

Though by no means an avowed Feminist, Carey's novels of the period once again reflect the preoccupations of those around her. Whilst continuing to both depict and advocate the domestic life, Carey infused her fiction with the awareness that many women were either unable or unwilling to fulfil the traditional female rôle. The New Woman novelists themselves recorded a dismal picture of women's frustration at their social and legal disability and depicted, in fictional form, the gender imbalance which meant that, not only was it impossible for all women to marry, but also that unmarried women could not rely on the good offices of male relatives for home comforts and subsistence. Yet Carey managed to represent this uncertainty in fairly positive terms. For example, whilst the eponymous heroine of Meredith's *Diana of the Crossways* (1885) fails to find happiness in a marriage of convenience and only as a second choice makes a career for herself as a writer, the heroine of *Uncle Max* (1887) not only escapes the shallow social round enjoyed by her aunt's family and takes up the profession she loves – nursing – but also gains the respect of the local doctor who initially accuses her of sentimentality and 'hysterical goodness'.[47] Ultimately, the heroines of both of Carey's books achieve one of the fictional New Woman's major aims: they are taken seriously, though without the need for suicide, marriage or repentance.[48]

Notably, Carey manages to carry her point without employing Meredith's themes of sex scandals and divorce, and without recourse to graphic portrayals of syphilis in the style of Sarah Grand in *The Heavenly Twins* (1893). Carey's depictions of any disease apart from consumption tend to be neither graphic nor explicit and her portrayals of mental illness (which appear to be largely based upon the work of Henry Maudsley) are, in general, confined to those cases that are treatable at home rather than in the asylum. Nor did Carey seem to need to express in her novels any kind of feminist – or anti-feminist – agenda. This is perhaps a more curious omission. The matter of women's rights appears to be broached only four times in the entire corpus of her work.[49] Yet, in her way, Carey was doing her own negotiations of the various concerns of her contemporaries. Though designated as conservative by reviewers she was far from reactionary. Her novels indicate that she was aware of the issues raised in

---

Woman fiction primarily as a product of the 1890s, see Pykett 1992, p. 3; for a critic who posits that the 'heyday' of the New Woman was 'the 1880s and 1890s', see Ledger 1997, p. 2.

47 R.N. Carey, *Uncle Max* (London, Macmillan, 1912), p. 52.

48 Suicide – Herminia Barton in Grant Allen, *The Woman Who Did* (1895); marriage – the eponymous heroine of George Meredith, *Diana of the Crossways* (1885); repentance – Angelica in Sarah Grand, *The Heavenly Twins* (1893).

49 In *Wooed and Married* (1875) there is a gently satirical portrayal of a women's rights activist; in *For Lilias* (1885) the major male protagonist teases his wife about women's rights being rubbish; in *Lover or Friend?* (1890) the major female protagonist is described as independent, though not militant about her freedom of action. The description of a 'New Woman' in *Our Bessie* has already been discussed.

the novels of the *fin de siècle* even if she chose not to dwell upon them extensively.

The 1890s, in addition to being the decade of the New Woman proper, saw the appearance of Oscar Wilde's 'gospel' of aestheticism, *The Picture of Dorian Grey* (1891), Bram Stoker's immensely popular horror story, *Dracula* (1897) and a small flurry of novels by the remaining sensationalists. However, Carey never seems to have been attuned to either aestheticism or horror and, although she still had her admirers and some of her best novels were still to be written, reviews indicate that her popularity was very much on the decline. The fragmented nature of the fiction market at the *fin de siècle* is highlighted in a review that points to both sustained sales and critical derogation:

> We are glad to see that a new and cheaper issue of Miss ... Carey's stories is announced by Messrs. Bentley, for the fact shows the existence amongst us of a taste too likely to be extinguished by the varied and piquant items in the menu now offered to readers of fiction.[50]

However, if the New Woman novel had been one such piquant item, by the first decade of the new century she had lost her topicality. For this was the decade in which Joseph Conrad wrote four of his best-remembered works and collaborated with Ford Maddox Ford on two others. Already substantially in print on his own account, Ford Maddox Ford's own best-known work, *The Good Soldier* (1915), was to be only a few years in the future. Experiments in form had come to replace perceptive characterization as the literary criteria of the day. Yet many of the popular Victorian novelists were still writing. Annie S. Swan still had the greater part of her career ahead of her; Marie Corelli still had several powerful and highly coloured romances to write, though she had reached the zenith of her popularity with *The Sorrows of Satan* in 1895; and, though the veteran writer of domesticity, Charlotte Yonge, died in the same year as her queen (1901), her books were widely available until at least the 1920s. Nor were novels by these writers mere anachronisms. For up-and-coming writers made their names in precisely these same genres. To give just two examples, in 1907 a new Sensation novelist, Elinor Glyn, delightfully shocked the world with an extravagant confection called *Three Weeks* and in 1908 a new domestic novelist, Florence Barclay, published her first work, *The Wheels of Time*.

In keeping with these trends, when Rosa Carey died in 1909, her novels – realist, chronological and, for the most part, concerning everyday events – continued to be simultaneously read by enthusiasts and reviled by reviewers. She continued in print until at least 1924 and her novels remained on library

50 Review of *Other People's Lives* in *Literature 2*, 16 April 1898, p. 449.

shelves until the eve of the Second World War. They virtually vanished from the minds of the critics and the imaginations of the readers thereafter.[51]

***

Rosa Nouchette Carey wrote forty-one novels over a period of forty-one years. Thus, it is impractical as well as undesirable to take the work-by-work approach. The sheer number of novels would make this approach unwieldy and methodologically repetitive; in addition, the division of Carey's *oeuvre* into discrete units would break up any continuity of subject matter between one novel and another. Instead, five recurrent themes in her work have been selected for consideration.

Chapter 1 deals with Carey's approach to insanity. A product of her own age and of the middle class, Carey inevitably reproduces the contemporary anxieties about irrationality and loss of self-control. Three particular aspects of this large subject are explored in this chapter: the 'unnaturally' assertive woman who is constructed as deviant and, rhetorically, as insane; the sufferer from the 'moral' and wholly literary illness called brain fever, whose inner mental conflicts manifest themselves in physical illness; and the passive victim of circumstance who, for what ever reason, cannot rise above poor physical health or uncongenial life-situation. Yet, in spite of her anxieties, Carey displays great compassion towards these sinners against the gospel of rationality and order, representing them in almost all cases as attractive miscreants, authors of their own painful dilemmas, potential heroines and wretched victims. This latter aspect of her writing is also taken into account.

The second chapter, 'Maiden Ladies', explores Carey's positive and creative responses to the demographic phenomenon of more women than men. She provides within her fiction positive role models for women of all ages, whether working entirely within the home or following an occupation elsewhere. In the main, she appears to wholeheartedly accept the images of womanhood provided by the dominant (male-powered and -empowered) discourses of the day. However, the boundaries of the dominant are interrogated. Carey actively engages with the proposition that single women are in any way 'redundant', advocating paid employment and decent living accommodation for lone women and condoning remunerative employment even for the more prosperous. Thus, in this chapter, aspects of Carey's indirect championship of the single state are placed in their contemporary context.

51 First-hand evidence of Regina Glick of Leeds (1912–99), who began to read and collect Carey's novels in the 1930s. See also Jane Crisp, *Rosa Nouchette Carey: A Bibliography*, p. 2, in which the author notes that her father bought her grandmother a complete set of Carey's novels in 'about 1928'.

Chapter 3 is concerned with Carey's construction of male characters. Given her class bias, the chapter compares the construction of her characters with texts constructing the English gentleman. It is contended that the conventions of 'gentlemanliness' are defined and regulated by, and exist solely for the benefit of, other men rather than women. Correspondingly, the vulnerability of female characters within the novels and the emphasis Carey places upon minor instances of male approval are also noted.

The fourth chapter turns to the stage upon which Carey's feminine dramas are performed: the home. In particular the chapter focuses upon the uneven nature of the nineteenth- and early twentieth-century home experience: men and children are serviced; women provide this servicing. Carey's evident adherence to the dominant domestic ideal is set against the various ways in which, consciously or unconsciously, she subverts it. As Carey may be termed a didactic writer, the role models she provides for the 'trainee' housekeeper are examined in some detail. In addition, attention is paid to the fictional rewards supplied to those who have done their domestic work well.

Carey's negotiations of the established religion are examined in the fifth and final chapter. Whilst Carey herself appears to have been a conventional adherent of the Church of England, her novels reveal a whole range of alternative or supplementary narratives to the Bible: sentimental heresies. The purpose of these narratives appears to have been largely that of dealing with the partings in families wrought by death. Whilst some of them have their counterparts in other sentimental fiction and poetry – indeed, some are even to be found in popular theological books – Carey appears to have developed her own.

Essentially, Carey's novels are viewed in this book in much the same way as Janice Radway has been compelled to view late twentieth-century romances: as experiential rather than purely intellectual texts. That is, as texts which are as important for what they *do* for the reader as for what they *say* to her. In her survey of romance-readers, Radway notes that she was obliged to 'give up [her] obsession with textual features and narrative details if [she] wanted to understand [her respondents'] view of romance reading':

> romance reading was important ... because the simple event of picking up a book enabled [respondents] to deal with the particular pressures and tensions encountered in their daily round of activities.[52]

---

52 In discussing her methodology, Radway notes that she had to relinquish her 'inadvertent but continuing preoccupation with the text' because the women she interviewed 'always responded to [the] query about their reasons for reading with comments about the pleasure of the act itself, rather than about their liking for the particulars of the romantic plot.' See Janice Radway, *Reading the Romance* (London: Verso, 1987), p. 86.

It is posited that Carey's novels function as romances in this sense.[53] It is not possible to interview Carey's original readership, as did Radway with her late twentieth-century romance-readers, and thus to find out why they enjoyed the novels. However, it is possible to find within the texts a number of themes that may have addressed themselves to such a readership. Thus, Carey's sympathy towards the fictional delinquent, her creative responses towards spinsterhood, her provision of vicarious male approval, her valorization of housework and her comfort for the bereaved may be seen as functions of the novels that lie beyond formal literary criticism. This is not to say that Carey's novels are devoid of literary value. However, the presence of these extra-literary features might well explain the popularity of the novels wiith their readership in spite of their undoubted lack of appreciation on the part of reviewers.

53 However, it would be to unnecessarily limit interpretations of them were they to be formally categorized as such.

Chapter 1

The Mad, The Bad and the Morbid

The Lady is Not Mad

> 'The lady is not mad; but she has the hereditary taint in her blood. She has the cunning of madness with the prudence of intelligence. I will tell you what she is, Mr Audley, she is dangerous!'[1]

> Or is her secret that "insanity" is simply the label that society attaches to female assertion, ambition, self-interest and outrage?[2]

Imagine Mary Braddon's novel, *Lady Audley's Secret*, which first exploded into the literary market place in 1862, as a Religious Tract Society publication. Needless to say, it is not. It seems a far cry from what might be classified as 'improving' literature, dealing as it does with a woman who fakes her own death, abandons her child, commits bigamy and attempts murder, all in order to gain and retain social position and material comfort. However, characters similar to Lady Audley may be met with in several of Rosa Carey's apparently innocuous tales of domestic life. It is therefore pertinent to begin by examining their apparent paradigm.

Braddon explains Lady Audley's behaviour in two apparently contradictory ways: criminality, with its attendant religious discourse, and madness, with its discourse of tainted heredity. The tension between the two is maintained virtually until the last. Only in the final chapters does the culpability of criminality overwrite the amorality of insanity. After all, repentance can only be urged upon a woman who is responsible for her actions. Yet if Lady Audley is sane, why is she certified? Somewhat problematically, she is certified on account of one kind of madness but is incarcerated because of another. The doctor signs the certificate on the formally-stated, though dubious, grounds that:

> 'There is latent insanity! Insanity which might never appear; or which might only occur once or twice in a life-time … [I]t would be *dementia*

1 Mary Elizabeth Braddon, *Lady Audley's Secret* (London: Simpkin, Marshall, Hamilton, Kent, undated [1862]), p. 292 (hereafter *LAS*).

2 Elaine Showalter, *The Female Malady* (London: Virago, 1991), p. 72.

> in its worst phase, perhaps: acute mania; but its duration would be very brief, and it would only occur under extreme mental pressure. The lady is not mad; but she has the hereditary taint in her blood." (*LAS*, p. 292)

Thus, Lady Audley is ostensibly certified on the grounds of what might happen rather than what has already occurred. However, members of the Audley family wish to incarcerate her for a very different reason. They believe her to be absolutely sane, but the alternative to the asylum – criminal proceedings followed by certain execution – cannot be contemplated because the resultant scandal would punish the innocent along with the guilty. By translating the discourse of criminality into a discourse of insanity the 'dangerous' woman may yet be contained, though without the adverse publicity. Notwithstanding his formal diagnosis, the doctor effectively colludes with them. When Robert Audley indicates that the family wishes to lock Lady Audley away, the reply is, 'I believe that you could do no better service to society than by doing this' (*LAS*, p. 294).

It is at this point that Elaine Showalter, as an (albeit twentieth-century) reader of the text, makes an alternative 'diagnosis' relating to Lady Audley. She posits that '"Insanity" is simply the label that society attaches to female assertion, ambition, self-interest and outrage.' According to this reading, the doctor's formal medical diagnosis may be seen as a legal fiction, resorted to because Lady Audley cannot be certified for having 'the cunning of madness' and for being 'dangerous'. Yet even this rhetorical construction of insanity yields a discourse of culpability if not actual criminality. Female ambition is madness but a woman can choose not to be ambitious. Conversely, the act of choosing madness may be construed as wilful wrongdoing. Ultimately, the madwoman is a criminal and the criminal is a madwoman; the closure is no closure.

Arguably, Braddon oscillated between these diagnoses of criminality and madness for two reasons: to create a sensational story which might be enjoyed for its own sake, and to create a discursive space within which to focus upon the late nineteenth-century construction of femininity. Presented with the apparently antithetical positions of criminality and madness in the novel, the reading subject is obliged to negotiate a personal synthesis or closure or, indeed, to construe some alternative reading. The conflicts and confusions which arise out of Braddon's dual explanation of 'deviant' womanhood certainly invite the reader to question the veracity of both discourses. However, there has been debate as to how well she manages to produce or permit viable alternatives to the dominant.

In *A Literature of Their Own*, Showalter admits that the appeal of the eponymous heroine lies in her transgression: '[a]s every woman must have sensed, Lady Audley's real secret is that she is *sane* and, moreover, representative'.[3] As evidence for this conclusion, Showalter cites known patterns of 'supportive identification' between middle-class women and such of their peers as are on trial for domestic murder (Showalter 1988, p. 170). However, she ultimately calls *Lady Audley's Secret* by its proper name: 'a carefully controlled female fantasy' (Showalter 1988, p. 163). Showalter's emphasis is decidedly upon the word 'controlled'. Lady Audley's criminality/madness must be paid for; the fantasy must come to an end and the 'real' world both assert itself and deal with the aberration. Thus, whilst acknowledging the achievements of sensationalists such as Mary Braddon in portraying the female condition, Showalter locates *Lady Audley's Secret* outside the explicitly feminist:

> even as they recorded their disillusion ... frustration ... anger [and] ... murderous feelings, the[y] could not bring themselves to undertake a radical enquiry into the role of women ... Anger is internalized or projected, never confronted, understood or acted upon ... Typically, the first volume of a woman's sensational novel is a gripping analysis of a woman in conflict with male authority ... By the second volume guilt has set in. In the third volume we see the heroine punished, repentant and drained of all energy. (Showalter 1988, pp. 162, 180)

According to this reading, the fictional Lady Audley's defeat simply replicates the power/gender–power relationships that obtained at the time when Braddon was writing. However, Showalter's assessment hierarchicalizes a twentieth-century reading over an (albeit reconstructed) nineteenth-century reading. That is, she attaches more importance to her twentieth-century feminist project of establishing a theory of women's writing than she does to understanding the nineteenth-century text and its reader on their own terms. Lyn Pykett, in providing a critique of Showalter, reverses the latter's priorities and provides an alternative thesis. Beginning with the assertion that interpretation is problematized by 'concentrating too much on endings at the expense of the complex middles of novels', Pykett goes on to say that:

> Showalter's ... desire to see women and women writers transcend the historical conditions of their oppression left her insufficiently ... alert to, the ways in which the women's sensation novels rework and negotiate, as well as simply reproduce, the contradictions of these conditions ... We need to see [the Sensation novel] not simply as either the transgressive or subversive field of the improper feminine, or the contained, conservative domain of the proper feminine. Instead we should explore [it] as a site in

3 Elaine Showalter, *A Literature of Their Own* (London: Virago, 1988), p. 167. (Hereafter Showalter 1988.)

> which the contradictions, anxieties and opposing ideologies of Victorian culture converge and are put into play ...[4]

In this passage, Pykett suggests that the capitulation to a more conventional standard which forms the closure to most Sensational novels is not to be regarded as the major site for investigation. This being the case, attention focuses on the initial assertiveness of the heroine and discussion thereby profitably returns to the stage at which Showalter suggests that '"Insanity" is simply the label society attaches to female assertion'. At the same time, it becomes possible to positively rate the nineteenth-century woman reader's pleasure in identifying with a successful Lady Audley. In gaining, through the fiction, a temporary (and safe) liberation from mundane reality, the reader additionally gained a space within which to try out an alternative female role without fear of the consequences.

Thus *Lady Audley's Secret* is not simply about the 'normal' and the 'deviant' female psyche. It is also about a woman who is able to pit her wits against the financial, social and legal disabilities suffered by women in the 1860s. Nor yet is the novel simply a humourless tract about the wrongs of women. Whilst the eponymous heroine is ultimately defeated, one must not ignore the appeal, to the reader, of a safely fictional woman who gets her own way most of the time and who is not, in the final reckoning, punished as severely as she might have been. Having identified these areas of potential reader interest relating to the construction of Lady Audley, it is pertinent to move on to a discussion of Rosa Carey's equivalents.

Although Carey was never perceived to be a Sensationalist novelist, several of her plots contain characters constructed similarly to Lady Audley. For example, Etta, the poor relation in *Uncle Max* [1887], is, like Lady Audley, culpable at law but never brought to trial. Her function in terms of plot, is that of controller and manipulator of others. One of only two real villainesses in Carey's writing, she is made to obstruct three marriages, to nearly drive one of the six victims insane and to incriminate an innocent man in the theft that she has herself committed.[5] Until the very end of the novel, she remains plausible to the male head of the household and so proceeds unchecked. Carey's creation differs markedly from Lady Audley on only two major counts: that Etta lacks the charm of the original and that she operates under her own name.

As Lady Audley's mental condition is discussed in one novel, so is Etta's in the other. The diagnoses differ but, rhetorically at least, the symptoms of the 'disease' and its 'treatment' are very similar. Though the diagnosis for Carey's

---

4 Lyn Pykett, *The Improper Feminine* (London: Routledge, 1992), pp. 50–51.

5 The only other real villainess is Madame Mercier in Rosa Carey, *Rue With a Difference* (London: Macmillan, 1914 [1900]). She is the least attractive of Carey's Lady Audley-type figures in that she mistreats a child.

character is supplied by a servant and not by a doctor who is attempting to certify her, the terminology used indicates more than a mere lay opinion:

> 'Somehow crooked ways come natural to her: the old mistress knew that, for she once said to me towards the last, "Leah, I am afraid that my poor child has got some warp or twist in her nature; but I hope that my nephew will never find out her want of straightforwardness".'[6]

In clinical terms, the expression 'warp or twist in her nature' connotes a blighted heredity. For the expression gains a kind of medical authority if it is allied to the alienist Henry Maudsley's comment that

> in consequence of evil ancestral influences, individuals are born with such a flaw or warp of nature that all the care in the world will not prevent them from being vicious or criminal, or becoming insane.[7]

If Carey was echoing Maudsley at this point, whether consciously or not, she was writing a diagnosis with multiple possibilities for the fictional Etta's mental state. For it is possible to find, within the character of Etta, evidence of all three of these outcomes. In spite of 'all the care in the world' Etta is, from a legal point of view, a criminal. In addition, she is vicious, meaning that she has a strong tendency towards depraved habits. She has an excessive love of fine clothes (this is the vice that leads her to crime) and she takes drugs for other than purely medical purposes (*UM*, pp. 442, 440).

As to whether Etta can, strictly speaking, be construed as insane, this is not so straightforward. With much discussion of her 'sin, – perhaps I should say crime' and the necessity for her future 'obedience and submission', it seems that, once again, 'the lady is not mad' (*UM*, pp. 141, 142). Yet, as in *Lady Audley's Secret*, even where discourses of sin and crime appear to prevail over the discourse of insanity, they do not furnish the novel with an absolute closure. Etta's 'hysterical state ... border[ing] upon frenzy' which lasts for 'some hours' after the discovery of her schemes is hardly emblematic of 'normal' feminine behaviour. Nor do the expressions 'my poor child' and 'warp or twist in her nature' indicate total culpability on Etta's part. In addition, the reader familiar with Maudsley's work is able to furnish Etta with a latent insanity

---

6 Rosa N. Carey, *Uncle Max* (London: Macmillan, 1912 [1887]), p. 425 (hereafter *UM*).

7 Henry Maudsley, *Body and Mind* (London: Macmillan, 1873), p. 76. The term 'alienist' denotes 'One who treats mental diseases.' *The Shorter English Oxford Dictionary* (reprinted 1991) gives the date of the term as 1864, though it was applied retrospectively to the earlier part of the nineteenth century and was probably going out of use by the 1880s. The terms 'alienism' and 'alienist discourse' refer to the texts and ideas of the prominent alienists – people such as Maudsley. The word 'psychiatry', meaning 'Medical treatment of diseases of the mind' is to be found in the *Nuttall's Pronouncing English Dictionary* [1879]. However, it does not seem to have been in use in popular medical texts from around this date.

commensurate with her criminality and viciousness. She, like Lady Audley, has a 'hereditary taint in her blood'.

Significantly, Carey uses this same diagnosis of 'a flaw or warp of nature' to explain the behaviour of another Lady Audley figure, Mrs Blake in *Lover or Friend?* [1890]. At point of discovery, Mrs Blake has dissociated herself from her husband, who is serving a prison sentence for fraud, and is passing herself off as a respectable bourgeois widow, under an assumed name.[8] On this occasion, too, the explanation is expressed in terms of pity as well as condemnation:

> Could she help it ... if her moral sense were blunted and distorted? There was something defective and warped in her nature – something that seemed to make her less accountable than other people. Truth was not dear to her, or her marriage-vows sacred in her eyes.[9]

It additionally seems to reflect Maudsley's contention that

> many persons ... without actually being imbecile or insane, are of a lower moral responsibility than the average of mankind; they have been taught the same lessons as the rest of mankind, and have a full theoretical knowledge of them, but the principles inculcated never gain that hold of their minds which they gain in a sound and well-constituted nature.[10]

Maudsley's reader might well be confused by the notion that an incorrigibly irresponsible person with a badly-constituted nature can be sane. However, arguably, his phrase 'without *actually* being ... insane' implies that such persons do not have a clean bill of mental health either. Notably, this category of 'lower moral responsibility' is the one into which Maudsley places the 'wicked' and 'habitual criminals' (Maudsley 1874, p. 25). Mrs Blake matches this paradigm exactly. Her unacceptable behaviour consists of transgressions against morality and class for which she may be blamed but for which she is not ultimately responsible. Thus Mrs Blake, too, is interpellated alternately into the discourses of criminality and madness.

Yet Mrs Blake is an altogether more complex figure than either Lady Audley or Etta in that a whole matrix of language relating to insanity is applied

---

8 Blake is the assumed name; her actual name is O'Brien.

9 Rosa N Carey, *Lover or Friend* (London: Macmillan, 1915 [1890]), p. 410 (hereafter *LoF*).

10 Henry Maudsley, *Responsibility in Mental Disease* (London: Henry S. King, 1874), pp. 24–5. The word 'moral' in this passage has two meanings: 'We can translate the term 'moral' as a rough nineteenth-century equivalent of the contemporary term "psychological" which at the same time retains certain ethical implications'. See Vieda Skultans, *Madness and Morals: Ideas on Insanity in the Nineteenth Century* (London: Routledge and Kegan Paul, 1975), p. 2 (hereafter, Skultans 1975).

to her throughout the novel. In the early chapters, emphasis is placed upon her embarrassing artlessness in conversation and upon her indulgence in obsessive bouts of a single activity: 'She never does things quite like other people. She likes either to work all day long ... or else to do nothing' (*LoF*, p. 58). In the later chapters she suffers two lengthy hysterical attacks, the first upon the discovery of her real identity and the second at the deathbed of her son (*LoF*, p. 375; p. 436). After the first of these another character, Michael, remembering what he 'ha[s] been told' about her, considers at some length whether she has finally reached a state of permanent mental alienation:

> he had been told that from her youth she had been prone to fits of hysterical emotion. She was perfectly unused to self-control ... Was there not a danger, then, that, the barriers once broken down, she might pass beyond her own control? He had heard and had read that ungovernable passion might lead to insanity. (*LoF*, p. 310)

However, this passage consists of mere conjecture. It is not an authoritative statement that Mrs Blake is, or will ever become, insane. Indeed, Michael destabilizes his own 'diagnosis' by glossing what he has read about 'ungovernable passion' possibly 'lead[ing] to insanity' with the comment that 'he almost believed it.' The 'myth' of Mrs Blake's insanity is also undermined as the invisible narrator, arguably Carey herself, repeats the local gossip on the subject:

> It was said and believed by more than one person that ... hereditary insanity [had been discovered] in the Blake family; indeed, one lady – a notorious gossip, and who was somewhat deaf – was understood to say that she had heard Mrs Blake was at that moment in a private lunatic asylum. (*LoF*, p. 418)

Even the ideal reader, who necessarily suspends disbelief in order to engage with the fiction, is obliged to doubt the veracity of a notorious gossip who is deaf.

The dubious medical diagnoses made in respect of Lady Audley and her fictional sisters, Etta and Mrs Blake, do not – and indeed cannot – constitute closures even though they are ostensibly used as such. By the time each diagnosis is made, the picaresque career to which it relates has drawn to a close but the interface between culpability and madness continues. An ambiguous diagnosis/judgement is followed by an ambiguous prescription of treatment/punishment. In each of the novels alluded to so far, the deviant woman is banished to some form of asylum or penitentiary, apparently in order to learn appropriate behaviours and values. Lady Audley proper is placed by the Audley family in a '*maison de sante*', with the recommendation that she repent; but Dr Mosgrave, the medical man who certifies her, speaks of mere incarceration:

> 'Whatever secrets she may have will be secrets for ever! Whatever crimes she may have committed, she will be able to commit no more. If you were to dig a grave for her in the nearest churchyard and bury her alive in it, you could not more safely shut her from the world and all worldly associations'. (*LAS*, p. 293)

Similarly, the wronged head of the household in *Uncle Max* banishes his 'unfortunate cousin' to where she can do no further harm. He tells her:

> I have found you a home far from here ... and tomorrow you will be taken to it. The Alnwicks are kind, worthy people – not rich ... or what the world would call refined ... and they promise to treat you like a daughter. You will be in comfort, but not in luxury; luxury has been your curse, Etta ... Let your future conduct atone to me for the past ... Your only course now must be obedience and submission. (*UM*, pp. 441–2)

This sentence of banishment, too, appears in the light of punishment. Etta is to be exiled from her current home and to have her expenditure curtailed. However, the Alnwicks have all the hallmarks of keepers of a private asylum. They are not her social equals but they are to have a kind of parental authority over her; and although Etta has nowhere else to go, she is to be delivered up to them rather than being allowed to travel to their home of her own free will.[11] As with Lady Audley proper, she evades criminal proceedings but her future is far from bright. The ultimate fate of Mrs Blake in *Lover or Friend?* only differs in that Carey has her choose seclusion of her own free will. Mrs Blake changes her religion from a nominal Anglicanism to Roman Catholicism and enters a convent with a very strict rule. This voluntary segregation places her in much the same position as her fictional peers. The convent may be viewed as another pseudo-asylum or penitentiary. Mrs Blake will be away from the world, under the tutelage of a Reverend Mother and a Mother Church, learning the ultra-feminine role of poverty, chastity and obedience.

---

11 In the nineteenth century private asylum-keeping was a low-status profession, both medically or socially. See Charlotte MacKenzie, *Psychiatry for the Rich: A History of Ticehurst Private Asylum* (London: Routledge, 1992), p. 193. However, even less status was accorded to the many medically unqualified persons who made a living from keeping a single insane patient in their own homes. (Carey's Etta appears to have been supplied with this kind of accommodation rather than entering an asylum as such.) Such keepers did not have to be licensed by the local authority and the single patient had little legal protection until the Act of 1890 (MacKenzie, p. 216). MacKenzie further suggests that 'it was those patients whose status before the law was most ambiguous ... who were likely to be confined in single lodgings' (ibid., p. 106).

However, not all of Carey's Lady Audley figures replicate this pattern of discovery followed by permanent exclusion from a former place in society. Joan, the eponymous heroine of *Only the Governess* [1888], feels compelled to leave her hypercritical husband and the sister-in-law who is trying to drive them apart; but she ultimately returns in triumph, to a renegotiated position within the marital home. She uses an assumed name but this is only a means by which she can both free herself from the constraints of marriage and gain safe employment.[12] An advantageous proposal of marriage from her employer's stepson brings about not bigamy (as with Lady Audley proper) but a full confession of her deception. The remainder of the narrative, in so far as it concerns her, is about reconciliation rather than punishment.

Nevertheless, Joan is, like the other Lady Audley figures, constructed alternately within discourses of insanity and transgression. She is 'undisciplined' and has a 'passionate and ill-disciplined nature,' these character faults being ascribed to her upbringing. Joan's father was 'one of those impulsive, hot-tempered Irishmen that one dreads to have much to do with'; and 'the aunt who brought her up was one of those worldly, scheming women that have so bad an influence on girls'.[13] Thus, the reader may deduce that Joan has not had the right kind of early environment in which to practice 'the wise development of the control of the will over the thoughts and feelings ... which makes strongly for sanity', as advocated by Maudsley (Maudsley 1874, p. 269).

Nor does this lack of moral development entirely free Joan from culpability for her actions, though her transgression is couched in a discourse of sin rather than criminality since she has committed no crime. Upon discovery, she is told 'you have done very wrong, for you have sinned against the truth', and she acknowledges the justice of this (*OTG*, p. 197). Elsewhere in the novel, Joan's employer tells her 'You must be very humble towards your husband, for your sin against him is very great' (*OTG*, p. 219; p. 229). Yet Joan's story differs from the other Lady Audley-style narratives in more than its ending. It is the most interesting of the three novels by Carey dealt with here because there lies within it a protracted discussion of the mitigating circumstances in the protagonist's unacceptable behaviour. The 'complex middl[e]' of this novel which, had it been a sensation novel as such, Pykett would have described as 'a site in which the contradictions, anxieties and opposing ideologies of Victorian culture converge and are put into play', contains the most even-handed discussion of the transgressive female to be found in any of Carey's Lady Audley-style novels.

---

12 As a governess, she uses the name Miss Huldah Rossiter; her name is actually Mrs Joan Thorpe.

13 Rosa N. Carey, *Only The Governess* (London: Macmillan, 1917 [1888]), pp. 30, 38 and 76; p. 75 (hereafter, *OTG*).

In placing her Lady Audley figures within the competing discourses of insanity and transgression, Carey was not merely emulating Braddon and creating a discursive space for the reader. In undermining a diagnosis of insanity in *Lover or Friend?*, and a diagnosis of incorrigible badness in *Only the Governess*, she may indeed have facilitated debate about suitable modes of feminine behaviour. However, she appears to have done far more than this with her material. The allusions to alienist texts, especially to those of her contemporary, Maudsley, appear to be far too plentiful if included solely for the purpose of encouraging an extra-textual debate on femininity. Arguably, Carey also had an explicitly didactic agenda: that of advocating the teaching of self-control from an early age and of warning about the dire consequences of neglecting such education.[14]

Thus the discursive space opened by the presence in the text of a woman placed within the competing discourses of insanity and transgression is, at least in part, closed by the didactic teaching embedded within those same discourses. However, the didactic subject matter placed within the novel and the discussion of the female role, potentially to be generated from without, only partially map over each other. Early training as a prophylactic against insanity is not an issue that relates solely to feminine behaviour. (As will be discussed below, Carey's male characters are equally susceptible to problems arising from defective education.) Moreover, Carey's focus, in the Lady Audley-style novels, upon the specific moral and social dilemmas experienced by female characters as they negotiate a potentially hostile society, are not totally founded upon the moral or mental health of the individual. Arguably, the two readings, utilizing the same source material, can run in parallel. However, if Carey's novels are not merely to be regarded as didactic, it is pertinent to explore other features of the texts which might have been of interest to the nineteenth-century reader.

Much of the enjoyment to be found in Carey's Lady Audley-style texts may be said to stem from the reader's identification with the Lady Audley-style character herself. Such an identification both gratifies the reader's narcissistic desire simply to see herself reflected in the text – however unfavourably – and provides the opportunity for her to engage with the competing discourses which

---

14 The general public was well equipped to detect the alienist discourses of self-control and self-culture for these discourses were present in both non-specialist medical books and general literature. See, for example, *Enquire Within Upon Everything to which is added Enquire Within upon Fancy Needlework* (London: Houlston and Sons, 1871), p. 256: 'children who have been the least indulged ... acquire more ... vigour of mind, than those who have been constantly favoured, and treated by their parents with the most solicitous attention: bodily weakness and mental imbecility are the attributes of the latter'. A popular general medical book which discusses mental disease, is J. M'Gregor-Robertson, *The Household Physician, A Family Guide to the Preservation of Health and to the Domestic Treatment of Ailments and Disease, with Chapters on Food and Drugs, and First Aid in Accidents and Injuries* (London: Blackie and Son, undated [c. 1888]). Maudsley is referred to by name in the section entitled 'Predisposing Causes' of insanity. See p. 106.

construct her now-fictionalized self.[15] However, the reader's compulsion to identify with the Lady Audley figure may also be profitably linked to Showalter's contention that '"insanity" is simply the label that society attaches to female assertion ... self-interest and outrage'.[16] That the nineteenth-century woman reader might have felt herself to be categorized as transgressive or otherwise abnormal if she challenged the minor mores of the dominant is all too plausible if analogies are drawn between women readers in the late nineteenth century and respondents in a study by Dale Spender in the late twentieth.[17] Spender notes that all of her respondents articulated anxiety about

---

15 Freud, quoting Paul Nacke, describes narcissism as 'the attitude of a person who treats his own body in the same way in which the body of a sexual object is ordinarily treated – who looks at it, that is to say, strokes it and fondles it till he obtains complete satisfaction through these activities'. See Sigmund Freud, *On Metapsychology: The Theory of Psycho-analysis*, The Pelican Freud Library Volume 11 (Harmondsworth: Penguin, 1987), p. 65. Freud suggests that, in adults, this extent of self-love is a perversion; but he also posits 'a primary narcissism in everyone' as a normal stage in human development (ibid., p. 82). Freud's own comment on supposedly deviant adult narcissism, given below, provides a useful starting point for a discussion of the reading subject as one who identifies with a character within the text:

> We have discovered, especially clearly in people whose libidinal development has suffered some disturbance, such as perverts and homosexuals, that in their later choice of love-objects they have taken as a model not their mother but their own selves. They are plainly seeking themselves as a love-object, and are exhibiting a type of object-choice which must be termed "narcissistic". (Ibid., p. 81)

Whilst disagreeing with Freud's classification of homosexuals as people 'whose libidinous development has suffered some disturbance' and whilst positing that a certain amount of adult narcissism is normal, if not socially acceptable, it is possible to formulate the theory that narcissistic readers can temporarily 'tak[e] as a model not their mother but their own selves'. In the private action of reading, readers are permitted to egotistically experience themselves as they believe they are portrayed in the novel rather than being obliged to look outside themselves and to emulate 'mother', who represents concepts such as society, duty and self-denial.

That Freud did not think that primary narcissism entirely disappeared in the 'normal' adult is evident. Perhaps unsurprisingly, he claims that many women after puberty experience 'an intensification of the original narcissism' (ibid., p. 82). Meanwhile, he suggests that 'A man who has exchanged his narcissism for homage to a high ego ideal [that is, the next stage of "normal" development] has not necessarily on that account succeeded in sublimating his libidinal instincts. It is true that the ego ideal demands such sublimation, but cannot enforce it' (ibid., p. 89).

16 For an affirmative discussion of reader identification with the 'heroine' in literature, see Janice Radway, *Reading the Romance* (London: Verso, 1987), p. 64. Showalter's notion of Lady Audley as 'representative' of all women has already been discussed. However, see also Kate Flint, *The Woman Reader 1837–1914* (Oxford: Clarendon Press, 1993), p. 36. It is argued in the present work that the reader gains most narcissistic pleasure from identifying with the character who is most like herself, regardless of that character's centrality to the plot, attractiveness or social and material conditions.

17 Spender's study posits that an absence of suitable language can negate the reality of female experience. She writes specifically about women in dialogue with men. However, an analogy can be made between speaking to men *per se* and the place allocated to nineteenth-century women in discourses of the patriarchal dominant. For Spender's study, see Dale

an indefinable problem, characterized only as 'the automatic classification of women as wrong'. The subjects in her study were thus 'obliged to resort to a description of the circumstances in which this experience arose because there [was] no ready-made name by which to label it'.

Whilst Carey does not 'name' this nameless problem of being female and thus wrong either, there is a strong sense of its presence in the Lady Audley-style novels. Many rational explanations for transgressive behaviour are given in the texts but somehow there lies beyond them all an ultimate classification of 'women as wrong' when measured against the dominant version of femininity. Joan and Mrs Blake in particular are too normal to be insane; too rational to be incorrigibly criminal; and too individual to be paradigms of the dominant. It is simply their misfortune that (fictional) nineteenth-century society finds their behaviour largely unacceptable.[18] The most self-aware of the Lady Audley figures, Joan, in *Only the Governess*, best sums up their plight:

> 'I can justify nothing. Everything is wrong, and the only pity is that I was ever born, to be the misery of myself and other people.' (*OTG*, p. 249)

Thus the potential was there for Victorian and Edwardian readers to find, in Carey's Lady Audley-style texts, 'description[s] of ... circumstances' in which characters attract the 'automatic classification of women as wrong' and to find parallels with their own experience.

Readers would also have been permitted to engage with issues of morality and conduct which were without analogy in the lives of the majority. For example, in identifying with Etta in *Uncle Max*, the reader could have decided whether or not it was reprehensible to take control of a household when the alternative was to live there as an obscure poor relation. Similarly, in identifying with Mrs Blake in *Lover or Friend?*, she could have decided whether the satisfactions of being honest were sufficient to compensate for the social ruin inherent in acknowledging that her husband was a felon. Carey facilitated this kind of debate in her novels by giving, on most occasions, at least two points of view.[19]

However, if Lyn Pykett's view of Sensation novels by women may be applied to Carey, the negotiations and reworkings of dominant viewpoints are not exclusively centred on the Lady Audley-style character herself. Although her madness or badness provides a focus in terms of plot, the competing

---

Spender, *Man Made Language* (London: Routledge and Kegan Paul, 1980), pp. 182–90. (The quotations that follow in the main text are from p. 187.)

18 There is no behaviour by Joan or Mrs Blake that has not its counterpart in *Moll Flanders*. However, the 'spirit of the age' in each case has determined both the writing and the reading of texts containing such characters.

19 Even Etta, the most censured of Carey's Lady Audley figures discussed here, is briefly represented sympathetically towards the close of the novel. See *UM*, p. 437.

discourses enabled by her presence are of equal interest. In *Only The Governess*, the initial antagonism displayed by other female characters towards Joan is rich in theoretically intersecting discourses which clash where they might be expected to map over each other. Yet, beyond this collision of ideas, there appears to be a unifying didactic agenda. For, rhetorically, the narrative critiques certain kinds of conduct and advocates others.

Thus, Rachel Thorpe, Joan's sister-in-law, lovingly and selflessly keeps house for her brother and donates both her time and her money to the administration of a charity. However, she operates within the letter rather than the spirit of divine law. As she herself admits towards the conclusion of the novel:

> Had she not made an idol of her brother? had she cared for aught in life but for him and for her work? What would it avail to her that she had fed the hungry and clothed the naked, when her cruelty ... had driven her sister-in-law away from her home – when her narrow jealousy ... had ... alienated Ivan from his wife, and had led to their separation? ... The life that had looked so pure and self-denying to others was full of hideous uncleanness to the Divine eyes of her Judge.[20]

Here, discourses of the religious and discourses of the conventional are shown to have disparate aims. Conventionally, a charitable woman is a good woman, and one who attracts the admiration of others. However, institutionalized charity is seen to be nothing without the old adage of charity beginning at home. Even Rachel's love for her brother is exposed as a selfish emotion as she will not place her brother's interests above her own.

On a strictly social level, *Only the Governess* debates whether an overbearing unmarried sister should take precedence over an inefficient wife. Simultaneously, the text poses the more general question as to whether a spinster should automatically leave her brother's home upon his marriage. It is pointed out that the aging Rachel has looked after her brother since he was a boy, and that brother and sister have a very close relationship. Besides, she has nowhere else to go and cannot afford her own establishment. However, the wife has both societal and religious entitlement to superior status, whether or not she receives it. Rachel might well believe of her brother that 'Joan does not love him; she makes him miserable' but she is told in no uncertain terms:

---

20 *OTG*, p. 325. The distinction between formal charity and charitableness of disposition is couched in biblical terms. See Matthew 25:35–6: 'I was an hungered and ye gave me meat … Naked, and ye clothed me.' But see also 1 Corinthians 13:3: 'though I bestow all my goods to feed the poor ... and have not charity, it profiteth me nothing'.

> 'This is your brother's house; his wife is its rightful mistress ... No sister has the right to come between a man and his wife.'[21]

Indeed, viewed as a usurper and a troublemaker within the home, Rachel may be regarded as a kind of Lady Audley figure herself. Rachel's sanity might be insisted upon throughout novel but she is certainly no different in virtue to the sister-in-law she disparages so often. Another female character whose dual standard is explored in *Only the Governess* is Madella, Joan's employer. She is constructed as a pure woman whose purity has been guaranteed by lack of temptation and who thus cannot empathize with the temptations of others:

> she was as innocent now ... as though she were in her teens. Length of years and many troubles had not taught her knowledge of the world ... Of course there were wicked people ... the criminal classes and others, but – but – she never cared to enter on the subject; with so much goodness in the world, it was foolish and morbid to dwell on the darker shades of life. (*OTG*, p. 97)

However, even before she shows a lack of charity towards the erring Joan, this supposed virtue is subjected to scrutiny. Though 'Her husband had adored this innocence', it is also stated that

> more than one strong-minded woman ... had been heard to express her opinion, that an old childhood was hardly a becoming age, and that there was something narrow and self-indulgent in a nature like Mrs Chudleigh's. (*OTG*, p. 98)

Whilst the 'strong-minded woman' is hardly praised in this passage, she does provide a foil for the extreme unworldliness of Madella. Even the stepson who adores her says that

> '... so long as she lives will Madella dwell in her own house, and pull down her blinds, and stop her ears with cotton-wool, that she may not hear the groans of human victims, or see how cruelty still stalks abroad.' (Ibid., p. 99.)

Yet Madella has been the ideal wife and is now the ideal widow. Her femininity and her motherhood are unquestioned. Her high but conventional standard of womanhood and her lack of experience in anything beyond it thus make her initial hostility to Joan inevitable. When Madella discusses Joan's delinquencies with her stepson, a predictable range of arguments is voiced by each of them. Madella's concern for her family, 'Think of the bad example to

21 *OTG*, p. 220.

our girls … A mother must first think of her own children' is more than countered by her stepson's retort:

> '… but a mother's duty need not stop there. That is the worst of you good women – you will mother your own girls, but you will not extend your guardianship and charity to a poor misguided young woman.' (*OTG*, p. 207)

Thus, even the approved paradigm of womanhood is seen to be inadequate if it excludes from its make-up charity towards those who cannot meet its standards.

In this broader exploration of the discourses of religion, convention, charity and female status, it may seem as though the Lady Audley figure herself has been left far behind and as though the argument has made a lengthy digression from the subject of insanity *per se*. On the contrary, the various issues are inxtricably linked. For, even within fiction, the individual cannot be divorced from her or his immediate social context. Each of the Lady Audley figures in Carey's novels is indeed constructed within the alienist discourse. However, as in the case of Lady Audley proper, it is not the alienist discourse alone that attempts to convict her of either clinical insanity or totally indefensible transgression. In each case, a jury of her fictional peers is made to deliver the verdict that 'The lady is not mad ... she is dangerous!' The danger may be seen to lie in permitting female ambition – or even self-preservation – to destabilize the existing structure of society.

'Thoughts too long and too intensely fixed on one object'[22]

However, it is not only assertive and ambitious female characters who are likely to be described in terms appropriate to insanity in Carey's novels. Another significant group of victims succumb to, or are only just saved from, a form of acute mental illness which she describes as 'brain fever'. By the late nineteenth century, this disease had been doubly dismissed by the general medical establishment even whilst it retained and renewed its place within fiction as diverse as Bram Stoker's *Dracula* [1897] and John Strange Winter's *A Blameless Woman* [c. 1896].[23] Medically speaking, the name of the complaint had been relegated to the realm of popular parlance and the symptoms had been transmuted from the psychological into the physical.

---

22 John Barlow, *Man's Power Over Himself to Prevent or Control Mental Disease* [1843]. Cited in Skultans 1975, p. 166.

23 Bram Stoker, *Dracula* (Oxford: Oxford University Press, 1983 [1897]), p. 99; see also note 30.

In late nineteenth- and early twentieth-century medical books, brain fever is most often conflated with simple meningitis. The *Cassell's Family Doctor*, published in 1897, contains a description of the illness as it was generally understood by the medical establishment of the day:

> Inflammation of the brain and its membranes is a very serious disease, and often terminates fatally ... the disease is called meningitis ... It is to this affectation that the title 'brain fever' is most justly due, although it is used in a popular sense to include all feverish diseases accompanied with brain symptoms ... [S]imple meningitis ... is caused by injuries to the head, disease of the ears, exposure to the sun, over-excitement of the brain, or excessive brain work.[24]

Thus it would seem safe to say that by the 1890s – and probably a decade or two earlier – 'brain fever' as a disease in its own right belonged to fiction alone. However, the fictional symptoms of brain fever are remarkably consistent throughout Carey's work and that of her peers: acute anxiety is followed by physical prostration and actual fever which often culminates in delirium.[25] No organic disease is present but the prognosis (albeit never realised) is that of chronic insanity or death. The passage below, from *Our Bessie* [1888–89], contains a typical description of the early symptoms. Here, the sufferer is still more or less *compos mentis* so she is able to speak about her condition to others:

> 'I have been thinking myself stupid; but I am still too restless to lie down. I feel as though I never want to sleep again, and yet I am so tired ... One seems on wires, and all sorts of horrid, troublesome thoughts keep

24 'A Medical Man', *Cassell's Family Doctor* (London: Cassell, 1897), p. 312. (Hereafter, *Cassell's* 1897.) See also *The Nuttall's Pronouncing English Dictionary* (London: George Routledge and Sons, 1879), p. 81: 'Brain-fever, s. An inflammation of the brain.' Whilst some of Carey's novels considerably pre-date these sources, it is possible to abstract from them the medical view of brain fever from earlier in the century.

I am indebted to Dr Bryce of Norfolk for more recent information on meningitis (interview 21 May 1992). It is not stress-related and is contagious. (Carey does not mention the latter.) In Dr Bryce's opinion, 'brain fever' is likely to have been a form of hysteria. To Sister L.C. Hartnell of Kent (an SRN), I am grateful for the suggestion that the general prostration was likely to have been akin to nervous breakdown (in its modern sense), and for the important reminder that any medical condition in which the body temperature goes above 105°F will produce delirium.

25 In Mrs Henry Wood's novel *Lady Adelaide*, Harry Dane broods himself into 'a long nervous fever, prostrating both mind and body' when he discovers that his fiancée has been unfaithful. See Mrs Henry Wood, *Lady Adelaide* (London: Richard Bentley and Son, 1896), p. 431. See also John Strange Winter, *A Blameless Woman*, 3rd edn (London: F.V. White, 1896), p. 55.

> surging through one's brain, and there seems no rest, no peace anywhere.'[26]

However, the outlook for an ill-treated child, in *Queenie's Whim* [1881], is even less auspicious. Examining unconscious little Emmie the doctor predicts that:

> 'When she wakes up ... she will not know [anyone]; brain fever is the least we can expect ... Acute terror on an exhausted system often leads to very sad results, especially with nervous children.'[27]

Fortunately, the fictional Emmie

> did not die, neither were her physician's worst fears verified; but for many a long week the frail existence hovered between life and death. When the lethargy had passed a long period of delirium intervened, and every symptom of severe brain fever manifested itself ... The child lay upon her pillow smiling idly and waving her emaciated arms to and fro upon the quilt; the fair hair was closely shaven, the eyes dilated and brilliant.[28]

Given that fictional characters who suffer from brain fever never have any underlying physical disease and that they always recover from the complaint, their creators cannot be said to reproduce even the popular conflation of brain fever with meningitis. However, the blurring of distinctions between a mental

---

26 R.N. Carey, *Our Bessie* (London: Office of the Girl's Own Paper, n.d. [1888–89]), pp. 165–6 (hereafter *OB*). (Where the date runs over two years, this indicates during which the novel was first serialized.) See also *Wee Wifie* (London: Richard Bentley and Son, 1894 [1869]), p. 189; *Robert Ord's Atonement* (London: Richard Bentley and Son 1898 [1873]), p. 396.

27 R.N. Carey, *Queenie's Whim* (London: Macmillan, 1898 [1881]), p. 59. (Hereafter, *QW*.) Cf. 'Sudden fear has sometimes acted beneficially ... more generally, however, its operation is the reverse, and many cases of epilepsy, mania, heart disease, &c., date from fright. In children, particularly of a nervous temperament, the influence of fear ... is most sedulously to be avoided ... further, if a child has been systematically frightened about the dark, &c., it may, if accidentally placed in it, suffer serious injury from fright.' See S. Thomson and J.C. Steele, *A Dictionary of Domestic Medicine and Surgery*, 34th edn, thoroughly revised and enlarged by A. Westland, G. Reid and J. Cantlie (London: Charles Griffin, 1899 [1882]), pp 265–6 (hereafter Thomson and Steele, 1899).

28 *QW*, p. 60. Here, as death is not the worst outcome to be feared, the ultimate threat is insanity. Emmie's treatment was typical of that for delirium in the late nineteenth century: 'the head should be shaved and kept cool ... the feet should be kept warm, the room darkened, and every source of excitement removed' (Thomson and Steele, p. 182). Her condition appears to be that of low delirium: 'In the low forms of delirium, the mental disturbance is equally complete as in the acute forms, but the violence of the inflammatory fever is absent; generally, the person lies in a dreamy state of incoherent thought ... the hands are tremulous ... and ... perhaps affected with convulsive startings' (ibid.).

condition and meningitis was useful to them in terms of plot. Authors had at their disposal both the cliffhanging, almost certain fatality, of meningitis and the advantage of not losing credibility if the victims recovered.

Fictional brain fever is always the result of 'over-excitement of the brain' rather than disease or injury. Thus it remains, in spite of its physical symptoms, what the Victorians would have called a 'moral' rather than a physiological disease. In an important sense, this word 'moral' simply alludes to the mental processes of the brain as distinct from its physiological entity. Yet the term cannot be divorced from resonances of moral conduct. Vieda Skultans glosses the word as 'psychological' but at the same time 'retain[ing] certain ethical implications' (Skultans 1975, p. 2). Today, writers would probably use the more common and less judgemental word 'functional'.[29] However, were this latter term to be used in this particular context, a major means of understanding why brain fever survived as a literary phenomenon long after it had ceased to be taken seriously by the medical establishment would be lost.

Seen as a 'moral', that is as a psychological, condition rather than as a physiological one, the causes and symptoms of fictional brain fever appear to parallel early nineteenth-century alienist thought. For example, in his treatise, *Man's Power Over Himself to Prevent or Control Mental Disease* [1843] John Barlow states that:

> Insanity from *misdirection* of the intellectual force ... has one very general character ... at first there are very few symptoms, if any, of structural disease ... the evil originates rather in the misuse than the impairment of the organ. Thoughts too long and too intensely fixed on one object, weary the part of the brain so employed, and we usually then seek relief by varying our occupation: if this is not done, the weariness may end in disease. (Skultans 1975, p. 166. Emphasis original.)

Barlow then illustrates the perils of brain-weariness with a case-study of a man who imposed upon himself the task of learning Greek grammar:

> he persevered in spite of weariness, but in a short time delirium came on. He took the hint, laid aside the Greek primitives, and recovered himself very quickly. Here the misuse of the organ had produced temporary disease: had the subject been one not so easy to lay aside, the temporary disease might have become permanent (Ibid.)

To an extent, this passage describes the experience of fictional brain-fever victims. First they dwell on something too long or too intensely; then they

29 As used in, for example, 'Mental Illness' in R.L. Gregory (ed.), *The Oxford Companion to the Mind* (Oxford: Oxford University Press, 1987), pp. 470–71: 'organic disorders ... and functional disorders'.

begin to suffer from temporary disease. The complaint eventually manifests itself as delirium and the prognosis is insanity or death. However, Barlow was far from being alone in assigning moral causes to mental diseases. Even the more physiologically-grounded Henry Maudsley grudgingly admitted that this was possible:

> To the argument that madness is produced sometimes by moral causes ... it is sufficient to reply ... that long-continued or excessive stimulation of any organ does notably induce physical disease of it, and that, in this respect ... the brain only obeys a general law of the organism ...[30]

Maudsley's categories of 'long-continued' and 'excessive' stimulation of the brain conveniently ally themselves to the two basic causes of fictional brain fever: protracted brooding and sudden shock. Thus Emmie in *Queenie's Whim* (whose illness has been described above), may be placed in the 'sudden shock' category. She succumbs to brain fever after the 'acute terror' of being locked up in a dark room. Similarly, Miss Bretherton, a character in Carey's novel *The Mistress of Brae Farm* [1896], is prostrated after witnessing the sudden and unexpected death of her fiancé.[31] In such cases, brain fever is merely a literary device utilized to bring colour and drama into the narrative. The nature of the illness excites the pity of the reader and potentially provides a catalyst in terms of plot.

However, Carey devotes more space in her novels to characters in whom 'long-continued' stimulation of the brain brings about disease. Characters who fall ill after protracted brooding generally suffer due to causes of the chronic kind, which are 'not so easy to lay aside', and their suffering generally has a more obviously moral or ethical dimension. Thus Gladys, in *Uncle Max* [1887], is an ideal candidate for brain fever. She fears that her adored twin brother has drowned and that the man she had hoped to marry no longer loves her; and, most importantly, she is out of charity with her elder brother. She has noone to whom she can confide her anxiety and sadness and so broods in unhealthy isolation.

Yet, in spite of its affinities with alienist writing, brain fever is deemed to be quite distinct from insanity. Neither Maudsley nor Barlow uses the term 'brain fever' at all and fictional texts tend to maintain a distinction between the two conditions. For Carey, brain fever is the potential cause of insanity, not a

---

30 Maudsley 1874, p. 16. From mid-century, the tendency was increasingly towards physiological rather than 'moral' explanations of mental disease. In particular, interest focused upon matters of heredity as opposed to environment.

31 R.N. Carey, *The Mistress of Brae Farm* (London: Hodder and Stoughton, 1920 [1896]), pp. 108–9.

manifestation of it.[32] As to the general opinion of the medical establishment, this can only be judged by its response to the symptoms of brain fever because the disease itself is accorded no real existence. Thus, it is necessary to look at medical views on its major manifestation, delirium.

Nineteenth-century physicians Thomson and Steele view delirium as 'a temporary disordered condition of the mental faculties, occurring during illness, either of a febrile or of an exhausting nature' (Thomson and Steele 1899, p. 181). They carefully distinguish it from insanity even whilst acknowledging the difficulties of doing so:

> In true delirium the presence of fever more or less, the acute disorder of the functions generally, such as digestion &c., and the disorder of the *whole* mind, generally sufficiently indicate its distinctness from insanity, in which the faculties of the mind are only perhaps affected or perverted, and disconnected ... Still, the two affections may nearly approach one another ... (Ibid., p. 182)

They additionally identify, almost as an aside, the most probable cause of brain fever. The passage continues:

> Still more difficult of discrimination are some cases of *hysterical delirium*, which, when long continued, might well be taken for insanity, unless subjected to medical judgement ... (Ibid. My emphasis.)

Brain fever was thus, in medical terms at least, deemed to be simply a manifestation of the chameleon-like pathology of hysteria. However, it might be asked why brain-fever sufferers *en masse* should be regarded as hysterical. The *Casssell's Family Doctor* provides a number of suggestions. Hysteria could be caused by

> many conditions which produce an exhausted, overwrought state of [the nervous] organs. Among these may be mentioned sudden fright, strong

32 In *Uncle Max*, the question of the sanity of Gladys, stricken with brain fever, is obliquely raised during a discussion about suitable medical care. Gladys's malevolent cousin Etta tells the nurse, 'Gladys's case is far too serious for me to be ... sanguine. I believe you have not nursed these nervous patients before. If Giles had taken my advice he would have had a person trained to this special work.' See R.N. Carey, *Uncle Max* (London: Macmillan, 1912 [1887]), p. 382 (hereafter, *UM*). The word 'person' suggests someone who is not a hospital-trained nurse; the phrase 'this special work' hints that the patient is suffering from something other than physical ill-health. These insinuations are immediately refuted by the reply that 'Gladys's case does not require that sort of nurse' (*UM*, p. 382). Similarly, in *Wee Wifie* [1869], Sir Hugh is raving and violent but he is treated by a 'well-known physician' and 'two hospital nurses' rather than by a specialist in nervous disorders. R.N. Carey, *Wee Wifie* (London: Richard Bentley and Son, 1894 [1869]), p. 193 (hereafter *WW*).

> religious impressions, unhappy love affairs, hope deferred, and other powerful emotional conditions ... (*Cassell's* 1897, p. 535)

For Rosa Carey's brain-fever victims, with the exception of the child Emmie, the common factor is that of thwarted sexual expectations: that is, they suffer 'unhappy love affairs' or 'hope deferred'. An explicit connexion between sexual anxiety and hysteria had been recognized at least as early as 1853, with the publication of Robert Brudendall Carter's influential book, *On the Pathology and Treatment of Hysteria.*[33] He writes at length about the woman whose hysterical condition has arisen due to her anticipation of licit sexual pleasures which then fail to materialize:

> it is evident that a young woman whose chief enjoyment rests either upon a complacent contemplation of her own perfections, mingled with an angry sense of the neglect shown to them by her associates, or else upon an imagined gratification of her sexual desires, is not in the best possible frame of mind for withstanding the pressure of a new temptation; such as is held out by the discovery that *she can, at will, produce an apparently serious illness*, and thus make herself an object of great attention to all around her, and possibly, among others, to the individual who has been uppermost in her thoughts. (Ibid., p. 203. My emphasis.)

Notably, in this early treatise, hysteria is viewed as a matter of 'moral' perversity, in both senses of the word. It is possible to make a large number of links between Carey's individual brain-fever victims and Carter's version of hysteria. For Sir Hugh in *Wee Wifie*, the lassitude following acute brain fever excuses his illicit desire to see his first love even though he is married to another; for Edna in *Our Bessie*, an hysterical cough and the first symptoms of 'brain fever' elicit the sympathy of her mother and friends after she has, of her own volition, dismissed the fiancé she was shortly to have married. Meanwhile, Gladys in *Uncle Max*, with her surfeit of problems, may be construed as pining in a carefully contrived manner in order to play on the guilt of her clergyman lover.

However, fictional brain fever, whether or not purely attributable to hysteria, is very much more than an illness; it not only provides pathos and aids plot development but also frequently carries with it heavily didactic overtones. Brain fever, as a 'moral' complaint, encompasses concepts of the ethical as

33 Unlike many of his peers, Carter posited that men as well as women were prone to hysteria and that in each the cause could be sexual frustration. He states that 'in many cases of hysteria in the male, the sufferers are recorded to have been "continent"'. Cited in Ilza Veith, *Hysteria: The History of a Disease* (Chicago: Phoenix Books, University of Chicago Press, 1965) p. 202. Thomson and Steele suggest that sexual frustration should predispose women to hysteria (Thomson and Steele 1899, p. 340). *Cassell's* (1897) reluctantly concedes that 'rare cases occasionally occur in very impressionable men' (*Cassell's* 1897, p. 535).

well as the purely mental. It indicates to the reader that the sufferer is wrestling with an apparently insoluble dilemma, perhaps one requiring an as yet unattained Christian forbearance or faith. It can also signify a point of personal crisis and an opportunity to change course in life. Rosa Carey makes full use of her brain-fever victims for this kind of didactic purpose, her favoured issue being that of appropriate Christian behaviour. Hence the ethical predicament of Gladys in *Uncle Max*. Gladys cannot forgive her elder brother, Giles, for his part in driving her rebellious twin, Eric, away from the family home. Consequently, she cannot forgive herself for her lack of charity: 'a sense of sin oppressed her; she must be more wicked than other people, or ... Providence would not permit her to be so unhappy'. In the same passage, Gladys goes on to express her feelings in explicitly doctrinal form, both 'blame[ing] herself with influencing [her younger brother] Eric wrongly: she ought not to have taken his part against his brother' and expressing her anxiety about her feelings towards her elder brother:

> '"He that hateth his brother is a murderer." Ursula, there were times, I am sure, when I hated Giles.' And, with this thought upon her she would beg him to forgive her when he next came into the room.[34]

Thus, the fictional Gladys is represented as being at least partially responsible for her own situation. She is represented as knowing that she must be reconciled with her elder brother in order for there to be a happy issue. Indeed, her recovery actually begins when she is able to ask Giles to kiss her good night *(UM*, p. 373). In another of Carey's novels, *Our Bessie*, a character called Edna becomes ill after she has dismissed her fiancé in a fit of ill temper and then begins to regret it. However, on this occasion, Carey takes the opportunity to enlarge upon the perils of neglecting early moral training in children. Edna's mother is made to say:

> 'I am afraid it is all my fault. I have indulged Edna too much, and given her own way in everything; and now she tyrannises over us all. If I had only acted differently.' (*OB*, p. 147)

And Carey's narrator somewhat sententiously adds:

> She had not taught her child to practice self-discipline and self-control. Her waywardness had been fostered by indulgence and her temper had become more faulty. (Ibid.)

34 All quotations from *UM*, p. 380; see also 1 John 3:15.

Yet *Our Bessie* does not merely deal with the shortcomings of an over-indulgent mother. Once again, a character cannot fully recover her health until she has taken some responsibility for her own behaviour. Explicitly, Edna must start to live as a Christian daughter and prospective wife. However, implicitly, she must learn self-control in order to improve her mental health and in order to ensure that illnesses such as brain fever do not recur. Her narrative concludes, not with her wedding, but when she has sought, and received, the forgiveness of both her fiancé and her long-suffering mother (*OB*, p. 224).

Given that *Our Bessie* was written for, and published by, the Religious Tract Society, it is likely that Carey had in mind the Old Testament injunction to 'Train up a child in the way he should go' that 'when he is old he will not depart from it' (Proverbs 22:6). Yet, in its preoccupation with the inculcation of self-control, Carey's writing is, at this stage, equally reminiscent of Maudsley's assertion that

> in the wise development of the control of the will over the thoughts and feelings there is a power in ourselves which makes strongly for sanity. (Maudsley 1874, p. 269)

In both *Our Bessie* and *Uncle Max*, the 'moral' aspect of brain fever is clear: the conduct of the individual is at variance with the professed creed of Christianity. For brain-fever victims such as these, a successful appeal to the conscience and the will is sufficient to bring about a full recovery. However, the greater complications experienced by the fictional Hugh in *Wee Wifie* yield further variations on the now familiar themes of religion and alienist thought. His sufferings begin when the woman he loves refuses to marry him because there is hereditary insanity in her family.[35] In a fit of pique, he marries someone

---

35 *Wee Wifie* is a novel about social and moral responsibility. Hugh tells Margaret, 'such things happen again and again in families, and no one thinks of them. If I am willing to abide by the consequences, no one else has the right to object.' (*WW*, p. 33). Carey's narrator adds, 'How could he think of the consequences to his unborn children, of the good of future generations of Redmonds, when he could hear nothing but the voice of his passion that told him no other woman would be to him like Margaret?' (*WW*, p. 34). In this passage there are further echoes of Henry Maudsley:

> When one considers the reckless way in which persons, whatever the defects of their mental and bodily constitution, often get married, without sense of responsibility for the miseries which they entail upon those who will be the heirs of their infirmities, without regard ... to anything but their own present gratification, one ... [thinks] ... that man is not the pre-eminently reasoning and moral animal he claims to be … He has persuaded himself ... that ... there is in the feeling of love between the sexes something of so sacred and mysterious a character as to justify disregard to consequences in marriage ... on the contrary, it is a passion he shares with other animals … (Maudsley 1874, pp. 276–7)

Ironically, Hugh's behaviour borders on insanity even though he is constitutionally sane, whilst the reverse is true of Margaret. She displays the sanity and social responsibility

else. Thus he drives himself to mental breakdown because he will not accept that the 'Divine Will' has forbidden the union of his choice and because he knows he has 'done a mean thing to marry [another] when his heart was solely and entirely Margaret's' (*WW*, pp. 34, 171). His symptoms are typical for the early stages of brain fever: an exhausting restlessness, morbid thoughts and lack of sleep; but this is not the entire sum of his physical and mental ills (*WW*, pp. 143–4):

> often he had yielded to the temptation to drown his inward miseries with pernicious drugs ... in those solitary vigils whilst his innocent child-wife was sleeping peacefully like an infant, his half-maddened brain conjured up delirious fancies that seemed to people the library with haunting faces. (*WW*, pp. 189–90)

The use of narcotics is not explicitly implicated in his eventual illness; there is an implied pre-existent state of 'nerves' (*WW*, p. 144). Rather, recourse to them is depicted as symptomatic of moral weakness: he is addicted to self-indulgence and he lacks self-control. Yet the picture of Hugh attempting to throw himself out of the window and that of his servants having to strap him down suggest, to the late twentieth-century eye at least, the withdrawal symptoms attendant upon drug addiction.[36] Unlike his fictional peers, Hugh is made to see his illness retrospectively as a point of personal crisis, as a vital opportunity to change his course in life and thus to avoid absolute destruction. He is made to wonder:

> What would have become of him ... if the hand of Providence had not laid him low before he had succeeded in ruining himself, body and soul? (*WW*, p. 189)

---

necessary to forbid the banns even though she is the one with the constitutional predisposition to insanity. However, she also represents the best that can be achieved by good moral training and strong religious faith in spite of a blighted heredity.

36 *WW*, p. 193. Nor would Maudsley have disputed this diagnosis. He suggests that 'it is possible to produce experimentally, by entirely physical causes, mental derangement exactly similar to that which is produced by moral causes' (Maudsley 1874, p. 16). Carey may have fictionalized a common phenomenon for her time without ascribing its biological cause. Some real-life instances of 'brain fever' in the nineteenth century may well have been caused by unwitting drug abuse. Drugs, in particular opiates, were more readily available and less was known about safe doses. Dr Bryce suggests that many women became addicted to narcotics through taking medication to relieve painful menstruation. Free availability of drugs which are now restricted is indicated by Thomson and Steele's list of suggested medicines for a '"domestic" materia medica'. On the list are ether, chloroform, chlorodyne, lead, mercury and four kinds of opium (Thomson and Steele 1899, p. 394).

Yet although Sir Hugh is Carey's only violent brain fever victim, his behaviour is within the expected bounds for someone suffering from delirium: 'In fever, and febrile diseases generally, delirium may be no more than a slight confusion of ideas on waking from sleep, or it may amount to furious and dangerous excitement' (Thomson and Steele, 1899, pp. 181–2.)

The implicitly Christian discourse at work here has as its underlying rationale that God works all things to the ultimate good, whether it is in preventing a marriage or in bringing about an illness. Margaret, his first love, is able to say from the first that, 'It is not I but the Divine Will that has interposed this barrier to our union.' However, Hugh cannot be brought to a proper understanding of the Divine Will until stricken by the 'hand of Providence'. However, he becomes a better person because of his sufferings. Eventually,

> there was ... in Hugh Redmond's face ... a nobler expression than it had ever worn in happier days ... there was a chastened gravity about his whole mien that spoke of a new and earnest purpose; of a heart so humbled at last that it had fled to its best refuge, and had found strength in the time of need.[37]

Only when he gains religious faith can Sir Hugh thank God for Fay, 'the wife He has given me' (*WW*, p. 412). Thus, he is ultimately made to acknowledge that his initial wilfulness was wrong and that his tribulation was not without good cause or happy issue.

The fictional condition of brain fever may thus be seen as a disease with two overlapping pathologies. In purely medical terms, one of these was obsolete and the other topical. By the late nineteenth century, no medical complaint called brain fever – whether physiological or purely psychological – was given serious consideration. Yet victims of brain fever were to be found in novels as late as the 1890s. Looking at the fictional symptoms from a medical aspect, the condition called brain fever seems to belong to the earlier part of the century. That is to say, the 'moral' aspects of the disease – in both senses of the word – as represented by early writers such as John Barlow rather than physiological or hereditary aspects as represented by Henry Maudsley are emphasized. The second pathology, that of clinical hysteria, seems to be a more appropriate paradigm for understanding the complaint because the novels under discussion are products of the later nineteenth century.

Yet why should authors have written novels which simultaneously suggested both of these historically distinct pathologies? The answer would seem to be that these discrete medical discourses served different but equally necessary ends. Case-studies of hysteria were fashionable or at least compatible with contemporary medical theory and practice. It may be argued that, to a certain extent, readers wanted to read, and writers wanted to write, about what they believed was a recognizable reality. However, nineteenth-century authors and writers also deemed the novel to be a suitable location for the discussion of

37 *WW*, p. 361. Cf. 'The sacrifices of God are a broken spirit: a broken and contrite heart, O God, thou wilt not despise' (Psalms 51:17). Cf. also 'God is our refuge and strength, a very present help in trouble' (Psalms 46:1 in the King James Bible. However, the *Book of Common Prayer* translates the word 'refuge' as 'hope'.)

moral issues. To quote Andrew Blake, author of *Reading Victorian Fiction* [1989]:

> The [nineteenth-century] novel ... was public property in a way in which family life and letters were not: it gave people a chance to discuss domestic ideology *in public* without touching upon their own domestic secrets. It is therefore a most important point of contact between the public and private.[38]

It would therefore seem that the disease called brain fever survived in fiction long after it had become obsolete in medical terms because it suited this requirement on the part of both writers and readers for a moral dimension. For Carey in particular, the illness was a didactic device through which she was able to debate matters of self-control and religious motivation. In her novels, brain-fever sufferers not only survive their illnesses but also live on to work through their dilemmas. The flirtation with something approximating insanity has a decidedly salutary effect.

'a mixture of mental and bodily disorder and irritability'[39]

Hitherto, discussion has focused upon Carey's 'unnaturally' assertive female characters, and upon those characters whose conflicting values lead to illness. However, three of Carey's novels include female protagonists who suffer psychologically in quite a different way. More than rhetorically insane, these characters cannot be assertive or criminal in order to improve their lot so they become depressive and introverted. In two instances this feeling of helplessness is due in part to ill health; in the third, the sufferer additionally experiences two bereavements in rapid succession. Thus the ailments are far from being simply fashionable ennui. Notably, in all three cases the end result is death rather than cure. Carey's treatment of these characters ensures that they are more realistic than the invalids portrayed in, for example, the novels of Charlotte Yonge. In Yonge's novel *The Clever Woman of the Family* it is said of the invalid, Ermine, 'No burthen is a burthen when one has carried it to her'; similarly, in

38 Andrew Blake, *Reading Victorian Fiction* (London: Macmillan, 1989), p. 72. Blake had, to an extent, been anticipated by Ian Watt, who posited that a striking feature of the novel *per se* was 'a controlling moral intention'. See Ian Watt, *The Rise of the Novel* (Harmondsworth: Penguin, 1968), p. 136.

39 Quotation from Thomson and Steele 1899, p. 416, from the section 'Nervous Disease, or Nervousness.' The complaint is 'indefinite' and 'generally the product of weakness'. Carey's characters discussed in this section of the chapter conform more nearly to this diagnosis than to insanity proper as they cannot be easily classified according to the College of Physicians' categories of mania, melancholia, dementia, paralysis of the insane, idiocy and imbecility. (For details of these classifications, see Thomson and Steele 1899, p. 357.)

her best-seller *The Daisy Chain*, the bedridden Margaret is taxed with the petty cares of the entire household:

> orders to butcher and cook – Harry racing in to ask to take Tom to the river – Tom, who was to go when his lesson was done, coming in perpetually to try to repeat the same unhappy bit of *As in Proesenti*, each time in a worse whine ... enter a message about an oil-lamp, in the midst of which Mary burst in ...[40]

However, far from creating idealized portraits on this model, Carey shapes her characters according to the more unsentimental picture of female invalidity to be found in one of Yonge's non-fictional works, *Womankind.* Here Yonge freely admits that:

> The invalid of books, who lies on the sofa ready to do everything for everybody, and to hear every care and trouble, is an excellent ideal for the invalid herself ... But all invalids have not the free head and nerves, lively spirits, and unfailing temper, required for such a post to be easily fulfilled. Heads and nerves will be shaken and need silence, backs will be jarred by hasty or heavy steps ... attention will flag to the best devised amusement, and the young brothers and sisters will go off declaring that their patient is so cross there is no pleasing her ...[41]

Carey's depressive invalids do indeed lack the 'free head and nerves, lively spirit, and unfailing temper' of Yonge's ideal. Indeed, none of them even approximates Yonge's 'invalid of books'. Yet they play an equally important role in the plots of their respective novels. Far from being mere shades to be acted upon by others, they have minds of their own, albeit disturbed ones. Carey is also very explicit about the reasons for their illnesses. She deals in well-founded physical impairment and psychological damage rather than in gratuitous sensibility. The constant feeling of wretchedness experienced by Hatty, a character in *Our Bessie*, is both mental and physical in its origin:

> All Hatty's failures, her miserable derelictions of duty, her morbid self-accusations and nervous fancies [were] bred of a sickly body and over-anxious temperament ... (*OB*, p. 33)

Hatty also tortures herself with guilt about not living up to the feminine ideal of quiet fortitude and amiability (*OB*, p. 15). As she tells her sympathetic sister Bessie:

---

40 C.M. Yonge, *The Clever Woman of the Family* (London: Virago, 1985 [1865]), p. 43; *The Daisy Chain or Aspirations: A Family Chronicle* (London: Macmillan, 1920 [1856], p. 102.)

41 C.M. Yonge, *Womankind* (London: Mozley and Smith, 1877), p. 261.

> 'I am always irritating some one ... I can't think how any of you can love me. I often cry myself to sleep, to think how horrid and disagreeable I have been in the day. I make good resolutions then, but the next morning I am as bad as ever, and then I think it is no use trying any more. Last night Tom made me so unhappy that I could not say my prayers. (*OB*, p. 31)

Thus her 'sickly' body and her 'over-anxious' mind prey upon each other. Her lack of health makes it impossible for her to participate in the expected norms of good temper and womanly service to others, whilst her self-perceived failure to live up to the ideal makes her depressed. As a result, she experiences a high level of anxiety and a consequent lack of sleep. She thus becomes even more physically debilitated and the cycle of decline continues.

At first glance, it seems that Hatty is hardly the stuff that heroines are made of. Yet she serves a number of important functions in the novel. In descriptive terms, she is a species of Everywoman. She reflects the fact that society has its Hatties as well as its more healthy and amiable characters. The general reader may simply view her as a probable inhabitant of the Lambert household, but the young invalid reader is able to enjoy the basic narcissistic pleasure of seeing herself reflected in the text, even though the portrayal is mainly unfavourable. In addition, the latter is able to vicariously participate in the praise given to Hatty for her positive talents. For example, Hatty is an accomplished needlewoman and eager to put this talent at her family's disposal (*OB*, p. 62). Moreover, she is described by Bessie as 'the purest, humblest little soul breathing' (*OB*, p. 34).

However, Hatty really comes in to her own in the overtly didactic content of the novel. As has already been noted, *Our Bessie* was a religiously-orientated book aimed primarily at the young.[42] Hatty therefore provides not just a mirror-reflection for the invalid reader but an active role model for all readers. For, although she is an invalid, she has the same opportunity to achieve salvation as her more active sisters. The work involved may differ but the basic process is the same.[43] Hatty's sister Bessie advises her accordingly:

---

42 Serialized in *Girl's Own Paper* 1888–89, it was published in book form in 1891. A second reprint appeared in the Religious Tract Society's series The Carey Library for Girls. See Jane Crisp, *Rosa Nouchette Carey* (University of Queensland, 1989) (hereafter, RNC Bibliography), pp. 38–9.

43 See, for example, Agnes Giberne's evangelical tale for children, *Floss Silverthorne or The Master's Little Handmaid* (London: John J. Shaw, n.d. [this edn c. 1905–10]), p. 120. The delicate nine-year-old, Gerald,

> ... th[at] other little servant had gone early to his rest. It was not much that he could undertake, but he could manage just as much as his Master gave him to do ... He was only told, perhaps, to stand still, and hold a heavy taper, and let its light shine around. And he had bravely, smiling at his weariness. (p. 120)

> '... why don't you look upon your unhappy nature as your appointed cross, and just bear with yourself as much as you expect others to bear with you? ... Why don't you say to yourself "I am a poor, weak little creature, but my Creator knows that ... and He bears with me. I cannot get rid of my tiresome nature ... but my one prayer and my one effort shall be to prevent other people suffering through me"?'[44]

However, Hatty is the subject of another didactic discourse besides that of religion. Their father, Doctor Lambert, advises Bessie on the most judicious treatment for Hatty from within the medical discourse. Too much indulgence is not good for her:

> It is not ... in the power of any man living ... to give that poor child health; but we may help her a great deal by teaching her self-control. Half her misery proceeds from her own nervous fancies; if we can help her to overcome them, we shall do more for Hatty than if we petted and waited on her.' (*OB* p. 91)

Once again, the emphasis is upon the inculcation of self-control and once again there is an apparent appeal to Maudsley's 'wise development of the control of the will over the thoughts and feelings ... which makes strongly for sanity' (Maudsley 1874, p. 269). Yet Hatty is not merely constructed as a case for treatment. She is also depicted as capable of heroism and self-denial at the last. Her behaviour is not of the kind that wins worldly fame but she nevertheless lives up to an approved nineteenth-century ideal of everyday heroism. In the words of Charles Kingsley,

> true heroism must involve self-sacrifice. Those stories certainly involve it ... which the hearts ... of [even] the poorest and the most ignorant, have accepted instinctively as the highest form of moral beauty – the highest form and yet one possible to all ... For it is nobler far to do the most common-place duty in the household, or behind the counter, with a single eye to duty, simply because it must be done ... than to go out of your way to attempt a brilliant deed ... [A]ny man or woman who *will*, in any age and under any circumstances, *can* live the heroic life and exercise heroic influences.[45]

---

44 *OB*, p. 66. Carey seems to have paraphrased Charlotte Yonge's *Womankind* here, though Yonge writes of purely physical ill-health: 'If ill-health does set in ... the only way not to be a burthen to ourselves and all around is ... submission to His will and doing it, first accepting the cross and then thinking of it and oneself as little as possible' (p. 259).

The notion of metaphorically carrying a cross is biblical – see, for example, Luke 14:27 and James 1:12.

45 Charles Kingsley, 'Heroism' (1880) in Charles Kingsley, *Sanitary and Social Lectures and Essays* (London: Macmillan, 1892 [1880]), p. 233, p. 243, p. 250.

Thus, when Hatty gains a small victory over her 'tiresome nature', this is as important morally as a general's victory on a battlefield. Bessie is away visiting a friend when Hatty enters into her final illness but Hatty will not have her recalled until absolutely necessary. She tells Bessie:

> '... of course I wanted you ... and that's just why I would not let them send. You know how unhappy I have always been because of my horrid selfishness, and I did want to be good for once, and I said to myself ... "Bessie shall not know how poorly I feel ... she shall be happy a little longer."' (*OB*, pp. 177–8)

However, Hatty does not merely deny herself in order to prolong her sister's enjoyment. Later she tells Bessie:

> "I am glad you went away and gave me something to bear ... it was something to do for you and something to bear for His sake." And Hatty dropped her voice reverently, for she was speaking of the Lord Jesus. (*OB*, p. 181)

Thus, through her self-denial, Hatty becomes a true Christian as well as a heroine. In terms of the pleasure to be gained from the text, if the socially unimportant and unproductive Hatty can become a Christian heroine, then this becomes a possibility for the invalid in the real world. Moreover, as a paradigm for identification, Hatty is within the realms of credibility because her heroism has its limits. Hatty's capacity for Christian fortitude and self-denial is, appropriately enough, curtailed by a happy and religiously-conceived death.

Yet if the narcissistic reader takes the dying Hatty as her model, the religiously-orientated consolations are actually twofold. Certainly she can share Hatty's certainty about the rewards of religion beyond the grave; however, extra enjoyment is to be had from sharing the religiously-motivated attention of Hatty's family. For, as one who is on the brink of eternity, Hatty is seen to represent to her family a direct interface with the Divine. Correspondingly, she becomes, in the period immediately before her death, a dispenser of wisdom rather than its recipient. Even the more ideal Bessie is made to say to her, 'It does me good to hear you' (*OB*, p. 182). Nor does Hatty's significance as medium between earth and Heaven subsequently diminish. For her death is permitted to cancel out the failures of her life. Once again it is Bessie who positions Hatty as one who is worthy of reverence:

> 'People are very proud when their relatives achieve any worldly honour or attain to any rank, yet no one seems to feel an added dignity when any dear one has finished his or her earthly conflict most gloriously, and has won a heavenly crown ... Somehow, it seems such an honour to me to

> feel that I have a sister as well as a brother in heaven; it makes one more careful not to do anything unworthy of them.'[46]

Thus the pleasures to be gained from identifying with even such an unpromising character as the physically and mentally tried Hatty are complex and, if analysed closely, contradictory. The reader can be at once bad-tempered and justified in being so; the centre of attention and satisfied in her own humility; and a thorn in people's flesh in life but assured of canonization after death. To sum up Carey's didactic methods here, it seems as though appeal is made simultaneously to personal vanity and to its exact opposite.

A character who is portrayed as having more to bear psychologically than Hatty is Belle in *Robert Ord's Atonement* (1873). Never actually described as insane, she attracts the epithets 'preoccupied' and 'failed ... in cheerfulness'. She is also unusually secretive, 'either evading ... questions or answering them with grave reserve' (*ROA*, p. 60). In her case, these mental characteristics are established before there is any indication of her physical decline. However, as with Hatty, the two factors are interactive. In the second half of the novel, the narrator comments upon 'the overwrought mind and body, reacting on each other so lamentably.' and Belle's brother-in-law is made to say that 'her mind is harassing her body, and both are alike sick' (*ROA*, p. 262; p. 379).

The key factors in Belle's illnesses, mental and physical, are her unhappy engagement, her lack of a definite role in life and a virulent form of consumption that is eventually fatal. Belle's history is that of a woman almost literally killed by inactivity and by the offices of a male tormentor. At the beginning of the novel she has been engaged to the eponymous hero for four years but, due to lack of means, there is no immediate prospect of them being married. Belle therefore lives with her sister Mary, who is married to Robert's elder brother, Austin:

> for [Robert's] sake [Belle] had renounced a project she had secretly cherished for securing her own independence, and, at his expressed wish, consented reluctantly to be a burden on her brother-in-law. (*ROA*, p. 79)

Even so, Belle is aware that she would have been mentally healthier had she been permitted to take up some form of remunerative work (*ROA*, pp. 413–14). She is treated kindly by the elder Ords but her position is far from easy. Robert

---

46 *OB*, p. 199. Cf also Ethel's sister Ella in Rosa Carey, *Heriot's Choice* (London: Macmillan, 1899 [1879]), p. 131. Ethel, whose baby sister has died many years before explains,

> '... I thought of Ella growing up in heaven ... schooled by angels ... and so strong was this belief, that when I was naughty or had given way to temper, I would cry myself to sleep, thinking that Ella would be disappointed in me ... [T]his childish thought has been my safeguard in many an hour of temptation.'

> would let both Austin and Mary know sometimes how it galled his pride to see his future wife dependent on their hands. He used to tell Belle so over and over again. It did not make her position more comfortable. (*ROA*, p. 60)

The reader is thus not surprised to learn that:

> There were times when Belle could almost have prayed to have loved Robert Ord less, that his troubles should not have so darkened her life to the exclusion of her own, but she never told him so. (*ROA*, p. 79)

The result is that she internalizes her own feelings and re-presents them as a series of psychological symptoms such as paranoia and inability to sleep and, implicitly, through progressive physical debilitation. In creating Belle, Carey may have had in mind Charlotte Yonge's expressed thoughts on the pernicious effects of a lack of gainful occupation:

> apart from the desire for usefulness, far more happiness is laid up for after years by a person who occupies her mind than by one who merely devotes herself to the pleasures of youth. Distresses, illness, nervous miseries, tedium, all may be mitigated by the power of being interested in some intellectual pursuit. (*Womankind*, p. 83)

It is not that Belle is addicted to pleasure or even that she neglects her duties in her brother-in-law's parish; rather it is that she has insufficient to occupy her mind in order to distract her from an untenable situation.

Belle's physical illness is interesting. The reader is left in little doubt as to its nature: the breathlessness and the pain; the hectic flush that makes its appearance in the evenings; her vain attempts to disguise her ashen cheeks with rouge at other times; the hard dry cough and the loss of weight; all symptoms indicate an advanced state of consumption rather than mere hysteria. Yet the illness is not named until very late in the novel. Until its presence is formally disclosed, the reader must rely on more oblique references. For example, the following passage appears in the eighth of the forty-two chapters:

> Lately the shadow of a fresh trouble had oppressed [Belle], and was making her nights dreary ... it never occurred to her to seek relief by imparting her fears. And so ... the strain on her harassed nerves had been aggravated by want of sleep and mental distress.
>
> Nor was it a mere shadowy foreboding of evil that was robbing her cheek of its bloom and depriving her of flesh. The thing, whatever it might be, was assuming tangible shape and reality. In the daytime she would rate herself for her cowardice, and would succeed in regarding it as purely imaginary … But at night she had no such relief; she would

> cower away from it with real terror and a real belief that made her nights dreadful to her. (*ROA*, pp. 77–8)

The formal clinical diagnosis is only given in chapter 33 and she dies in chapter 37.

By focusing primarily upon the psychological aspects of Belle's condition for most of the novel, Carey manages to frame her as a sentimental heroine; one who is pining away under the weight of inner mental conflict rather than through the ravages of physical disease. Whether Carey introduced the physical disease to deflect criticism from her use of the melodramatic device of maidenly decline or whether she actually believed that mental dis-ease could produce or aggravate serious physical disease is a moot point. Certainly when Mary interprets the words of Belle's doctor, it seems that the latter is the case:

> 'all this strain and anxiety has been killing her … if it had gone on – this concealment and strain, I suppose he meant – she could not have lasted three months' (*ROA*, pp. 370–71).

Mary's artlessness in 'suppos[ing]' what the doctor meant by 'if it had gone on' opens a space in which the reader can generate her own meaning for the words. Belle has indeed been concealing severe physical pain and a desperate fear of dying. However, as importantly, she has been concealing her purely psychological agonies of humiliating dependency and her feelings of social failure on account of her endless engagement.[47]

Of equal interest is the contrast between the portrayal of Belle's psychological state and that of Robert. For what is explained as illness in her is simply described as frustration with regard to pecuniary circumstances in him. This is even though he attracts some weighty alienist terminology in his own right. Robert has been disinherited by the wealthy aunt who brought him up and so is obliged to take a low-paid clerkship, though this is beneath both his dignity and his original expectations. Equally galling to him is the fact that his aunt's former paid companion inherits the whole estate with the proviso that she live in the same town as Robert and his family. Yet his obsessive hatred of the heiress, Rotha Maturin, seems to be out of all proportion to her supposed crime of having influenced her employer to make a will in her own favour. Even when other members of the Ord family are convinced of Rotha's innocence, Robert is not. In his obsession, he even refuses Rotha's offer to pay

47 The journalist W. R. Greg's article, 'Why Are Women Redundant?', which appeared in the *National Review* in 1862, embodies the contemporary belief that unmarried women were somehow failures. He deemed that those 'not having the natural duties of wives and mothers' had to 'carve out artificial and painfully sought occupations for themselves' rather than 'completing, sweetening and embellishing the existence of others'. Cited in Mary Poovey, *Uneven Developments* (University of Chicago Press, 1988), p. 1.

for life-saving medical treatment for Belle because he will not tolerate the burden of obligation. Yet, ironically, it is he and not his victim who is made to muse upon the notion that he might be literally going mad:

> Sometimes in the dead of night he would start up and ask himself ... was it a mistake – a morbid fancy? He had heard that dwelling on a single thought creates monomania; had his brain become diseased with brooding over his wrongs?[48]

When most other characters speak to him or of him, they use the alienist idiom metaphorically, thereby negating any suggestion of insanity. For example, Rotha immediately converts a speech by Robert, which is disturbing if taken at face value, into something more reassuring for all concerned:

> 'Why do you look at me like this, Miss Maturin? Do you think I am mad to-night?'
>
> 'I think you are,' she returned softly. 'God help you! Mad with pain and disappointment and remorse ...' (*ROA*, p. 373)

In other words, Rotha colludes with the man who has been so unjust to her, in order to maintain a fiction of his normality. Yet in spite of the language used to define him, the nearest Robert gets to a formally diagnosed mental illness is when he exhibits the early symptoms of brain fever.[49]

Little is said amongst the Ord family about Robert's hatred of Rotha but, sane or insane, his assumed right to take his ill temper out on Belle does not go completely unchallenged. Mary in particular is made to criticize him for further undermining Belle's precarious psychological state:

---

48 *ROA*, pp. 224–5. Clinically speaking, 'Monomania consists of firmly held but false beliefs. In contemporary terms, they would be called delusions.' (Skultans 1975, p. 6.) However James Cowell Prichard, writing in 1847, details conflicting beliefs about the condition in the nineteenth century:

> Monomania is the name by which physicians now designate the disorder ... termed partial insanity ... [However, n]othing ... can be more remote from the truth than the opinion that madmen of this description have their whole disorder centred in, and restricted, to one delusive idea. One illusive notion or set of notions ... occupies his attention to the exclusion of almost all other subjects ... but careful enquiry will generally shew that his whole mind is diseased.

See J.C. Prichard, *On the Different Forms of Insanity in Relation to Jurisprudence* (London: Hippolyte Balliere, 1847), cited in Skultans 1975, p. 169. Carey's version of monomania seems to consist entirely of a single idea (not necessarily a delusion) which is perpetually on the mind of the sufferer.

49 *ROA*, p. 398. Robert's near attack of brain fever is attributed by Austin to the death of their brother Garton. However, the reader can once again posit an alternative interpretation. It may be seen as the culmination of his irrational hatred of Rotha. This latter interpretation is given some weight in that Robert is saved from full-blown brain fever by a visit from Rotha, who has long ago forgiven him.

> 'I don't see – I have never seen – that her engagement has brought her any happiness. The fact is this ... you do not study her enough. When she wants soothing, you excite her; you try her patience with your ill-humours. When she is at her brightest you depress her; and yet you have no patience with her little moods. In spite of your goodness, Robert, there is something selfish in your love ... You talk about her dependent position ... while all the time your pride is making her bread so bitter to her, she can hardly endure to swallow it.' (*ROA*, p. 175)

Thus, some kind of justice is done to Belle. That is to say, her mental state is not simply written off as due to gender, innate mental weakness or physical ill health. It is notable that Belle herself is the only character besides Robert to suggest that he is at all 'warped' without some kind of mitigating phrase or resort to metaphor. However, she is only permitted to speak out about her ill-fated engagement when she is near to death. What she says may be regarded in same light as a deathbed confession; it is the final opportunity to make an honest appraisal of her short but unhappy life:

> '... my beauty faded ... and he grew warped and weary, and then he began to misunderstand me and doubt my love; and at last it was all doubt and wretchedness ... I sometimes think I am not so much to blame after all; for if he had let me do what I wished – earn my own living, I mean – I should not have lived all those years dwelling on one idea, and growing morbid over my very love ...' (*ROA* pp. 413–14)

A number of alienist terms are reiterated here: 'warped ... dwelling on one idea (monomania) ... morbid'. Implicitly, Belle is saying that the engagement has made them both mad. Significantly, she does not take all the blame upon herself. Unfortunately, this positive statement on the part of a hitherto passive character can hardly called a victory for Belle. She cannot utilize the understanding she has gained because she dies within two days of its utterance. Carey thus seems aware of the problems that a young woman in Belle's position might experience but is unwilling to let her character live on to work out a solution. Perhaps death is the most eloquent statement of all; perhaps observation without didactic or even feminist comment is more powerful than any overt protest. Carey's portrayal of the fictitious Belle constitutes in itself a powerful social commentary on the negative authority of the male and the stultifying effect of Mrs Grundy.

However, as Jane Crisp points out, it is Mrs Haldane, the mother in *But Men Must Work* (1892), who takes the internalized notion of helplessness to its absolute limit. This woman

> retreats from a suspected murder within the family and the attendant disgrace into a death-like semi-comatose state from which she never

> emerges, thus taking as it were woman's forced inaction to its logical extreme – significantly, it is not her daughters but the two men who love them who take the action necessary to solve the case and release them from their self-enforced seclusion. (*RNC Biography*, p. 21)

For the mother, the eventual happy reversal of circumstances comes too late. She enjoys no earthly consolation and her 'recovery' is couched in the biblical terms of her being, after death, 'sitting, clothed and in her right mind, at her Master's feet'.[50] Possessed of a single sensational plot and devoid of the attention to detail to be found in Carey's other novels, *But Men Must Work* nevertheless foregrounds the domestic circumstances of its main female characters. It is a sympathetic portrayal of an entire family under stress. The text emphasises the fact that all of the main protagonists have their burdens to bear, not just the invalid herself. Hence, the elder daughter has

> the hushed footstep and subdued voice of one who has long ministered to a nervous invalid ... look[s] ... wan and delicate ... her eyes somewhat sunken; and ... there [a]re dark lines under them … (*BMMW*, pp. 45–6)

Meanwhile, the younger daughter is made to say that 'It is a very distressing form of illness ... for it affects other people's lives so much.', fretting that her sister is 'growing gray at six-and-twenty … All this nursing and shut-up life is killing her' (ibid., p. 43; p. 47) Jane Crisp, writing in more general terms about the mentally unbalanced characters in Carey's novels, suggests that they can be interpreted from a modern perspective as

> the casualties of middle-class Victorian patriarchal values – values that their author may not question, but the cost of subscribing to which she frequently seems all too well aware of. (*RNC, Bibliography*, p. 20)

To this we might add that not all victims are on the official casualty list.

Conclusion

The only two characters who appear to be certifiable in Carey's novels are Mrs Haldane in *But Men Must Work* and Cousin Everhard in *Cousin Mona*; and only the latter has a physiologically delimited condition: 'softening of the brain'.[51] However, the entire range of non-certifiable mental illnesses seems to be covered in the course of Carey's writing. That several texts contain more

50 R.N. Carey, *But Men Must Work* (London: Richard Bentley and Son, 1892) p. 182 (hereafter, *BMMW*). See also Luke 8:35.

51 R.N. Carey, *Cousin Mona* (London: Religious Tract Society, 1897 [1895]), p. 192.

than one victim of mental illness is especially interesting. In *Wee Wifie* there are to be found a victim of hereditary insanity, a woman whose uncontrollable temper leads her to blind a man, and a man who suffers from acute brain fever on account of his wilfulness and lack of Christian resignation. Similarly, *Our Bessie* contains one character who lacks sanity due to her poor upbringing and another whose mental imbalance is due to ill health. In *Robert Ord's Atonement* a woman is driven into a morbid condition by a man whose own behaviour is far from normal; whilst in *Uncle Max* the warped Etta persecutes the already mentally frail Gladys and they have an equally unbalanced poorer neighbour. It is possible that, by including such characters, Carey was simply reflecting and endorsing the opinion of the alienist Andrew Wynter regarding the prevalence of poor mental health. The latter argues that:

> When we remember the number of persons in the country whose insanity is undoubted ... there must be a very large number of individuals who inherit either the disease direct, or are saturated with the seeds of nervous disorders, which only require some exciting cause to force them into vigorous growth ...[52]

It might also be conjectured that Carey shared something of Henry Maudsley's anxiety about how little of the misery of mental illness could be prevented or remedied. After all, in his book *Responsibility in Mental Disease*, Maudsley depressingly states that, in most cases, neither prophylaxis nor cure is possible:

> [The sufferer's] character, developed as it has been, will not assimilate advice that is counter to its affinities. We cannot efface the work of years of growth, cannot undo his mental organisation, and it is borne in upon us that advice, if it was to do any good, should have guided the direction of education. (Maudsley 1874, p. 275)

Nevertheless, Carey's outlook is a little less bleak. For, where Maudsley suggests that even a proper education cannot prevent or cure poor mental health, the rhetoric of her novels is at variance with this assumption. Maudsley states that:

> Education can plainly act only ... within the conditions imposed by the species, and within the conditions imposed by the individual organization: can only ... determine what is predetermined in the organization of the nervous system and of the bodily machinery in connexion with it ... (Ibid., p. 20.)

---

52 Andrew Wynter, *The Borderlands of Insanity* (London: Robert Hardwicke, 1875), pp. 45–6. Cited in Skultans 1975, p. 214.

By comparison, Carey not only aligns specific forms of training with good mental health but also insists that at least some re-education of the poorly-trained individual is possible. It seems that, rather than dwelling exclusively – or even extensively – upon the issue of hereditary physiological weakness, Carey enthusiastically embraces Maudsley's one small concession to the power of the human will. For, in spite of his pessimism, Maudsley ultimately admits that, by painful and relentless effort, character can change:

> No one can resolve successfully by a mere effort of will to think in a certain way, or to feel in a certain way, or even, which is easier, to act in accordance with certain rules; but he can ... imperceptibly modify his character: he can ... by calling external circumstances to his aid, learn to withdraw his mind from one train of thought and feeling, the activity of which will then subside, and can direct it to another train of thought and feeling, which will thereupon become active, and so by constant watchfulness over himself and by habitual exercise of will in the required direction, bring about insensibly the formation of such a habit of thought, feeling and action as he may wish to attain unto. He can make his character grow by degrees to the ideal which he sets before himself.[53]

Yet, to encounter what may be taken as a recognizable alienist discourse in Carey's novels is not to encounter Carey's approach to mental illness in its entirety. For there seems to be an inherent contradiction in the way in which she approaches her unbalanced characters. On the one hand, the novels appear to countenance only conduct that is commensurate with creating and maintaining sanity through self-control; on the other, with two exceptions, the ill-advised, the faithless and the maladjusted are dealt with sympathetically. Nor is Carey consistent in her application of the alienist discourse *per se*. Her appropriation of this register of language is neither wholly literal nor wholly metaphorical. Rather, it seems, she uses the vocabulary creatively in order to establish a conceptual framework that cannot be articulated by any other means. It seems that, interesting though diagnoses of abnormal mental conditions could be, her interest was in sketching the diverse behaviours and motivations of all character types, both normal and abnormal.

She certainly possessed a more general interest in matters of the psche than the heavily-used alienist discourse to be found in her novels initially suggests. In an interview with the journalist Helen Black, published in 1893, Carey lists her favourite books as:

> *Amiel's Journal*, Currer Bell's works, George Eliot's, and biographies; also psychological works, the study of mind and character[54]

53 Maudsley 1874, p. 273.

54 Helen C. Black, *Notable Women Authors of the Day* (London: Maclaren, 1906 [1st edn. 1893; original article in the *Ladies' Pictorial* c. 1891]), p. 155.

Both the specified fictional works and the unnamed biographies indicate an interest in personal motivation whilst *Amiel's Journal* is, quite literally, a man's diary. It, too, focuses upon its author's mental, as opposed to physical, life.[55] The 'psychological works' suggest similar preoccupations. However, this list is puzzling in that it does not explicitly mention alienist texts at all, even though the discourses in Carey's novels suggest that they should be present. The only category in which they might be included is that of 'psychological works'. Yet, if the writings of people like Maudsley are indeed included here, Carey's decision to use the word 'psychological' to describe them would seem to imply a specific agenda. For the word 'psychiatry' was to be found in ordinary dictionaries from at least the late 1870s.

Both terms are listed in the *Nuttall's Pronouncing English Dictionary* [1879], the word 'psychiatry' being defined as, 'Medical treatment of diseases of the mind.' By comparison, 'psychology' is deemed to include 'The doctrine of the soul or mind; a treatise on the soul; mental philosophy; [and] metaphysics.' It is easy to see from these definitions why the latter cluster of synonyms might have appealed to the religiously devout Carey more than the clinical term. For the word 'psychological' posits a version of the human psyche which is far more than a potential medical problem.

Upon this evidence, it may be conjectured that, though Carey was indeed interested in things medical, she was rather more interested in viewing the individual as a Christian soul; as a subject for salvation first and for treatment next. Yet, by combining a religious framework with notions of moral management in her fiction, Carey seems to have given a new dimension to each. Religion attracts an additional air of pragmatism whilst physiologically-based medicine regains its soul. Perhaps this is Carey's ultimate reply to Maudsley's pessimism: effort of will alone cannot secure sanity; however, individual effort enhanced by Divine Help is sure to bring about mental and spiritual peace on earth as well as salvation for eternity.

55 Henri-Frederic Amiel, *Amiel's Journal,* ed./trans. Mrs Humphrey Ward (London: Macmillan, 1901 [Vol. 1, 1882; Vol. 2, 1884; trans. 1885]). Carey quotes from it in at least two of her novels: *Our Bessie* [1888–89] and *Basil Lyndhurst* [1889].

Chapter 2

Maiden Ladies

Spinster of this Parish

> [Tina's mother] wondered ... whether the invitation was the outcome of politeness or whether it meant – *Tina*. But Tina, alas ... was getting perilously near to that age when a feminine creature who has been called a girl by courtesy for a long time suddenly develops into a woman of a certain age ... It was borne in upon her reluctant mind ... that it was useless to speculate any longer about Tina's future. Tina's future was fairly well assured, or, at least settled. It would be a future with a modest income, a house shared with her elder sister; she knew positively for the first time that Tina had overshot her mark, a fatal impediment to what may be called the turn-over of business. Poor Mrs. Mornington-Brown! ... There must come moments in such lives when the chief thought is the wild wish that they had brought up their daughters to some other profession than that of marrying. Everybody cannot marry ...
> (John Strange Winter, *A Magnificent Young Man*, 1896)[1]

The fictional Tina Mordington-Brown is a woman with many problems. Not least amongst these are the depressing facts that she has failed to ensnare a husband and that she has reached the age at which she is unlikely to attract one. As a result, mother is unhappy. But then, as the passage concludes, 'Everybody cannot marry.' However, her final humiliation is that her story is told by a smug narrator whose apparent sympathy for her plight is more than a little tinged with spiteful amusement.

Tina's fictional experience of single blessedness reflects the real-life experience of many Victorian and Edwardian women: like her, they were obliged to survive in a society where '[e]verybody c[ould] not marry'; and like her they were the object of embarrassment or amusement because of a situation over which they had little control. For, throughout the Victorian era, there was

1 John Strange Winter [Mrs Arthur Stannard], *A Magnificent Young Man* (London: F. V. White, 1896), p. 73. Cf. 'Queen bees or working bees', *Saturday Review*, 12 November 1859: 'Married life is a woman's profession; and to this life her training... is modelled. Of course by not getting a husband, or losing him, she may find that she is without resources. All that can be said of her is, she has failed in business', cited in Patricia Hollis, *Women in Public: The Women's Movement 1850-1900* (London: George Allen and Unwin, 1979), p. 11 (hereafter, Hollis 1979).

a significant gender imbalance in the population as a whole; an imbalance which became more marked as the century progressed. As the numerical excess was in terms of women, it meant that between an eighth and a quarter of all women would never marry.[2] However, unlike the fictional Tina, few of these unmarried women could count upon 'a future with a modest income'. Nor was it always economically viable for them to remain remuneratively unproductive within a family home, even if one were available.

The demographic phenomenon of significantly more females than males was over two centuries old by the time the Victorians began to designate these supposedly 'redundant' women a problem. However, the censuses dating from 1851 made the imbalance strikingly quantifiable.[3] With or without statistics, the phenomenon was indeed a problem to all concerned, though not all viewed it from the same perspective. For many of the single women themselves, the anxiety rested in questions of survival. Even amongst the few who managed to obtain professional status in their employment, life was hard. A governess might earn as little as £20 per year and be forcibly retired at any age from thirty-five to fifty-five, with nothing to look forward to but years of penury.[4] However, for those who were not part of the 'problem', the perplexity was in how to deal with an embarrassing surplus of non-wives who did not fit into a society that almost exclusively valued marriage and maternity. As the popular author Dinah Mulock Craik saw it, the married woman had 'realised to a greater or lesser degree the natural destiny of our sex' but the confirmed spinster necessarily lived in 'an unnatural condition of being'.[5] Other writers defined the problem and then moved on to suggest radical solutions.

In a blatantly androcentric article bearing the proleptic title 'Why Are Women Redundant?', W.R. Greg openly condemned single women who were obliged to 'earn their own living instead of spending ... the earnings of men', suggesting that those 'not having the natural duties of wives and mothers' had

---

2 For statistics on single women, see Hollis 1979, p. 33; Martha Vicinus, *Independent Women: Work and Community for Single Women 1850–1920* (London: Virago, 1985), p. 26 (hereafter, Vicinus 1985); Jalland 1986, pp. 254–5; Sheila Jeffreys, *The Spinster and Her Enemies* (London: Pandora, 1985), p. 86 (hereafter, Jeffreys 1985); Mary Poovey, *Uneven Developments* (London: Virago, 1989), p. 4 (hereafter, Poovey 1989).

3 Pat Jalland, *Women, Marriage and Politics 1860–1914*, (Oxford: The Clarendon Press, 1986), p. 254 (hereafter, Jalland 1986).

4 Vicinus 1985, p. 25; see also 'The Governess Question', *English Woman's Journal*, November 1860, cited in Hollis 1979, p. 90.

5 *A Woman's Thoughts About Women* [1858], in Elaine Showalter (ed.), *Christina Rossetti: 'Maude', Dinah Mulock Craik: 'On Sisterhoods' and 'A Woman's Thoughts About Women'* (London: Pickering Women's Classics, Pickering and Chatto, 1993). (Hereafter, *WTAW*). Quotations from p. 63. Craik addresses 'the single women, belonging to those supernumerary ranks, which, political economists tell us, are yearly increasing' (ibid.). Initially serialized in *Chambers Journal*, the book was frequently reissued throughout the nineteenth century.

an unbearable vacancy in their lives. Greg assumed that such women were obliged to 'carve out artificial and painfully sought occupations for themselves' rather than 'completing, sweetening and embellishing the existence of others'. Thus, in his view, the 'redundant' woman was an unhappy creature, one who was 'compelled to lead an independent and incomplete existence'.[6] His solution was to 'remove five hundred thousand women from the mother country ... to the colonies', in order to provide wives for male emigrants.[7]

Yet Greg was not merely viewing the 'problem' from an egotistical and non-participatory point of view. He was also making a statement about the mechanisms of society as a whole. As Mary Poovey observes:

> When Greg argues that unmarried women constitute the problem to be solved, he not only mobilises assumptions about women; he also alludes to an entire social organisation that depends upon naturalising monogamous marriage, a sexual division of labour, and a specific economic relation between the sexes in which men earn and women 'spend' ... the earnings of men. (Poovey 1989, p. 2)

That exponents of the 'social organisation' in question were prepared to go to extraordinary lengths in order to maintain the *status quo* is strikingly illustrated by the historically-authenticated case of Edith Lanchester. When, in 1895, she opted to cohabit with a man from a lower social grouping than her own, her father and brothers kidnapped her and placed her in a lunatic asylum. Though released by the Lunacy Commissioners five days later, she had been formally certified, the cause of her insanity being diagnosed as 'over-education'. The physician who signed the certificate, G. Fielding Blandford, later explained that he adjudged her insane because 'he believed that her opposition to conventional matrimony made her unfit to care for herself'.[8] Yet even such visible evidence of the power of patriarchy was insufficient to prevent middle-class women from seeking alternatives to the proffered (and proscribed) paradigms of normative wifehood or less well-defined though emphatically marginalized spinsterhood.

The preoccupation of society with the redundant women 'problem', the desire of single women to gain an authentic existence, and the response of an existent patriarchal establishment to these perceived challenges are concerns expressed at length in the literature of the day. Etiquette books, medical treatises, devotional handbooks and the periodical press are full of conflicting views about what was regarded as a crisis situation. However, the complexity

6 Cited in Mary Poovey, *Uneven Developments*, p. 1.

7 Poovey 1989, p. 5.

8 Elaine Showalter, *The Female Malady* (London: Virago, 1991), pp. 146–7; Charlotte MacKenzie, *Psychiatry for the Rich: A History of Ticehurst Private Asylum* (London: Routledge, 1992), p. 208.

of the debate about the position of single women within society is also accessible through the medium of fiction, and few novelists of the period position themselves within the debate without reproducing viable alternatives to their own point of view.

Yet in spite of this spirit of open discussion, one factor remained more or less unexamined: that of class. To focus upon the novels of Rosa Carey in particular, the domestic servants and deserving poor who fill her pages do not function significantly as individuals and the author seldom discusses their duties or their conditions of work. They are, on the whole, either plot-functional in terms of verisimilitude or illustrative of the quasi-maternal or philanthropic 'instincts' of their 'betters'. For example Rotha, in Carey's novel *Robert Ord's Atonement* [1873], works with her maids to make clothes for the poor; whilst Ellison in *The Mistress of Brae Farm* [1896] supervises her maids' morals, marriages and free time. Indeed, in certain respects it seems that Carey's female servants are not even regarded as 'working women'. Conservative in their behaviour and, most often, devout in their religious practice, they are also entirely incorporated into domestic establishments; they are the fabric rather than the ethos of the domestic sphere. More completely than any other characters from the 'lower orders', they take upon themselves the middle-class ideal of the domestic whilst at the same time knowing their place and earning their keep. Thus they are omnipresent but comfortably invisible. However, many members of the Victorian middle classes appear to have viewed (or ignored) domestic servants in this way. W.R. Greg, in the article cited above, both praises and dismisses them simply because they fulfil their 'natural' female functions:

> they are fully and usefully employed; they discharge a most important and indispensable function in social life; they do not follow an obligatory independent, and therefore for their sex an unnatural, career:– on the contrary, they ... fulfil both essentials of a woman's being: *they are supported by, and they administer to*, men ... Nature has not provided one too many ... and scarcely any portion of their sex is more useful or more worthy. (Emphasis original)[9]

Nor was Carey at all unusual in focusing upon the concerns of the middle classes in her novels. For, to quote Malcolm Bradbury, the novel *per se* may be 'identified with the social eminence of its main reading public, the bourgeoisie'.[10]

---

9 Hollis 1979, pp. 11–12. See also Vicinus 1985, pp. 3–4.

10 Malcolm Bradbury, 'Novel', in *A Dictionary of Critical Terms*, ed. R. Fowler, (London: Routledge, 1991), p. 163 (hereafter, Fowler 1991). However, he qualifies this definition, suggesting that it is apt for the nineteenth-century realist novel but problematic for later works.

This middle-class focus being the case, the matter of remunerative employment, or even gainful occupation, takes on a rather different complexion than it would otherwise. For the majority of working-class women, remunerative work and the obligation to be self-reliant were burdens to be lived with rather than privileges to be fought for. To quote a Fabian tract published in 1914, the working-class woman demanded 'not independence and the right to work, but rather protection against the unending toil which ha[d] been laid upon her.'[11] Conversely, the dominant middle-class ideal, for the nineteenth century and beyond, was that women should not undertake any form of remunerative work or any kind of employment that removed them from the domestic sphere unless absolutely necessary.[12] In keeping with the latter ideal, Carey often portrays the impecunious 'lady' wage-earner as unfortunate rather than as independent.[13]

Yet Carey was more sympathetic than many of her contemporaries towards more prosperous middle-class women who sought remunerative employment or extra-domestic stimulus. From a late twenty-first-century perspective at least, she certainly compares favourably with Charlotte Yonge.[14] The latter's novel, *The Clever Woman of the Family* [1865], begins promisingly enough with the

---

11 M.A., 'The Economic Foundations of the Women's Movement', *Fabian Tract No. 175*, 1914, cited in Hollis 1979, p. 335 (section 10.1).

12 The boundary between the domestic sphere of the home and the public sphere of remunerative work is difficult to locate. Philanthropy Sunday school teaching and professional nursing necessarily took place outside the home. However, they were regarded as employments suited to women's 'natural' abilities. As Ruskin comments in *Sesame and Lilies* (London: George Allen, 1906 [1865]) (hereafter, *SL*): 'a woman has a personal work or duty, relating to her home, and a public work or duty, which is the expansion of that' (*SL*, p. 130). As early as 1877, Charlotte Yonge was writing about women's work without enthusiasm but apparently without condemnation either:

> And for the young who need support, it would be well, if they have no special talent, to try to learn to be telegraph clerks, or even dress-making, or whatever is possible in their station.
>
> "The Year Book of Women's Work" will point to the means of getting instruction and employment, and there is much less every year of the fear of losing caste by absolute labour.

C.M. Yonge, *Womankind* (London: Mozley and Smith, 1877), pp. 237–8 (hereafter, *Womankind*).

However, the qualifications, 'in their station' with regard to the type of employment and 'much less', added to the phrase 'fear of losing caste', indicate her ambivalence towards remunerative work. In addition, considering that *Womankind* is supposed to be about 'the duties and opportunities placed in the hands of her sex' (p. 1), Yonge allocates very little space to paid employment.

13 For example, the widowed Nea Trafford in *Wee Wifie* [1869] is deemed worthy of sympathy even though she manages to earn enough as daily governesses to maintain a modest home. Upon the marriage of her daughter to a wealthy man, she becomes 'leisured' but undertakes voluntary work in an orphanage.

14 Carey's novel-writing career spanned from 1868 to 1909; Yonge's from 1844 to 1901. They were therefore contemporaries for over thirty years.

heroine, Rachel, openly rebelling against the behavioural restrictions and limited expectations inherent in being a young lady:

> 'And here am I, able and willing, only longing to task myself to the uttermost, yet tethered down to the merest mockery of usefulness by conventionalities. I am a young lady forsooth! – I must not be out late; I must not put forth my views; I must not choose my acquaintance; I must be a mere helpless, useless being, growing old in a ridiculous fiction of prolonged childhood ... why? Is it for no better reason than because no mother can bear to believe her daughter no longer on the lists for matrimony?'[15]

However, Rachel's point of view is in turn undermined, ridiculed and censured before she is rehabilitated through marriage.[16] Yet Yonge did not object to the single state *per se* – she herself remained single – rather, she was strongly opposed to notions of female autonomy and sex-equality. Her views are expressed plainly as the hapless Rachel's faults of character are analysed:

> Many of her errors had ... arisen from want of some one whose superiority she could feel, and her old presumptions withered up to nothing when she measured her own powers with those of a highly educated man … Rachel having been more than usually removed from the influence of superior man, had been affected by the more feeble and distant power, a leading that appeared to her the light of her independent mind … (*CWF*, p. 337)

Initially, this passage appears simply to be a comment on Rachel's lack of educational opportunity, 'error' implying poor teaching and 'superiority' being genderless. However, further into the passage, the reader learns that Rachel is innately deficient; that women need 'the influence of superior man'.[17] Implicitly, an independent woman is a danger to herself and to others, or else she is simply ridiculous. Yet the most powerfully-rendered expression of Yonge's belief in female inferiority is to be found in the novel's almost confessional conclusion. Rachel herself is made to acknowledge the cardinal errors of her youth:

---

15 C.M. Yonge, *The Clever Woman of the Family* (London: Virago, 1985 [1865]), p. 3 (hereafter *CWF*).

16 Other rehabilitated subjects in Yonge's writing include Ethel May in *The Daisy Chain* [1856] who, with much self-denial, becomes a useful daughter and the self-styled Sister Mena in *Modern Broods* [1900], who submits herself to the discipline of a regular sisterhood and abandons the one she has herself started.

17 At its plainest, this belief is communicated in her non-fictional work *Womankind*, p. 2: 'I have no hesitation in declaring my full belief in the inferiority of woman, nor that she brought it upon herself.'

> 'I really do not think I was ever such a Clever Woman ... I should have been much better if I had had a father or brother to keep me in order.' (*CWF*, p. 367)

Many of Carey's heroines share with the fictional Rachel yearnings for other than the prescribed and proscribed life of a 'young lady' but they are not held up to such ridicule for their pains. Indeed, Cathy, in Carey's novel *Queenie's Whim* [1881], even articulates her dissatisfaction with life in terms analogous to those of Rachel:

> '... this little corner of the world stifles me; I get so tired of it all, the trying to be good and keep down my restlessness ... I do so object to be tamed down, and be made submissive to mere conventionality ... I want ... to have a life of my own to live, not tagged on to other people.'[18]

However, there are notable differences between the two characters as they are subsequently developed. Most importantly, Carey's Cathy makes a great success of the nursing work for which she leaves home, even though she does not have the wholehearted approval of the brother who stands *in loco parentis*. Another difference is that, when Cathy finally opts for marriage to the middle-aged vicar of her home village, it is out of self-knowledge and love for her future husband rather than from any experience of humiliation or failure. As she tells her friend Queenie on the last page of the novel,

> 'we poor women cannot escape our fate after all. I am tired of running away from myself and him, and pretending not to care for his liking me; so I just told him he must put up with me, faults and all, for I won't promise to mend; but if I am not the better for being with him– ' (*QW*, p. 477)

The end of the clause is left for the reader to fill in for herself. Thus, Cathy's 'confession' differs greatly from that of Rachel. Her only disclosure is that she loves her man too much to be apart from him. However, she has not only made her own decision, independently of external circumstances; she has also laid down the parameters of her expectations within the marriage. She has not promised to conform to the stereotype of the submissive wife but she does expect to grow within her marriage and to become a better person. In Carey's novel, one of the most powerless of women, a spinster with limited private means, is invested with not only success in her chosen work but also a real choice between a career and matrimony.

18 R.N. Carey, *Queenie's Whim* (London: Macmillan, 1898 [1881]), p. 251 (hereafter, *QW*).

Carey's fiction reflects society's preoccupation with the disproportionate number of single women in a number of ways. However, her novels seldom give the impression that there is such a person as a truly redundant woman. Significantly, not all of her eligible heroines marry. For example, the beautiful, rich and intelligent Ellison in *The Mistress of Brae Farm* does not consider matrimony until she is in her late twenties and ultimately never marries. Some single female characters, for example Frances in *No Friend Like a Sister* [1906], actively seek career alternatives; others, such as Elizabeth and Dinah in *Herb of Grace* [1901] enjoy their non-marital domestic circumstances. All of these characters provide positive role models for the reader. In addition, whilst Carey nominally adheres to the notion that women are better off if they have menfolk to keep, advise and protect them, the reader is not told that all other modes of life are 'incomplete'. Nor does Carey consistently represent marriage as an ideal state; indeed, many of her fictional marriages are far from successful. The ideal of 'completing, sweetening and embellishing' the lives of others may well be important to the characters in Carey's novels but she permits the reader to see that this work is not always successful or even possible.[19]

Carey appears to enter into dialogue with the male-dominated ideologies of the day, in part, at least, condoning the actions of the rebellious and deconstructing the myth of the domestic. There is nothing in the novels to suggest that she consciously wrote from a feminist perspective. However, one most certainly gains the impression that she felt obliged to valorise the spinster existence – even spinster existence outside the governance of 'superior man' – for she, like Charlotte Yonge, never married.

Part of a Domestic Establishment

In much Victorian and Edwardian fiction, representation of the ideal woman, whether single or married, is premised upon the twin notions of middle-class social mores and total identification with the domestic or private sphere. If a fictional woman is intended to be middle class, she fits into this mould; if she is not, then she is compared with the ideal and approved of or condemned according to the success of her attempts to emulate it. Thus, to take two examples from Carey's novels, the gauche 'lower-class' Australian, Nell, in *At The Moorings* [1904], not only fails to achieve acceptance but also causes her middle-class husband to lose caste. Conversely, in *The Household of Peter* [1905], the pleasant-mannered and restful ex-companion, Hannah Burke, who

19 However, she is under no illusions about the single state either. The eponymous heroine of *Averil* [1890–91] both finances and services her stepmother's family, but they are neither grateful nor co-operative.

is the daughter of a 'factory girl' and a carpenter, both marries well and mixes freely with members of her newly-acquired higher social class.

When Carey was writing, middle-class single women, both in fiction and in reality, were expected to live with their parents or, if this were not possible, in the home of a close relation such as a brother or married sister. However, due to the demographic imbalance between men and women, the heads of many households were actually female. This was usually deemed respectable, especially where an older woman provided chaperonage to any younger females or where a lone householder was deemed to be beyond marriageable age. However, as will be demonstrated, there was a general ambivalence towards households without adult men and this may even be detected in the novels of the pro-woman Rosa Carey.

Wherever they lived, single women were not expected to spend their time in remunerative work but they were expected to be 'useful' to both their families and their parishes. Carey's own life provides a concrete example of someone who, at least nominally, acted according to societal expectation. As Jane Crisp points out, such biographical details as are available 'present a fairly familiar picture for the times ... one that would not be out of place in her own novels'.[20] Carey always lived with close relatives: first with her parents, then with a brother, bringing up his motherless children. After his death and when the children had left home, she moved in with a married sister. When she finally set up her own establishment, at around the age of fifty, a recently widowed sister came to live with her. Notwithstanding her work as a professional writer, Carey also performed the requisite duties of a leisured single woman. For example, she was a Sunday school teacher for many years. However, even this important work was secondary to the needs of her large family. A journal article from about 1891 indicates how Carey was viewed by her close friend and house-mate, Helen Marion Burnside:

> 'She has so consistently lived her religion ... that family duty and devotion to its many members have always come first. She never hesitates for a moment to give up the most important professional work if she can do anything in the way of nursing or comforting any of them ... '[21]

Whether or not Burnside was telling the literal truth, the appropriate sentiments for the age had been expressed. Nor did Carey contradict her. Indeed, this ideal of womanly service for single women seems to have been fully endorsed by Carey in her fiction if we take into account the number of instances where a

---

20 Jane Crisp, *Rosa Nouchette Carey*, Victorian Fiction Research Guides 16 (Queensland: Victorian Fiction Research Unit, 1989), p. 2.

21 Helen C. Black, *Notable Women Authors of the Day*, (London: Maclaren, 1906 [1893]), pp. 153, 156.

sister or a daughter's entire life's work, certainly during the years when she might have been expected to consider marriage, is the maintenance of her family's comfort. For example, the officious Dora, in *Queenie's Whim*, for all her faults,

> fulfilled all her duties admirably. She married both her sisters ... and she soothed her father's declining years with the utmost dutifulness. When he was dead, and she was no longer young ... she married a wealthy widower ...[22]

However, in real life, large numbers of bereaved women were compelled to leave the parental home without moving on to the comparative security and status of marriage. Seeking a home with more distant kin was one option for the very young or those left in poor financial circumstances. Yet even if a family could afford to maintain an extra individual within the household, it was inevitable that relations sometimes became strained. For example, a young women who wrote to the *Girl's Own Paper* in 1896 evidently found herself at odds with her benefactor on the grounds of religious observance. It was the policy of the *Girl's Own Paper* not to publish letters from correspondents, but much may be deduced from the reply she received:

> We feel sorry for your present position, as your relative is endeavouring to upset your deceased parents' teaching and wishes. But you are still very young, and you are under her care; and it is your duty to conduct yourself humbly, and show respect for her, and endeavour not to aggravate her by saying all you think and acting as you feel ... True religion bears fruit in obedience, humility, respect to those who (in the Providence of God) are placed over you ...[23]

Such circumstances in real life are paralleled by the many depictions in literature of a 'poor relation', whose fictional dependence means frequent humiliation if not actual ill-treatment. Classic examples of such characters are to be found in Charlotte Bronte's *Jane Eyre*, and in Jane Austen's *Mansfield Park*. Carey's novels are unusual in that a new home with relatives is generally a haven of rest after an encounter with the hostile world.[24] For example, in *Averil* [1890–91], two young women who are destitute find shelter in the household of the eponymous heroine. Though it costs some effort for the frail

22 *QW*, p. 475. Cf. also Aunt Milly in *Heriot's Choice* [1877–79]; Lettice in *Mary St John* [1882]; and the eponymous heroine of *Cousin Mona* [1895].

23 'Answers to Correspondents', *Girl's Own Paper*, 7 November 1896, Vol. 18 [October 3 1896–September 25 1897], p. 96 (hereafter, title abbrieviated to *GOP*).

24 One major exception is Christian in *A Passage Perilous* [1903]. However, the book is primarily about her life after to her marriage.

Averil to prevent her stepmother from exploiting the first to arrive, Lottie, both are considerably better provided for than previously.[25]

The prior circumstances of the second arrival, nineteen-year-old Annette, are given in some detail and, in the process, the motivations behind Averil's offer to her of a home are made clear. Annette has been supporting herself by mending lace, but it is a subsistence income at best and the work does not permit her to fulfil the duties of her gender and class. At the outset of the novel, she is living unchaperoned in a French lodging house after the death of her mother. In spite of her poverty and her long residence in a foreign land, Annette knows what is appropriate to her English birth and breeding:

> '... it is dreary to walk in the dusk; besides, there are *les convenances* – what you would call the propriety – one would not willingly offend against that.'[26]

But this is the only overt reference to the subject of morality. Averil couches her reasons for taking Annette into her home in quite different terms:

> 'Tell her ... that my home is hers – that I am ready to welcome her as a sister ... it is my duty to befriend my cousin. What does it matter what she is like? It is enough for me that she is unhappy and desolate.'[27]

However, implicitly, there are three determining factors in Averil's decision: gentility (what is appropriate to class); philanthropy (what is owing to duty on the part of the benefactor); and respectability (considerations of youth and gender). In all, Averil's good will extends well beyond the dispassionate advice to householders in *Everybody's Book of Correct Conduct* [1893], that '**It is the correct thing** ... To be invariably civil to all dependents and servants'.[28]

Yet, in *Cousin Mona* [1897], Carey also represents sympathetically the problems which may be encountered by the well-meaning benefactor who, whilst aware of her/his duty and philanthropic enough to perform it, is not able to provide a suitable home for a destitute relative. In this book, the eponymous heroine provides eighteen-year-old Rufa with a home that is both genteel and

25 Lottie is Averil's step-mother's ward but Averil, as mistress of the household and financial provider, shelters Lottie from much of the stigma and work attached to being a poor relation.

26 R. N. Carey, *Averil* (London: Office of 'The Girl's Own Paper', n.d. [1890–91]), p. 36 (hereafter, *Averil*).

27 *Averil*, p. 15. Cf. also R.N. Carey, *The Mistress of Brae Farm* (London: Hodder and Stoughton, 1920 [1896]), p. 17, (hereafter, *TMOBF*), in which Ellison gives similar reasons for inviting a destitute cousin to live with her.

28 M.C., *Everybody's Book of Correct Conduct, Being the Etiquette of Every-day Life*, (Whitstable and Wallsall: Pryor Publications, 1996 [1893]), p. 90. Note the bracketing of dependents with servants.

respectable, but she can neither afford it financially nor provide a comfortable atmosphere in which to live. With the best of motives, Mona conceals from Rufa the real problem: that the brother who lives with her and who requires her constant attention, is slowly losing his mind. Thus, not understanding the real situation, the youthful Rufa thinks to herself, 'Neither of them wanted me … What distorted sense of duty had induced them to offer me this meagre and grudging hospitality?'[29]

However, towards the end of the book, Carey permits her fictional benefactor the right of reply. Once Rufa has discovered the truth about Cousin Everhard, Mona is free to explain her true motivations and feelings:

> 'More than once I sat down in my room and had a good cry about you. "How is that child ever to love me?" I would say to myself, "and how am I to look after Everhard and make her happy?" ... it is a dreary life for you to lead; I knew that when you came; but how was I to shut my door upon a homeless orphan? I said to myself that Providence had sent you here, and that it was one more duty …' (*CM*, p. 192)

To the fictional Mona, the necessity for sheltering the orphaned Rufa in a family home by far outweighs the unsuitability of the environment for a young woman of eighteen.[30]

Throughout Carey's novels, middle-class notions of propriety and duty are represented as a transparent discourse.[31] But if the twin ideals of single womanhood – accommodation in a suitable domestic establishment and adherence to middle-class social mores – remain applicable throughout, it in no way means that all female characters are made by Carey to respond to these ideals in a uniform way. As has already been noted, a large number of women, whether by fictional accident or design, live in all-female households. Their material circumstances vary too: some are wealthy whilst others live in penury; some women choose the single life, others do not have the personal attractions or the opportunities to attract a partner. Carey's forty-one novels suggest a similar proportion of spinsters to that found in the non-fictional world, so there is room for a great deal of variety.

---

29 R.N. Carey, *Cousin Mona* (London: Religious Tract Society, 1897 [1895]), p. 68 (Hereafter, *CM*).

30 In *The Old, Old Story* [1894], two penniless upper-middle-class orphans are offered a different kind of 'unsuitable' home. They are taken in by their aunt and uncle who are 'lower-class' shopkeepers. Whilst the reader is led to sympathize with both parties, most pity is given to the two young people who have lost status.

31 That is, as something that is self-evident or unmediated 'fact'; as if no discourse (meaning a register of language emanating from an institution), were present at all. Cf., for example, 'linguistic transparency', or 'a flawless mirror to the world' as a description of the realist novel. See Peter Mercer, 'Realism' in Fowler 1991, pp. 201–2.

The popular stereotype of the fussy or embittered 'old maid' with neither menfolk nor children is certainly present in Carey's writings but she is nearly always a minor character and nearly always has a foil in another single woman who has no such characteristics. The lonely Miss Bretherton in *The Mistress of Brae Farm* is in many ways a typical portrayal. Eccentric due to 'brain fever', occasioned by the death of her fiancé, her 'queer' temper leads to a second great disappointment in her life – that of failing to secure the affection of her young nephew, whom she wishes to adopt. She cannot forgive his childish rebellion and thus, by cutting off his entire family, spends her old age alone.[32] She has as her foil the energetic and intelligent Ellison who carries no grudges even though the poor relation to whom she gives a home wins the love of the man Ellison had hoped to marry.

However, both Miss Bretherton and Ellison are assertive in their manner and comfortably provided for in terms of this world's goods. The same cannot be said of the four spinster sisters to be to be found in *Queenie's Whim* (*QW*, p. 127). The eponymous Queenie, who is visiting their home village, initially receives the following tart explanation as to why none of the Misses Palmer has married:

> They have lived in Hepshaw all their lives; they could not possibly have met any gentlemen except the Vicar, and I daresay he was married. You would not have a lawyer's daughter commit the unpardonable crime of entering into a *mesalliance* with the innkeeper or the chemist ... ' (*QW* p. 115)

However, when Queenie ventures to say 'How very sad', her companion even more sharply replies: 'Not at all ... people are just as well without marrying. For my part, I think men are a mistake' (ibid.). The two speakers come to no synthesis of their points of view, they simply change the subject. Thus, the conversation is one of many in this particular text that the reader can interpret in her own way. Strictly speaking, the conversation is no advertisement for the single state. The first speaker, Cathy, is constructed as young, impetuous and impatient with convention (she also eventually marries). This would enable an older woman reader to disregard Cathy's speeches on account of her youth and lack of experience. However, Queenie's words may be equally easily disregarded as they are spoken with 'a girl's involuntary pity for the

32 *TMOBF*, p. 109. Oddly enough, many of Carey's elderly female characters who attempt to adopt children but who end up alienating their families and spending their last years alone are the long-widowed and childless, for example Mrs Hazeldean in *Nellie's Memories* [1868]; Mrs Ord in *Robert Ord's Atonement* [1873]; and Mrs Hartree in *At The Moorings* [1904]. However, they are represented in much the same way as unmarried women. Peevish older spinsters who antagonize others include Miss Faith in *Life's Trivial Round* [1899–1900], Miss Brookes in *Robert Ord's Atonement* and Prudence Palmer in *Queenie's Whim*.

monotonous existence of single blessedness' (Ibid.). Once again, a 'girl's' point of view may be seen as uninformed. Yet the two speakers embody two popular views of the single state and, indeed, they provide the starting point for a much longer textual dialogue on the subject.

Notwithstanding their impeccable, if dull, gentility, the Palmer sisters' lack of both gainful occupation and pecuniary means is very obvious. Of the four, the aptly-named Prudence has the unenviable task of '[holding] the purse-strings of the little household, and ... guard[ing] the proprieties' (*QW*, p. 145):

> Poor Miss Prudence! there was still a warm woman's heart beating under the harsh, unloving exterior, though it seldom found utterance. Her one object in life had been to eke out a narrow income, and bring down her own and her sisters' wants to the limits of penury ... the low standard had dwarfed her moral stature; petty cares had narrowed and contracted her ... yet ... Miss Prudence's faults were only caricatures of virtues. She was miserly, but it was for her sisters' sakes more than her own. To keep the little house bright and respectable she toiled from morning till night; but I do not know that any of them loved her better for it. (*QW*, p. 345)

Poor 'grim' Miss Prudence![33] The narrator also enlightens the reader as to Miss Prudence's thoughts on men and marriage:

> [she] was much given to expatiate in the domestic circle on the evils of matrimony, and to thank heaven that she and her three sisters had not fallen into the hands of the Philistines; a peculiarly happy state of resignation for an unattractive woman, with a cast-iron exterior; and endowed besides with a masculine appendage of the upper lip.[34]

This portrait tends towards cruel caricature but it invites the reader to sympathise with Prudence rather than to ridicule her. Moreover, her sisters are equally savagely portrayed. The crippled Charity is a 'talkative little woman' who wears out her sister Faith with her incessant demands for 'improving reading' (*QW*, p. 147). By comparison, Hope is 'vigorous and loud-voiced' as well as 'cosmopolitan in her charities' and 'a little shaky in her church principles'(*QW*, p. 271; p. 127). Meanwhile, Faith's 'sweet lovable face' is coloured only by 'pallid neutral tints' and there is a 'certain sadness of repression on it – the shadowing of an over quiet life' (*QW*, p. 126).

---

33 *QW*, p. 272.

34 *QW*, p. 278. There is more than a tinge of irony in the suggestion that Miss Prudence lives in 'a peculiarly happy state of resignation'; and her point of view is certainly not constructed as the preferred position for the reader. However, her fictional voice adds weight to the notion that spinsterhood is not the worst condition for a woman.

However, Faith possesses redeeming qualities that are absent in some of the more lively characters in the novel. In many ways she compares favourably with the eponymous heroine, who has been alone in the world since the age of seventeen and who has hitherto been exploited by her employer:

> Queenie fell in love with [Faith] on the spot ... The unsophisticated freshness of the simple woman, her tender voice, her old-fashioned ways, and the little quaint pedantries, charmed the young governess, grown bitter with the hard edge of life. (*QW*, p. 127)

Certainly the fictional Faith appears to be more capable of 'completing, sweetening and embellishing the existence of others' than her counterpart, Queenie. But although Carey's narrator similarly considers lack of sophistication attractive, Queenie is not censured for her cynicism. Any bitterness on her part is merely attributed to unavoidable circumstances. The Misses Palmer have been provided for (albeit not luxuriously) by their deceased father; Queenie must work or want:

> 'Other women had a strong arm to lean upon, other women had fathers and brothers or husbands to work for them, and shield them in the battle of life; she had to work for herself and her helpless little sister, that was all.' And so she took up her burthen bravely, neither repining that such things were, nor wasting her best energies with fruitless regrets for impossibilities.[35]

Once again Carey enters into dialogue with the invisible but pervasive imperative that women should be provided for by men. The result is that the reader is permitted to admire both women: the one for having retained her 'unsophisticated freshness' and the other for her bravery in dealing with a basically hostile world. Nor does this end the dialogue about the supposed emptiness of the single state.

For Faith is eventually made by Carey to marry the lover that she had been obliged to leave ten years previously. Her doctor husband then regulates the domestic arrangements of the remaining sisters from the home he shares with Faith, which happens to be next door. The resultant improvement in their circumstances appears to be a comment on the disadvantages of all-female households and a vindication of Yonge's theory that women need to be managed by 'superior man'. However, Carey never explicitly gives credence to

35 *QW*, p. 191. Cf. J. Boyd-Kinnear, 'The Social Position of Women' in Josephine Butler (ed.), *Woman's Work and Woman's Culture* [1869], cited in Hollis 1979, p. 54: 'Many women have fathers, brothers, or husbands, who provide for them. But ... there are many women who... have not only to work for themselves, but have to work for the maintenance of others dependent on them'.

this notion and there are to be found throughout her fiction many other all-female households in which there is neither need nor place for male authority.[36]

The reader is also frequently warned that, although single blessedness can be stultifying, matrimony can be far worse. An interesting discussion on the latter theme is to be found following the retrospectively-related history of the eldest Palmer sister, Charity. For notwithstanding the assertion that Charity 'could not ... have met any gentlemen except the Vicar', she was, at one time, to have been married to a local farmer. However, after the accident which made her a confirmed invalid, she 'was obliged to give him up' (*QW*, p. 149). Thus, ostensibly, Charity's accident has debarred her from both the best and the second best in life: she enjoys neither marriage and maternity nor active spinsterhood. However, the fact that her fiancé was, at the time, 'strongly suspected' to be 'addicted to intemperance' problematizes this assumption of loss (*QW*, p. 150). The conclusion reached by the two young women discussing Charity's single state is that, even though she cannot walk, she is better off than she would have been as an unhappily married woman. As the more outspoken of the two speakers, Cathy, concludes:

> 'Of course ... the poor thing has suffered a good deal ... but how do you know that it was not all for the best? ... Think if that accident had never happened, and she had married him ... To be tied for life to a man, and then to see him sink lower and lower, to despise one's own husband! ... If it were I, I know I should get to hate him. Nothing should make me live with such a man; I would beg my bread first ...' (Ibid.)

As might be expected for unsensational fiction of the period, the passage is limited to an articulation of the psychological aspects of despising a husband who is a drunkard. Yet subjects such as poverty and physical violence remain implicit, mainly through Cathy's assertion that it would be better to beg for bread than to live with such a man. Cathy's comments are also likely to have highlighted for the original readership the difficulties inherent in escaping such a marriage. Even if divorce or separation had, in itself, been practicable, a woman would have had difficulty in gaining permanent custody of any children and would have had no legal right to her own previous earnings or property.[37] The low social status accorded to separated and divorced women would have

36 For example, the Challoner sisters in *Not Like Other Girls* [1884] set up the dressmaking business that will keep the entire family whilst all their male advisor can do is to lament their impoverished state.

37 *QW* was first serialised between 1880 and 1881, before the Married Women's Property Act; and only since 1873 had it been legally possible for a mother to retain custody of her children until the age of sixteen.

Figure 3: Frontispiece to *Merle's Crusade* (date unknown)

provided an additional deterrent. In the circumstances, Carey can hardly be viewed as an advocate of marriage at any price.

Domestic and Quasi-Domestic Employment

As has been noted, Miss Bretherton and the Misses Palmer do not need to seek remunerative employment. However, Carey indicates an awareness that not all women had the option of being stay-at-home spinsters, however desirable this might have been to the arbiters of middle-class taste, or indeed to the women themselves. Her forty-one novels all contain sympathetic portraits of middle-class working women, the vast majority of whom are located in some kind of domestic or quasi-domestic employment. For middle-class women, remunerative domestic work generally entailed the performance of duties which would otherwise have fallen to the leisured female occupants of a household. Such employments might have included those of companion and governess and, latterly, those of child's nurse and social secretary. However, in the second half of the nineteenth century, other employment opportunities became available that were distinguishable from domestic work, in degree if not in type. Such posts seem to have developed from trained or otherwise directed specialisms within the range of domestic duties and by the orientation of such specialisms towards both professional status and employment beyond the immediate boundaries of the home. The work of teachers, nurses, philanthropists and mission-workers may be described as quasi-domestic in this sense.

Carey does not appear to use her novels in order to question the supposed natural aptitudes of women for domestic and quasi-domestic work but this is hardly surprising.[38] There were plenty of commentators to make the myth of female domesticity appear to Carey as an unimpeachable fact of existence. The enormously influential John Ruskin, though careful not to imprison women in their own homes, certainly rhetoricized them into a sphere of activity which did not compete with that of men:

> Now the man's work for his own home is ... to secure its maintenance, progress and defence; the woman's to secure its order, comfort, and loveliness.
>
> Expand both these functions. The man's duty as a member of the commonwealth, is to assist in the maintenance, in the advance, in the defence of the State. The woman's duty, as a member of the commonwealth, is to assist in the ordering, in the comforting, and in the beautiful adorning of the State ...
>
> [W]hat the woman is to be within her gates, as the centre of order, the balm of distress, and the mirror of beauty: that she is also to be without her gates, where order is more difficult, distress more imminent, and loveliness more rare.[39]

Yet Ruskin's view is by no means a mid-century aberration. Joseph Johnson, writing some twenty years later, if anything expands upon the theme. In his book, *Noble Women Of Our Time* [1886], Johnson concedes that 'There is scarcely a walk in life, however abstruse and absorbing, that has not been adorned by a woman.' However, he rhetorically draws his readership into collusion with a rather different proposition:

---

38 Education and vocational training are commented upon; but even though the North London Collegiate was founded in her lifetime and women had started to attend university, none of Carey's heroines actually attend either. Nursing appears to have interested Carey but she was markedly less interested in settlements or Sisterhoods. She virtually ignores other kinds of work, for example the clerical work, which became available in the late nineteenth century. However, *Girl's Own Paper* frequently answered correspondents' queries about such work and it appears to have been greatly sought after. See, for example, 'Answers to Correspondents' in the issue for October 3, 1896, and 'Questions and Answers' for May 29, 1897, *GOP* Vol. 18, pp. 15, 559.

39 John Ruskin, *Sesame and Lilies* (London: George Allen, 1906 [1865]), pp. 130–31.

> 'All ... will admit that woman is in her true sphere, about her own work, when administering to the sorrowing and ameliorating suffering ...'[40]

Johnson's book, framed by its preface and introductory chapter as a book about working women, is about famous and saintly women employed in the fields of nursing, teaching, charity work and mission work. Thus in spite of the occasional genuflection towards the adaptability and ingenuity of women, his notion of what constitutes women's work does not appear to extend beyond the domestic and the quasi-domestic. It is notable that neither Ruskin nor Johnson alludes to pecuniary matters at all.

In Carey's novels the majority of middle-class women in remunerative work remain within this continuum of domestic and quasi-domestic employment. Such characters are generally conventional both in their choice of work and in the execution of their duties. For example, Miss Mewlstone in *Not Like Other Girls* [1905] is the perfect companion:

> 'Oh, yes, she can talk, and very well too ... but she knows that I do not care about it; her silence is her great virtue in my eyes. And then she has tact, and knows when to keep out of the way ...'[41]

However, Carey also focuses upon the problem of women who are obliged to undertake remunerative employment of a domestic or quasi-domestic nature even though they have neither the temperament nor the aptitude. For example, in *Aunt Diana* [1885] the thin-skinned and aging Patience Leigh means well and knows her place. However, she cannot cope with the boisterousness and newly emerging assertiveness of her eldest pupil, Missie. By contrast, Dympha in *Wooed and Married* [1875] is too young and too inexperienced to cope with a subordinate position in a household and the constant necessity for curbing her tongue in the presence of an employer.

Carey also seems to have understood that the quest for employment was far from being an easy one. The fictional Dympha, first thrown onto the employment market at the age of seventeen, is introduced to the reader only after she has gained, and lost, several posts. In describing her plight, Carey uses the occasion to enlarge upon the crisis in the women's employment market generally:

> Dym tried Haverstock Hill and even Hampstead, but the market seemed overstocked. A great commercial panic had taken place in the City a few months previously, and scores of girls, younger and less well educated than Dym, had been thrown upon their own resources: girls luxuriously

40 Joseph Johnson, *Noble Women of Our Time*, (London: T. Nelson and Sons, 1886), NWT, pp. 10–11 (hereafter, NWT).

41 R.N. Carey, *Not Like Other Girls* (London: Macmillan, 1905 [1884]), p. 152.

> brought up, and taught everything but to govern themselves and teach others, were driven from the fastnesses of happy homes and launched suddenly upon the world. Incompetence seeking competence ... Dym's neat little figure traversed miles of pavement in answer to countless advertisements, but she never found anything to suit; her youth was against her.[42]

This particular 'great commercial panic' may well have been fictitious but the overcrowding of the teaching profession was an actual fact of life.[43]

Carey articulates a genuine concern for the plight of women who are obliged to compete for work whether or not they have the requisite qualities. However, in *Queenie's Whim*, she appears to take her concern further. She puts into the mind of her irrepressible character Cathy, the notion that all women, regardless of their background or expectations, should be trained for some kind of remunerative work. Significantly, she has the fictional doctor in *Queenie's Whim* agree with her:

> 'I like your idea of every woman trained to a definite employment; I never could understand the enforced helplessness of the sex. I have known pitiable examples of women being left dependent on overtaxed brothers, or turned upon the world absolutely without resources.' (*QW*, p. 264)

Cathy's original argument is not stated at this point in the text; the reader only knows of her beliefs by virtue of the doctor's reply. However, in this way, the notion of training for all women is given a more emphatic endorsement: that of the approval of a professional male. Yet even this endorsement is not represented as being free from debate; even the quasi-domestic is disputed territory. Mr Logan, the gentle clergyman who opposes Cathy's ambition to train as a nurse, and who is possessed of the 'old-fashioned notion that woman's mission, in its perfectness, very rarely lies beyond the threshold of the home', is politely decried by everyone present. Yet he continues to put across the alternative viewpoint (*QW*, pp. 265–6):

> 'How about Florence Nightingale?' interrupted Cathy.
> 'Or Sarah Judson?' from Langley.
> 'Or Mrs Fry? or Joan of Arc?' commented Dr. Stewart.
> 'Or we might add Grace Darling, and a score of others,' put in Garth.
> 'All typical women, raised up in their generation to perform a certain work, and performing it right nobly. The world calls them heroines, and

42 R.N. Carey, *Wee Wifie* (London: Macmillan, 1894 [1869]), pp. 76–7. See also *Not Like Other Girls*, p. 65. There are also many competent governesses in Carey's fiction, e.g. Eden in *My Lady Frivol* [1899]; Huldah in *Only the Governess* [1888]; and Miss Osbourne in *But Men Must Work* [1892].

43 Cf. Vicinus 1985, p. 23.

> with reason. They are heroines in the true sense of the word, for they have discovered the needs of the world, and, recognising their own power to remedy them, have fearlessly dared to cross the threshold of home duty for the larger arena, where only the strong prevail and the weak go to the wall.'
>
> 'Cathy does not pretend to be Florence Nightingale,' put in Langley quietly.
>
> 'I thought you always told us to elevate our standard?' a little defiantly, from Cathy.
>
> 'The higher the better,' with a benign glance at her; 'but it must be a true standard, unselfishness and self-sacrifice for its base, and built up of pure motives. If it be one-sided it will topple over.' (*QW*, p. 266)

Thus the vicar neutralizes the examples given to him, of women who have worked outside the home, by categorizing them as self-sacrificing, exceptional and heroic, and by divorcing their motives from those of the unexceptional Cathy. Effectively, Cathy's motives, whether those of self-development or pecuniary advantage, are rendered unacceptable.

Once again, opposing points of view expressed by two of Carey's characters are akin to opposing schools of thought in the real world. The perspective of Dr Stewart and Cathy is to be found not only in the writings of the feminists of the day but also in relatively conservative periodicals such as the *Girl's Own Paper*, a Religious Tract Society publication, and *The Woman At Home* which had as its editor the Evangelical writer, Annie S. Swan.[44] By comparison, the views of Carey's fictional vicar are more akin to those expressed in the spate of articles by self-interested male writers such as W.R .Greg, which had found their way into mainstream journals in the 1850s and 1860s. The vicar does not insist that marriage is the only career for a woman but he as surely interdicts any means by which a woman can earn a living wage. Effectively, his position is little different from that of the writer for the *Saturday Review* in 1859, who posits that, if women become economically independent, men might be reduced to doing their own housework:

> Men do not like, and would not seek, to mate with an independent factor, who at any time could quit – or who at all times would be tempted to neglect – the tedious duties of training and bringing up children, ... keeping ... tradesmen's bills, and mending ... linen, for the more lucrative returns of the desk or counter …
>
> Married life is a woman's profession; and to this life her training – that of dependence – is modelled. Of course by not getting a husband, or losing him, she may find that she is without resources. All that can be

44 The *Girl's Own Paper* had always run letters pages and articles on 'Girls' Employments'. See Wendy Forrester, *Great Grandmama's weekly* (Guildford: Lutterworth Press, 1980), pp. 164–5. *The Woman At Home* (hereafter, *WAH*) similarly printed a series of articles entitled 'Women's Employments.' See, for example, *WAH* Vol. 3 [1895], pp. 397–8.

> said of her is, she has failed in business; and no social reform can prevent such failures.[45]

According to such rhetoric, Cathy should stay at home with her domestic duties and pray that her brother will be able to keep her until she can capture a husband. To return to the home-versus-work debate in *Queenie's Whim*, once again Carey declines to provide a definitive pronouncement on a matter which might have been of great female concern. The fictional Cathy defiantly ignores the emotive appeal for her to take up woman's perfect mission in the home but the scene does not have a comfortable conclusion. In the following passage, the vicar, Mr Logan, is the first speaker:

> '... About your plan [to become a nurse], now?'
> 'I will not hear a word against it,' she returned wilfully ... 'It is bad enough having to argue with all one's home people; but to be lectured in public, and before Dr. Stewart – no, indeed, Mr Logan.'
> 'Very well, I will reserve what I have to say in private,' he returned, looking [at] her with a sort of indulgent tenderness ...
> The circle broke up after this ... (*QW*, p. 266)

Cathy is ultimately vindicated in her choice of a career: she inconveniences no-one when she leaves home; and her professional nursing skills are put to good use when her beloved sister is taken ill. Yet, at this early point in the narrative, the silencing of Mr Logan is no victory. It seems that, even whilst Carey advocates training and employment opportunities for women, such advocacy is still in tension with the culturally-prescribed wholly domestic ideal.

Nurses' Homes and Homes from Home

The problems faced by middle-class women seeking remunerative employment were manifold. They were hampered in their selection of work by appeals to their femininity and by threats to their marriage prospects if they worked at all. By no means all applicants were suited to domestic employments and relatively few had the education or training required for the quasi-domestic posts. At the same time, long before the end of the nineteenth century, many areas of female employment were massively oversubscribed.[46] Yet, as authors such as Martha Vicinus indicate, the importunity of the impecunious and the determination of the unwillingly leisured resulted in both greater employment opportunities for

45 'Queen bees or working bees', *Saturday Review*, 12 November 1859, cited in Hollis 1979, p. 11.

46 See, for example, 'Women's Employments' in *WAH* Vol. 3, 1895, pp. 156–7; 'Questions and Answers' (reply to Elspeth), *GOP* Vol. 18 , p. 256.

women and a greater general acceptance of the validity of remunerative women's work.

The fictional Cathy's chosen career, nursing, was one of the first occupations for ladies to gain general acceptance. In spite of its remunerative potential, it began to capture the public imagination when stories about Florence Nightingale and her hospital work were relayed back from the Crimea. Nightingale was an ideal advocate for the work. Born a 'lady', she was a public figure who embodied for many the ideals of selflessness and pious womanhood. She thus set an example which it was possible for other middle-class single women to follow, though the respectability of the calling was not allowed by all quarters overnight. By the end of the nineteenth century, nurses (though not necessarily 'lady' nurses) became one of the largest occupational groups of working women.[47] An almost accidental result, arising from the formalization of training for nurses, was that some women had access to affordable and respectable living accommodation.[48]

Yet nursing only gained acceptance by emulating in a number of ways the very situation that many women were trying to break with. As Poovey has argued, the development of the nursing profession was based on a contradictory role for many of the women concerned:

> A calling or a profession? This was the pertinent question for those who advocated that women nurse. Those feminists who supported opening nursing to women of all classes argued that nursing should be a profession, with some form of regular training, adequate wages and sufficient provisions for retirement. Other[s] ... however, advocated conceptualizing nursing as a vocation. (Poovey 1989, p. 176)

In designating nursing as a calling or vocation, as indeed did Nightingale herself, commentators appealed to middle-class social mores (the insistence upon feminine piety, selflessness and modesty) and located the work, at least nominally, within the domestic sphere (through the notion that it should not compete with male occupations and that it should be unwaged). However, too few idealistic women of the right calibre were available to work on a purely voluntary basis. As a result, a hybrid system of training evolved, in which the requirements of both middle-class ideology and hard economics were taken into account. As Vicinus notes:

> Although some of the new training schools ... had begun with a single course for everybody, they all soon had a two-tier system ... Lady probationers paid £1 per week for up to one year's training, while regular

47 Vicinus 1985, p. 96–7.

48 Alas, this accommodation was often uncomfortable. See Vicinus 1985, p. 109. However, Carey seems to have approved of the idea of nurses homes. See below.

> probationers were paid £12 to £20 per year during their three years' training. (Vicinus 1985, p. 97)

Thus, nursing was theoretically open to all and at least some impecunious women had access to a living wage in a relatively high status job. Moreover, all those who had undergone training could use their skills in a variety of posts other than those offered by the big teaching hospitals.

Judging from her novels, Carey was interested in both the vocational and the practical opportunities afforded by nursing work. However, in *Our Bessie* (1888–89) her commitment to the notion of vocation is uppermost. This novel, which is explicitly directed at younger readers, makes the heavily didactic point that nursing training must be undertaken in a spirit of humility and self-sacrifice. Thus, when the fictional Edna wishes to train as a nurse following her broken engagement, she is gently and earnestly admonished for selfishness by the eponymous heroine:

> 'If it were not for Mama, I would go to some hospital and learn nursing; it is too dreadful living like this just to amuse oneself, and try to forget. I must do something, something for the good of myself, if not for my fellow creatures.' ...
>
> 'Oh, my dear ... I have learnt that we must not run away from our trouble; girls often talk like that ... about going into a hospital, but they do not know what they want. Nursing is too sacred a work to be done from such a motive. What good would such a work, undertaken in a selfish, self-seeking spirit do them?[49]

Nevertheless, in four of Carey's other novels, there are to be found nurses who do not appear undertake their work from purely idealistic motives.[50] Ursula in *Uncle Max* certainly seems to have a vocation. However, as she reflects upon her career to date, the reader discovers that she prefers hard-working independence to the more conventional behaviour for her age and class, that of living with her wealthy aunt:

> I remembered the dear old rectory life, where every one was in earnest, and contrasted it with the trifling pursuits that my aunt and cousin called duties ... And then came emancipation in the shape of hard hospital work ... when under the stimulus of useful employment and constant exercise of body and mind, I slept better, fretted less, and looked less mournfully out on the world.[51]

49 R.N. Carey, *Our Bessie* (London: Office of 'The Girl's Own Paper', ?1914 [1888–89], p. 203.

50 *Queenie's Whim* [1881], *Uncle Max* [1887], *Other People's Lives* [1897] and *No Friend Like A Sister* [1906]; *The Key of the Unknown* [1909] has a nurse as a minor character.

51 R.N. Carey, *Uncle Max*, (London: Macmillan, 1912 [1887]), p. 13 (hereafter, *UM*).

Clearly, nursing is also an antidote for boredom and lack of purpose. Moreover, Ursula can afford her idealism; she has a private income and her ultimate occupation, nursing the sick poor in an uncle's country parish rather than in a hospital, is reassuringly similar to that of district visiting. It also seems that she has completed her training as a 'Lady probationer'. At the beginning of the novel, she has 'spent the past year in the wards of St Thomas' but '[Her] work [i]s over ... and [she] ha[s] come home again' (*UM*, p. 3; p. 2).[52]

Similarly, Cathy and Faith, the nurses in *Queenie's Whim*, can afford to be idealistic. Though regarded as relatively poor, the former has a brother to support her and the latter a small income inherited from her father. Cathy's motives for training – in order to see life outside her own small village and in order to be able to keep herself if the need should arise – have already been stated. Meanwhile, Frances in *No Friend Like A Sister* [1906] has even less need for a wage and even more reason for taking up a career. Initially taking up nursing as a means of moving out of the home she shares with her overbearing sister, Augusta, she eventually opens a private nursing home. Yet, in running what is a profit-making concern, her gains are not essentially financial: she already has 'seven hundred a year of her own'.[53] Rather, she gains both emancipation from family ties and the social sanction to live in her own establishment. It seems that, if Carey was trying to popularize nursing as a means of remunerative employment, she was advocating it as an occupation for the middle-class woman of slender means rather than for the working-class woman of no means at all.

The only description of hospital-type accommodation for nurses to be found in Carey's novels is of that provided by Frances at her nursing home in *No Friend Like A Sister*. However, it is very much idealized and its salient features appear to have been lifted straight out of Florence Nightingale's paper, *Suggestions on the Subject of Providing, Training, and Organising Nurses for the Sick Poor in Workhouse Infirmaries* [1867]. In this paper, Nightingale argues that hard-working nurses deserve not only a home but a lifestyle in keeping with their calling:

> a home which gives what real family homes are supposed to give – materially, a bedroom for each, dining and sitting-rooms in common, all meals prepared and eaten in the home; morally, direction, support,

52 Carey's trained nurses all appear to be lady probationers. Frances in *No Friend Like A Sister* clearly has the correct social background as well as the finances. The nurses in *Queenie's Whim* seem to regard their time at the hospital as temporary (neither trains for three years) and Nurse Clare in *Other People's Lives* has a private income. Sister Rose in *The Key of the Unknown*, though of the right class, is a poor and childless widow and hence the only one of Carey's nurses who may be constructed as having earned a wage whilst training.

53 R.N. Carey, *No Friend Like A Sister* (London: Macmillan, 1906), p. 4 (hereafter, *NFLAS*).

> sympathy in a common work; further training and instruction in it; proper rest and recreation; and a head of the home, who is also and pre-eminently trained and skilled head of the nursing; in short, a home where any good mother, of whatever class, would be willing to let her daughter, however attractive or highly educated, live.[54]

Carey's fictional Frances runs her nurses' home on exactly these principles. With regard to the sleeping accommodation:

> Each cubicle ha[s] its window, and beside the bed, chest of drawers, and washstand there [i]s also room for an easy-chair and small writing-table and bookcase. (*NFLAS*, p. 3)

There is also 'the nurses' sitting room, with its Chesterfield couch and deep easy-chairs and well-filled bookcase'; and the meals supplied are 'good and well cooked, [with] plenty of vegetables and fruit' (ibid., pp. 3–4). Frances herself is the 'head of the home.' Like the wise surrogate mother-figure obliquely suggested by Nightingale, Frances 'never begrudges anything to her nurses', so it is '[n]o wonder [they love] and appreciate her'.[55] However, like any other kind of approved parent figure, 'with all her indulgence, Sister Gresham [i]s a strict disciplinarian'; she provides the moral direction and support required by Nightingale's model. She also protects her staff from overwork even though her district nurses are 'in such request that [she] ha[s] some difficulty in securing them needful rest' (*NFLAS*, p. 5). In addition, Frances' establishment, which consists of in-patients, 'house' nurses and domestic servants, as well as boarding district nurses, is explicitly run along domestic lines. As she tells a friend from her training days at Guy's Hospital, 'I prefer to take fewer patients and fewer nurses, and make it practically a Home' (*NFLAS*, p. 3).

In adding imaginative depth to Nightingale's bare outline, Carey emphasises the fact that few such comfortable homes from home were available to women working away from their families. Frances is made to state that her nursing home is intended to be 'a sort of pattern and object-lesson for other Homes', this implying that other nursing homes were not run on these lines, if indeed such small organizations existed at all (*NFLAS*, p. 3). The narrator then adds that 'Young nurses were almost piteous in their appeals to be taken in; for their very soul was sick with envy' (ibid.).

Carey was evidently interested in the respectable and affordable accommodation that hospitals and other nursing establishments could provide

54 Cited in Poovey 1989, p. 190

55 *NFLAS*, p. 4. Frances is also 'anxious to start a Pension Fund for superannuated or sick nurses whose health is broken down, and it is the general belief that every penny of profit [from the nurses home and the paying patients] goes towards that fund' (ibid.).

for the single woman. However, she may well have been attempting to popularize independent living for all single working women who required it. Two of her other nursing characters, Ursula in *Uncle Max* and Clare in *Other People's Lives*, live in comfortable and well-serviced lodgings, as do two of her fictional governesses. Whilst the loneliness of living apart from members of their own class is not ignored, the advantages of the single life are also ungrudgingly emphasized. Miss Osbourne, the governess in *But Men Must Work* [1892] is delighted that she is in a position to keep her pet dog, Mousquetaire, something that would have been impossible had her post been residential; and Eden, the governess in *My Lady Frivol*, is equally well pleased. The latter happily tells her brother that, 'It will be so delightful to be free and to have my evenings to myself'.[56]

Even in the earlier novels, Carey furnishes her single female characters with alternatives to traditional family homes or domestic employments. For example, in *Robert Ord's Atonement* [1873], Meg Carruthers lives for some time with her friend and benefactor, Rotha. However, when the latter marries, Meg moves 'by her own desire' into the Children's Home where she has hitherto worked on a daily basis.[57] By comparison, Margaret in *Wee Wifie* [1869] becomes a Sister of Charity following her brother's marriage. For each of these women, the individual nurturing role that they have hitherto undertaken is at an end and they need to seek fresh work in order to avoid redundancy. Each thus exchanges family life for community life. However, the need for change extends beyond the simple need to find fresh interests for themselves. In accordance with the social mores of the time, the marriages also signal a considerable loss of status for these single women within their respective households. Before her brother's marriage, Margaret is the mistress of his home; afterwards, that status automatically transfers to his wife. For Meg Carruthers, friendship must give way to the societally prescribed exclusivity of the relationship between man and wife.[58] Moving out of someone else's marital home is thus an altogether more comfortable option. Female hierarchies within the middle-class household are such an important feature of Carey's novels that the subject is taken up at greater length in chapter 4, 'Hearth and Home'.

---

56 R.N. Carey, *My Lady Frivol* (London: Hutchinson, n.d., [1899]), p. 18.

57 R.N. Carey, *Robert Ord's Atonement*, (London: Richard Bentley and Son, 1898 [1873]), p. 464. Meg is, by this stage a widow. However, throughout the novel she is a deserted wife with no family and thus is in the position of a single woman.

58 Cf. *A Woman's Thoughts About Women*, p. 140: 'After marriage, for either party to have or to desire a dearer or closer friend than the other, is a state so inconceivably deplorable ... that it will not bear discussion.'

Conclusion

Discussion has centred on the variety of images of single womanhood to be found in Carey's novels: daughters joyfully wearing out their youth in the service of their families; fussy or acid old maids; 'ladies' employed in wholly domestic establishments; and nurses and others who pursue careers away from family homes. Carey thus represents a variety of responses to the demographic phenomenon of more women than men. Within the novels, residual notions of women remaining in family homes under all circumstances are found alongside dominant notions about women in domestic or quasi-domestic work, though only when financially necessary or until marriage; and both coexist with emergent notions of women in careers, this work being undertaken for its own sake, or even as a positive alternative to marriage. Nor does Carey ignore the voice of the financially solvent woman who enjoys a life at home and who has no desire to undertake remunerative work.

In Lyotardian terms, the crystallized boundaries of the domestic exist alongside the real stakes in the game, public sphere employments for women. In the main, Carey appears to wholeheartedly accept the images of womanhood provided by the dominant (male-powered and -empowered) discourses of the day. However, even from within the bounds of the dominant, its prescriptions and proscriptions are interrogated. Carey does more than to advocate paid employment and decent living accommodation for lone women and to condone remunerative employment for the more prosperous. She also appears to rebel against the notion that women can be redundant.

Even where Carey portrays those who, through no fault of their own, are denied both home duties and gainful occupations, she utilizes their plight to articulate protests against the enforced isolation of women within the domestic sphere. Thus, it is explicit that Agnes, in *No Friend Like A Sister* [1906], would gladly change places with the busy farmer's widow, Mrs Keith, because the latter is happy in her work. By comparison, Violet in *The Old, Old Story* [1894] is permitted a veritable tirade in protest against her enforced, rather than innate, redundancy. As she tells a sympathetic friend, a single woman who is forced into idleness and who is only permitted to invest her hopes in a future married state which may never come to pass, effectively has no life to call her own:

> 'But what if [a suitable man] fail to put in an appearance? Is there to be no life for a single woman? I am seven and twenty ... the best and sweetest part of my life is over, the bloom of youth gone, and I am necessary to no one. Yes, that is the sting, the hateful secret sting – that I am not necessary to a single human being![59]

59 R.N. Carey, *The Old, Old Story* (London: Macmillan, 1899 [1894]), p. 119. Cf. also *No Friend Like A Sister*, p. 178.

These characters, Violet and Agnes, do not attempt to liberate themselves from the restrictions imposed upon them by society but they suffer because it is impossible for them to conform to the prescribed behaviour. Implicitly, Carey, too, is railing against the impossibility of the standard. Nor was she alone in doing so. In this protest, Carey reflects the non-fictional words of Frances Power Cobbe from a few decades earlier in the century:

> The private and home duties of such women as have them are, beyond all doubt, their first concern, and one which, when fully met must often engross all their time and energies. But it is an absurdity ... to go on assuming that all of them have home duties, and tacitly treating those who have none as if they were wrongly placed on God's earth. (Cited in Vicinus 1985, pp. 15–16)

Cobbe's paper was published several years before any of Carey's novels found their way into print and there is no evidence that Carey ever read it. However, her novels seem to be a vindication of the single state based upon precisely this contested premise.

Part of this vindication lies in the fact that very few of Carey's characters without home duties are left wanting. Both Violet and Agnes marry, though not until around the age of thirty, and a number of other heroines marry even later in life. For example, in *The Key Of The Unknown* [1909], Aunt Felicia becomes second wife to the sweetheart of her youth at the age of fifty-eight. Faith Palmer's marriage at the age of thirty-five has already been mentioned. Carey also allows the most unlikely of characters to marry. The slightly deformed Nest in *Barbara Heathcote's Trial* [1871] marries a baronet; whilst Mattie in *Not Like Other Girls* [1884], who is not only thirty but also plain, garrulous and ill-dressed, ends up marrying a millionaire. Thus, in Carey's novels, with the exception of career women and severely physically disabled characters such as the eponymous heroine of *Averil*, few women are represented as incorrigibly unmarriageable. Romance does not remain the prerogative of the young and no woman is confirmed in her (societally determined) redundancy. This concept of late blessing may well have boosted the morale of older and encumbered readers and it is possible that Carey herself hoped for such a reward.[60]

However, Carey was also a practical working woman, though it is difficult to tell from the biographical evidence available whether she wrote purely for pleasure or out of stern necessity. It seems that, besides writing romance, she wished to popularize, in her novels, ideas with regard to the autonomy of single women. This she did by providing positive role models for women of all ages,

---

60 Her older sister married for the first time in her late thirties.

whether they lived entirely within the home or whether they followed an occupation elsewhere.

Generally Carey gives high status to a group of characters, single women, who are given low status in other fiction. If she does not appear very radical by today's standards, it was because her beliefs in the capabilities and natural aptitudes of women differed greatly from those of feminists today. As Vicinus observes:

> Very few feminists fought for women as human beings who were potentially equal to men in intellect, instincts, and morals – a radical message unacceptable until the early years of the twentieth century. (Vicinus 1985, p. 16)

Carey was not, in any case, explicitly a feminist. She was also trapped within her own class bias. As a social construction, she was bound, to an extent, to reproduce the society that had made her.[61] However, her achievement was in her subversive questionings of that society. She did not argue for sex-equality; her agenda was rather more modest in its scope. Rather, she posited that some kind of permanent space should be permitted to single women, who were, at that time, especially short of space to call their own.

61 Cf. J.-F. Lyotard, *The Postmodern Condition: A Report on Knowledge*, (Manchester: Manchester University Press, 1987), p. 15: 'even before [birth] ... the human child is already positioned as the referent in the story recounted by those around [them], in relation to which [they] will inevitably chart [their] course'.

Chapter 3

Women and Children Second

Gentlemen may be Rude to their Sisters; or, 'so like a girl'

The Enlightenment left as its legacy to the Western world a theory of gender difference based upon the perceived ability or inability to reason. Rationality, with its concomitant facility for making moral judgements, was deemed to be characteristic of men; a diametrically opposing state of 'nature' and thus amorality was deemed to epitomize the disposition of women, children and animals. Such ascriptions, occasionally based upon questionable empirical evidence, may be observed in the works of philosophers as disparate as Rousseau, Kant and Swedenborg.[1] However, times do not seem to have changed very much by the late nineteenth century and Carey's novels contain many characters who, broadly speaking, conform to these powerful gender stereotypes.

Victor Seidler's late twentieth-century analysis of the masculine power-base suggests, by analogy, something of the impact that this institutionalized sexual inequality may have had upon both the men of Carey's day and upon Carey's own construction as a subject and a writer. Taking a specifically Kantian perspective, Seidler analyses Kant's construction of the subject and concludes that this construction leads to the normalization of a 'universalized' kind of male experience:

> [Men] have inherited a historical identification of masculinity with reason and morality ... It is an identification with which it is crucial to come to terms, if [one is] to grasp what it means to grow up as a man in modern western culture. Kant's philosophy offers ... an account of the human subject as split irrevocably between reason and desire, in which it

1 See Jean Jacques Rousseau, *Emile* (London: J.M. Dent and Sons, 1963), p. 323: 'though swayed by ... passions man is endowed with reason to control them. Woman is also endowed with ... passions; God has given her modesty to restrain them'; Immanuel Kant, *Anthropology from a Pragmatic Point of View*, cited in E. Kennedy and S. Mendus (eds), *Women in Western Political Philosophy* (Brighton: Wheatsheaf, 1987) p. 35: 'the woman should reign and the man should rule; because inclination reigns and reason rules'; Emanuel Swedenborg, *Compendium of Swedenborg's Theological Writings* (London: Swedenborg Society, 1909), p. 446: '*From disposition* ... the man acts from reason, and the woman from affection' (italics original).

> is ... reason, and not ... [inclination] ... that guarantees [a man's] capacity for morality. It is ... reason that allows [men] to calculate the rightness of action, through a process of abstracting from particular situations and working out whether an action is in principle universalizable. Yet the claim to objective rightness, as well as the fragmentation of the self on which it is built, and the shifting of questions of morality into the realm of abstraction, can be argued to be itself a normalization of a particular kind of masculine experience.[2]

In short, if the only admissible kind of reason is a universalized masculine reason, then collective male experience becomes 'a norm against which others are to be judged and found wanting' (Seidler 1989, p. 3). Seidler then moves on to outline the far-reaching consequences of this enforced dichotomy within the male self:

> Ever since the Enlightenment, men have sought to silence the voices of others in the name of reason. Men have taken control of the public world and sought to define the very meaning of humanity in terms of the possession of reason. The experiences of women, children and animals have been closely identified as lacking reason, and being closer to nature. Women were forced to subordinate themselves to men to anchor themselves in the new world of reason and science. (Seidler 1989, p. 14)

By the late nineteenth century, this normative male rationality had become clothed in a number of conventional psychological and behavioural guises. A significant cluster of these conventions crystallized into a system which produced an almost standardized end-product, the English gentleman. However, this notion of a standard product needs to be heavily qualified. For whilst certain elements of the gentleman's composition were deemed desirable in men of all classes, the expectation of their realization was, in reality, fixed entirely upon those of the middle and upper classes. The very meaning of the word 'gentleman' was – and is – biased in this way. Leaving aside vernacular,

---

2 Victor Seidler, *Rediscovering Masculinity*, (London: Routledge, 1989), pp. 2–3 (hereafter, Seidler 1989). Kant does indeed posit a schism in the subject between nature and reason. However, with the exception of one line in his *Anthropology from a Pragmatic Point of View*, his attribution of rationality to males and 'naturalness' to females is impressionistic rather than explicit. Seidler appears to have adopted this view from Susan Mendus, 'Kant: An Honest but Narrow-Minded Bourgeois ?' in Kennedy and Mendus 1987, pp. 21–43 (full reference in note 1). Seidler cites her in his Bibliography. However, even Mendus says that the view is not easy to pin down (see p. 39).

To avoid the kind of universalization he considers to be so damaging to both men and women, Seidler writes much of the book in the first person. However, as the address of the book is exclusively male, he also occasionally uses the term 'we' in order to 'encourage ... mutual recognition and identification' amongst the readership. As this multiple address makes certain passages difficult to read when they are taken out of their greater context, all passages from Seidler 1989 have been rendered into the third person.

complimentary and professional meanings, the word 'gentleman' is glossed by the *Oxford English Dictionary* as:

> A man of gentle birth; prop., one entitled to bear arms, though not noble, but also applied to any person of distinction ... A man of chivalrous instincts and fine feelings ... A man of superior position in society; often, a man of money and leisure.[3]

In this cluster of definitions, notions of privilege and exclusion (heredity, money and leisure) are promiscuously mixed with what are theoretically more universal psychological factors (distinction, chivalrous instincts and fine feelings). Yet even the latter imply a heritage of 'gentle' blood and access to education and opportunity. Thus, the attribution of morality (via reason) to all men becomes transmuted into the notion that morality is the exclusive preserve of men in the middle and upper classes. In effect, 'silenc[ing] the voices of others in the name of reason' becomes not just a silencing of women but the silencing of large numbers of supposedly 'ungentlemanly' men.

It must also be borne in mind that however standardized the procedure for constructing the gentleman-product, there is no guarantee that he will conform to type in all respects. It is possible to abstract from the the dictionary definition a recognizable notion of 'gentleman' based solely upon the external factors of opportunity and lifestyle. The vast majority of Rosa Carey's fictional male protagonists are gentlemen in at least this latter respect. However, she continually interrogates the psychological and thus moral aspects of the ideal.

Though not so blatant as many of her contemporaries in her expression of sexual difference, Carey typically portrays men and boys dictating to, and disparaging the experience of, women and girls. For example, in *Lover Or Friend?* [1890], sixteen-year-old Kester scathingly dismisses his younger sister Molly's experience of their meeting with a hitherto unknown man:

> 'I was so afraid of him at first; his eyes seem to look one through and through, even when he says nothing. But he is kind – very kind.'
> 'Is that all you found out about him?', returned her brother contemptuously. 'That is so like a girl! Who cares about his eyes? Do you know what he is? He is a hero – he has the Victoria Cross ...' [4]

The disparity in their responses indicates that the speakers dwell in separate worlds; worlds hierarchically placed with regard to one another, in which the inhabitants necessarily have different preoccupations. The girl is initially

3 *The Shorter Oxford English Dictionary*, 2 vols., (Oxford: Clarendon Press, 1991), p. 843.

4 R.N. Carey, *Lover or Friend?* (London: Macmillan, 1915 [1890]), p. 65 (hereafter, *LoF*).

frightened of the unknown man – she is portrayed as one who has already learnt to fear the capriciousness of the opposite sex – but is finally convinced that he is kind. Her brother does not even entertain this point of view; Molly is 'so like a girl' and thus her opinion may be dismissed. Kester's interest in their visitor centres on the latter's status as a soldier and a holder of the Victoria Cross (masculine/universal [pre]occupations) rather than on any individual traits or characteristics.

However, the outcome of the conversation is that the two young people '[elect] Captain Burnett to the position of their favourite hero' (*LoF*, p. 62). Thus, their points of view are reconciled and Carey's narrator questions neither Molly's initial timidity towards Captain Burnett nor Kester's ungentlemanly speech towards his sister. This seems to imply that, for Carey, there was nothing noteworthy in either character's response. Nor was she alone in accepting that such taunts were the prerogative of brothers. Her contemporary, Charlotte Yonge, sums up the relative positions of brothers and sisters thus:

> Boys are apt to be jealous of anything that engrosses their sisters to the exclusion of their lordly selves, and to have a strong love of teasing, which inspires banter after they have grown too old for the bodily tortures to which they put their little sisters ... [A boy insists] on his sister's coming up to his idea of the perfect lady … He wants to be proud of his sister ... and is determined to have her refined and well dressed.[5]

A brother who fits this paradigm very closely is to be found in Carey's novel, *Not Like Other Girls* [1884]. One of the major protagonists, 28-year-old Archie, finds it beyond his capacity to even 'take a proper amount of interest' in six of his seven sisters:[6]

> He tried to ... be serenely unconscious of their want of grace and polish; but the effort was too manifest ...
>
> Isabel and [D]ottie might be tolerated, but he could easily have dispensed with Susie and Laura and Clara; he had the happy knack of forgetting their existence when he was absent from them, and when he was at home he did not always care to be reminded of their presence. He was one of those men who are very exacting to their woman-kind, who resent it as a personal injury if they fail in good looks or are not pleasant on the eye. He did not go as far as to say to himself that he could dispense with poor Mattie too, but he certainly acted on most occasions as though he thought so.[7]

5 C.M. Yonge, *Womankind* (London: Mozley and Smith, 1877), pp. 138–9 (hereafter, *Womankind*).

6 R.N. Carey, *Not Like Other Girls* (London: Macmillan and Co., 1905 [1884]), p. 118 (hereafter, *NLOG*).

7 *NLOG*, pp. 118, 231. Carey's use of the expression 'woman-kind' is suggestive of Yonge.

Plainly, the fictional Archie does not feel obliged to inhabit his sisters' world; he tries to ignore its existence. Nor, indeed, does he feel constrained to give them more than the most perfunctory attention. However, it is thirty-year-old Mattie, the sister who keeps house for him, who bears the brunt of his ill humour. She is made to suffer for simply not being his only truly favoured sister, Grace, who cannot be spared from the family home. Many of Archie's most scathing remarks to Mattie relate to her poor dress sense, though his motives are far from aesthetic or altruistic:

> 'Oh Mattie! ... I am positively ashamed that anyone should see you. That hat is only fit to frighten the birds … If you have no proper pride, you might at least consider my feelings. Do you think a man in my position likes his sister to go about like an old beggar-woman?' (*NLOG*, p. 140)

Archie also takes Mattie to task for other forms of 'unladylike' behaviour, though his priggish self-righteousness is not always left unchallenged. For example, on the occasion when he makes the condemnatory assertion, 'I am not a gossip like you, Mattie', his position is rapidly undermined (*NLOG*, p. 140). His rapt attention when Mattie nevertheless proceeds to talk about their new neighbours is followed, some pages later, by the narratorial comment that 'gossip was to [Archie] as the sin of witchcraft, unless he stooped to it himself, and then it was amiable sociability'.[8] Thus, Carey both reproduces the institutionalized power relationship, whereby men have the right to freely criticize their sisters, and subverts it by adding that men are guilty of precisely those faults they condemn in women.

In the manner of romantic fiction, Carey's Mattie ultimately gains a measure of respect from Archie but even this approval remains within the bounds of the power relationship already outlined. Her initial success is due to her discovery of a good dress-maker. Though qualified, Archie's praise of her new dress contrasts noticeably with his earlier speeches:

> 'I like it excessively,' was Archie's comment; and then he added, with the delicious frankness common to brothers, 'It makes you look quite a different person, Mattie; you are almost nice-looking tonight.' (*NLOG*, p. 247)

However, Mattie's crowning achievement is her engagement to a millionaire who is also a baronet. Archie's reaction to her news is a triumph for her:

> '… what will mother say?' finished Mattie ...
> 'Good heavens, Mattie!', gasped Archie … 'I tell you what ... I will take you down myself to Lowder Street, and see what she says ... upon

8 *NLOG*, p. 183. See also p. 289.

> my word, Mattie, I was never so pleased about any-thing in my life. He is a straight-forward good fellow, I am sure of that; and you are not such a bad little thing yourself, Mattie. There!' (*NLOG*, p. 470)

Yet this is clearly fantasy rather than mimesis. For Mattie, the outward trappings change: new clothes and the prospect of a titled husband turn the supposed old maid of the family into a person of consequence. Archie, her sternest critic, does not have to change his perspective or repent of his previous behaviour at all. She has become what he has demanded from the first: well-dressed and worth knowing. Moreover, Carey appears to have thoroughly internalized the intense androcentrism of the day and, at times, to have reproduced it without question. For example, in *At the Moorings* [1904], the heroine is made to express pity for her brother even though she shares his disadvantages:

> 'It must be deadly dull for a man of his intellect never to mix with his equals ... A woman can inure herself to monotony far more easily ...' [9]

Yet portrayals of self-depreciating women who give priority to their brothers' concerns are not always simple. Mattie in *Not Like Other Girls* infers from her brother's perpetual snubs that somehow the fault is always her own. However, in the following passage, narratorial rhetoric obliquely suggests that Mattie is accusing herself excessively, if not needlessly:

> Mattie was of the opinion that – well, to put a mild term – irritability was a necessary adjunct to manhood. All men were cross sometimes. It behoved their womankind, then ... to speak peaceably, and to refrain from sour looks, or even the shadow of a frown. Archie was never cross with Grace, therefore it must be she, Mattie, on whom the blame lay. She was such a silly little thing, and so on. There is no need to follow the self-accusation of one of the kindest hearts that ever beat. (*NLOG*, p. 185)

To summarize, Carey depicts a difficult world for women: a world which men control but decline to share; a world in which men purport to live up to a gentlemanly code but in which reality is shaped by a self-referential group which uses, adapts or abandons this code according to its requirements of the moment. However, Carey also introduces into her novels therapeutic and compensatory strategies in order to boost the self-esteem of an implicitly female reader: strategies such as subversion of male speech, inflected narratorial comment and vicarious fulfilment of fantasies. Given that the comfort of women living in this male-constructed world is contingent upon a

---

9 *At The Moorings* (London: Macmillan, 1914 [1904]), p. 21 (hereafter, *ATM*).

code which may or may not be kept, it is necessary to examine what it meant to be a man and a gentleman in the late nineteenth- and early twentieth centuries.

The English Gentleman

From the middle of the nineteenth century, a major component in the construction of the gentleman was the assurance and prestige to be gained from having attended a public school. According to Eve Kosofsky Sedgwick, the middle-class gentleman, unlike the aristocrat, was obliged to rely upon such abstract indicators of status in lieu of more tangible kinds of inheritance:

> Unlike title, wealth, or land, the terms that defined the gentleman [as opposed to the aristocrat] were not clearly and simply hereditary but had somehow to be earned by being a particular kind of person who spent time and money in particular ways. But the early prerequisites for membership in this powerful but nebulous class – to speak with a certain accent, to spend years translating Latin and Greek, to leave family and the society of women – all made one unfit for any other form of work, long before they entitled one to chance one's fortune actively in the ruling class.[10]

This is to say, the gentleman-product was obliged to produce as his 'pedigree' an extended and economically unproductive 'childhood' and the inability to engage in any work outside the parameters of the class for which he had been educated. This view of a public school education makes intelligible a remark made by Tom O'Brien, the retired shopkeeper in Carey's novel *Lover or Friend?* Humbly and without irony, the financially secure though unwillingly leisured Mr O'Brien tells his friend, Audrey:

> 'I was fond of the shop – its no use denying it – and it takes a special sort of education to fit one for idleness. Even now – would you believe it, ma'am? – I have a sort of longing to finger the oats and peas again.' (*LoF*, p. 81).

Tom O'Brien thereby defines himself as a member of a respectable – and respectful – working class. However, in the real world, not all working people made good were satisfied with their place. Many wanted their children to have the 'education to fit one for idleness' even if they could not themselves wholly acquire the concomitant status.

---

10 Eve Kosofsky Sedgwick, *Between Men: Literature and Male Homosocial Desire* (New York: Columbia University Press, 1985), p. 177 (hereafter, Sedgwick 1985).

For at least the first half of the nineteenth century, public schools were unwholesome places, major defects being 'the prevalence of killer epidemic diseases, the schools' own admissions concerning the probability of moral contamination, and ... the cruelty involved in public-school life'.[11] Nevertheless, many parents were undaunted; there was more to be gained than lost, especially by families with social pretensions. The opportunity to board sons at suitable establishments away from home was in itself a major consideration:

> Where families were using these schools as part of a process of upward social mobility, a measure of discontinuity between home and school was essential: claustration of their sons in institutions which must be as near 'total' as possible was a necessary guarantee of their losing the values, manners and speech-patterns of their home background and taking on those of the classes they were entering. (Honey 1977, p. 208)

The impact of such an education upon an aspiring family is dramatized in Carey's novel *Not Like Other Girls*. The fictional Dick Mayne, with his standard English accent and his excellent though unforced company manners, represents a sharp contrast to his wealthy manufacturer father. Dick is on far better terms with his middle-class neighbours than either of his less educated parents. In spite of affectionate family relationships, his father freely admits to his mother that '[t]he lad's a cut above us both, though he has the good taste to try and hide it' (*NLOG*, p. 14). This discontinuity with his home background, allied to his father's wealth, ultimately gains for Dick the opportunity to marry into a family that has never been in 'trade'.

Yet not all families sent their sons to public school wholly for the purpose of social advancement. For, as the nineteenth century progressed, the public school became valued as something more than a vehicle through which social status was acquired or retained. According to Honey, there emerged 'a powerful new value in Victorian society which the family ... was powerless to generate: *manliness*'.[12] This new value required the development of a specific range of male behaviours. To use Honey's somewhat quirky terminology:

> The *machismo* which gripped the later Victorians embraced three interwoven strains: 'anti-effeminacy, stiff-upper-lippery, and physical hardness.' (Honey 1977, p. 209)

---

11 J.R. de Symons Honey, *Tom Brown's Universe* (Millington, 1977), p. 203 (hereafter, Honey 1977).

12 Honey 1977, p. 209. For discussion about nineteenth-century versions of 'manliness,' see David Newsome, *Godliness and Good Learning*, (London: John Murray, 1961), especially pp. 195–200. (Hereafter referred to as Newsome 1961). Newsome also attempts to chart the reasons behind the emergence of this new priority in education. See pp. 216–27.

It was deemed that these desirable attributes could only be instilled into a boy in a setting both devoid of womenfolk and away from the supposed excess of affection to be found in the home. The presence of all-male teaching staffs and the inherent austerity and brutality of the public school system, made the public schools the ideal venue for such work (Honey 1977, p. 222). Edward Thring, headmaster of Uppingham between 1853 and 1887, certainly endorsed both the asset of manliness and the notion that the public school was the appropriate location for its inculcation. In a letter dating from the early 1870s, he emphasises 'manliness' more strongly than social considerations, arguing that the recipient of a 'manly' education has a much-respected and universally-applicable training for later life:

> There is a very strong feeling growing up among the merchant class in England in favour of the public schools; and hundreds go to schools now who thirty years ago would not have thought of doing so. The learning to be responsible, and independent, to bear pain, to drop rank, and wealth, and home luxury, is a priceless boon. I think myself that it is this which has made the English such an adventurous race; and that with all their faults ... the public schools are the cause of this manliness.[13]

Thus, a sojourn at public school seems to have been viewed as far more than an indulgence that rich parents bestowed upon their sons. It was, additionally, an essential education in the foremost values of the age.[14] By implication, the man who did not undergo this lengthy and expensive training somehow lacked not only a vital ingredient in the making of a gentleman but also a vital ingredient in the making of a man. Another great advocate of 'manliness', Charles Kingsley, certainly felt that in being deprived of a public school education, he had lost a great deal. His biographer relates that:

> Dr Hawtrey ... was anxious to have him at Eton; and Dr Arnold would have welcomed him at Rugby; but his parents decided otherwise. Charles deeply regretted this decision in after life, as it was his own conviction that nothing but a public school education would have overcome his constitutional shyness.[15]

---

13 Letter, c. 1873, cited in Honey 1977, p. 146. See also Newsome 1961, p. 222.

14 What Seidler says of men in the late twentieth century is likely to have been true in the nineteenth: 'If we live in a "man's world", it is not a world that has been built upon the needs and nourishment of men. Rather, it is a social world of power and subordination in which men have been forced to compete if they are to benefit from their inherited masculinity' (Seidler 1989, p. 21).

15 See F.E. Kingsley, *Charles Kingsley: His letters and Memories of his Life* (London: Macmillan, 1890 [1883]), pp. 6–7.

On a similar though fictional note, Rosa Carey's early novel *Barbara Heathcote's Trial* [1871] contains the very pointed moral that a less 'manly' education leaves its subject dangerously unsophisticated and insular. When the eponymous heroine's favourite brother, Leigh, is rusticated from his university for a year on account of a drunken brawl, the local squire notes that Leigh's innocence rather than his innate wickedness has been his downfall:

> the lad ... never went to school, never mixed much with other fellows; learnt from his sister's governess, or what [his father] and the vicar ... could teach him ... [T]o turn a fellow like that, with all his ignorance of the world, into the midst of a gay university! – well, if he hadn't gone to the wrong ... it would have been a miracle ...[16]

By not attending public school, the fictional Leigh has lost something in terms of his development which would have permitted him to pass through university creditably. However, as this passage and the one relating to Charles Kingsley make abundantly clear, the *savoir-faire* to be gained from a public school education was deemed to have very little to do with academic achievement. That conventional scholarly activity was accorded a somewhat low priority in the curriculum may be illustrated by reference to that classic tale of school life, *Tom Brown's School Days* [1857]. Early in the novel, the father of the eponymous hero meditates thus:

> 'Shall I tell him to mind his work, and say he's sent to school to make himself a good scholar? Well, but he isn't sent to school for that – at any rate, not for that mainly. I don't care a straw for Greek particles, or the digamma; no more does his mother ... If he'll only turn out a brave, helpful, truth-telling Englishman, and a gentleman, and a Christian, that's all I want.'[17]

The attributes that the fictional Squire Brown hopes will be acquired by his son appear innocuous enough. However, they imply the cultivation of a wide range of attitudes and behaviours. For neither the mindless regime of 'anti-effeminacy, stiff-upper-lippery, and physical hardness' outlined by Honey nor the purely intellectual ability to deal in 'Greek particles' are sufficient in themselves. Bravery suggests the need for confronting danger, possibly culminating in fighting for one's country; helpfulness and truth-telling suggest

---

16 R.N. Carey, *Barbara Heathcote's Trial* (London: Macmillan, 1915 [1871]), p. 34 (hereafter, *BHT*).

17 'An Old Boy' [i.e., Thomas Hughes], *Tom Brown's Schooldays* (London: Macmillan. 1898 [1857], pp. 60–61. Hughes' tale was based upon life at Rugby though, according to Honey, Hughes' view of the school was somewhat idiosyncratic (see Honey 1977, pp. 1–2). Hughes is quoted here because his book gained great popularity and came to represent the public school discourse in itself.

the ideals of chivalry; Englishness implies racial awareness and patriotism; and Christianity a type of diffused moral and social conduct. Yet, in spite of the strong rational/moral tone running through the passage, the quality of cultivated intelligence is notably absent from the final list. It seems that reason, far from being a deductive process based upon formally learnt principles, is largely represented as the will to conform to certain approved modes of 'moral' conduct.

Many of Carey's public school products appear to fulfil the requirements of the fictional Squire Brown, even to the extent of not betraying an excessive amount of intellect. For example, twenty-year-old Dick, in *Not Like Other Girls*,

> was quite of his mother's opinion, that an honest, God-fearing young fellow, who spoke the truth and shamed the devil; who had no special vices but a dislike for early rising; who had tolerable brains, and more than his share of muscle; who was in the Oxford eleven, and who had earned his blue ribbon – that such a one might be considered to set an example to his generation. (*NLOG*, p. 28)

Far from disputing the rationality of the public school style of education, Carey uses its peculiar canons of achievement, taste and precept as an indicator of class between men and of learned sexual difference in mixed company.[18]

Notwithstanding the fate of the fictional Leigh in *Barbara Heathcote's Trial*, fighting was an accepted part of public school life. At best, it rested easily amidst notions of sporting fairness and gentlemanly honour as well as having affinities with the perpetual wars and challenges to single combat to be found in Latin textbooks. In addition, the notion that fighting was 'natural' in men had a powerful advocate in Thomas Carlyle:

---

18 Nor was she alone in viewing the presence or absence of a public school education as a social indicatior. See also H.C. Davidson, gen. ed., *The Book of the Home* (London: Gresham, 1901), p. 145:

> One of the most conspicuous positive characteristics of the public school is its high social rank. This, combined with the organization and regime characteristic of boarding schools ... has given education there a peculiar and special character which leaves its stamp on most of those who are brought under its influence.

Not all of Carey's heroes have been to public school but she is ambivalent about those who have not been so educated. In *No Friend Like a Sister* [1906] an architect who was a 'day-boarder at a private school' marries well. However, his mother was the cast-off daughter of an earl and his uncle, who has succeeded to the title, is to 'give him a helping hand' in the near future (p. 381). In *At The Moorings*, public school educated Ned teaches at a grammar school. However, this is financial necessity rather than choice. In *The Old, Old Story* public-school-boy Harvey moves to a grammar school when his father dies penniless. He objects that the boys there are 'cads ... and not a gentleman amongst them'. However, his sister replies,'not everyone of our rank in life can afford to send their sons to public school' (p. 43).

> Man is created to fight; he is perhaps best of all definable as a born soldier; his life 'a battle and a march', under the right General. It is for ever indispensable for a man to fight: now with Necessity ... Scarcity ... Bogs, tangled Forests ... now ... with the hallucinations of his poor fellow men. Hallucinatory visions ... in the head of my poor fellow man ... make him claim over me rights which are not his. All Fighting ... is the dusty conflict of strengths, each thinking itself the strongest, or, in other words, the justest ...[19]

Nor did Carey fail to portray this supposedly innate bellicosity in her male characters, whether children or adults. In *Lover or Friend?*, the war hero Michael Burnett is made to discuss the theory and practice of fighting with the baby-faced schoolboy victor of one such altercation. The boy tells him 'Jefferson minor fought me, and I licked him. You may ask the other fellows, and they would tell you it was all fair. He is a head taller than me.' Michael Burnett's reply condones the fight, rewards the victor and embodies the conventions of such a contest:

> 'I hope you shook hands afterwards; fair fight and no malice, Willie. There's a shilling for you because you did not show the white feather in the face of the enemy.' (*LoF*, p. 314)

A set of rules and the act of shaking hands afterwards make fighting acceptable rather than disgraceful. However, Michael Burnett's final remark to Willie is of the greatest interest here, for it links the boy of the present with the man of the future, and the bravery shown in the playground with the prospect of a military career once school-days are over: 'You will be at the head of a brigade yet, my boy' (ibid.). If the Duke of Wellington did not literally remark that 'The Battle of Waterloo was won on the playing fields of Eton', it must have at least sounded plausible to Carey's generation.[20]

Yet, by today's standards, the narratorial comment that follows Michael's remark is somewhat chilling, even allowing for the untried enthusiasm of young boys:

> all Dr Ross's lads were bitten with the military fever ... each boy nourished a secret passion and desire to follow the Captain's foot-steps,

---

19 Thomas Carlyle, *Past and Present*, ed. A.M.D. Hughes (Oxford: Clarendon Press, 1927 [1843]), p. 172 (hereafter, *Past and Present*). The correlation between believing oneself to be right and attempting to enforce this view on another accords with Seidler's notion of 'silenc[ing] others in the name of reason. See above.

20 Cited in M Girouard, *The Return to Camelot* (New Haven: Yale University Press, 1981), p. 233 (hereafter, Girouard, 1981). Cf. also Henry Newbolt's poem, *Vitaï Lampada*, in which a game of cricket at school is paired with a military battle in later life. For the text of Newbolt's poem, see Girouard, pp. 233–4.

> [all] were ready to be hewed and slashed into small pieces if only the Victoria Cross might be their reward. (*LoF*, p. 314)

Nowhere in her writing does Carey refute the logic or the fitness of this enthusiasm. However, in her 1903 novel, *A Passage Perilous*, which is set in the Boer War, she has the heroine, Christian, make a flippant speech on this very subject. Newly married to a soldier about to go on active service, Christian articulates her anxiety in a piece of savage humour:

> 'I have a friend ... and I shall ask her to keep me company until ... until' – here Christian's eyes gleamed rather dangerously through her glasses – 'Jack has fought all his battles, and come back minus an arm or a leg, and with the Victoria Cross.'[21]

The fictional Christian does not question the premises underlying such 'bravery'. Indeed, she struggles to accommodate them. However, the factor that makes Christian's outburst even more emotive than the narratorial comment about 'military fever' in *Lover Or Friend?* is that Christian is speaking from a specifically female point of view; she is displaying personal emotions instead of reproducing the appropriate patriotic/patriarchal and thus universalized discourse. Her speech when someone ventures to criticize her husband is quite a different matter. She leaps to his defence and, quite without irony, justifies his actions according to the dominant ideal: 'A soldier must do his duty' (p. 53). In *A Passage Perilous*, there is a clear disparity between the emotive feminine response and the articulation of the dominant, even though both are expressed by the same person. This is contradictory but it is also identifiably human. A great deal of Carey's appeal as a writer lies in her ability to give voice to this kind of ambivalence. She writes the text of pleasure – containing that which is constructed by men but familiar to, and popular with, women – whilst simultaneously making visible, in fictional terms, the psychological cost to women of adherence to such masculinist ideals.

In spite of the advantages of a public school career, a man's education in the nicer points of combat, as well as upon a host of other essential gentlemanly refinements, was not gained merely by drawing analogies with sporting events and reading Latin books. Nor did the would-be gentleman wholly take as his paradigm the modern war hero, whether alive or recently dead. For the early nineteenth century saw the re-emergence and restoration to favour of the mediaeval ideal of chivalry, a phenomenon which was initially a means of conspicuous consumption for the rich, but which became a diffused mode of thought and conduct which permeated a much larger proportion of society as

21 R.N. Carey, *A Passage Perilous* (London: Macmillan, 1906 [1903]), p. 47.

the century progressed.[22] Mark Girouard summarizes the diffused phenomenon thus:

> [H]ow gentlemen lived and died was partly determined by the way in which they believed knights had lived and died. All gentlemen knew that they must be brave, show no sign of panic or cowardice, be courteous and protective to women and children, be loyal to their comrades and meet death without flinching. They knew because they had learnt the code of the gentleman ... through advice, through example, through what they had been taught at school or by their parents, and through endless stories of chivalry, daring, knights, gentlemen and gallantry ... told by way of history books, ballads, poems, plays, pictures and novels. (Girouard 1981, p. 7)

Carlyle was one of the many nineteenth-century writers who helped to create an intellectual environment in which the chivalric ideal could flourish as practice. Having encouraged men to believe that it was in their nature to fight, he also gave them a rationale for viewing their bloodletting in positive terms:

> Under the sky is no uglier spectacle than two men ... hacking one another's flesh; converting precious living bodies, and priceless living souls, into nameless masses of putrescence ... How did a chivalry ever come out of that; how anything that was not hideous, scandalous, infernal?
>
> ... let us remark ... how, in these baleful operations, a noble devout-hearted Chevalier will comfort himself, and an ignoble godless Bucanier and Chactaw Indian. Victory is the aim of each. But deep in the heart of the noble man it lies forever legible, that, as an invisible Just God made him, so will and must God's Justice ... ultimately prosper in all controversies and enterprises and battles whatsoever. Blessed divine Influence, traceable even in the horror of Battlefields and garments rolled in blood: how it ennobles even the Battlefield; and, in place of a Chactaw Massacre, makes it a Field of Honour! (*Past and Present*, p. 172)

Thus, according to Carlyle, the chevalier or knight may assure himself that victory is assigned to the righteous by a beneficent God. This conviction of 'God's Justice', to be found 'deep in the heart of the noble man', transforms any battle, brawl or skirmish into a Christianized version of the Jihad.[23]

---

22 Key nineteenth-century manifestations included the popularity of Scott's novels and, for the few, the conversion of their stately homes into baronial halls. Emblematically, there was, in 1839, the Eglinton Tournament, a mediaeval jousting match which attracted thousands of visitors. See Girouard 1981, chapters 4 and 7, *passim*. The chivalric ideal was not a coherent set of beliefs, practices or even texts. Rather, there was built onto a much earlier corpus of illustrative ballads and tales a further body of commentary and artistic output. See below.

23 Carlyle assumes that knights always fight from 'right' motives. However, once again, a notion of male rationality may be seen to 'silence others in the name of reason'.

Carlyle's *Past and Present*, written in 1843, was immensely popular throughout the nineteenth century. However, Carlyle was not the only person to write about chivalry; nor, indeed, was he the first. Kenelm Digby's influential attempt at codifying chivalric behaviour, *The Broadstone of Honour*, had been published in 1822 and continued in print in various editions until at least 1877.[24] In turn, this book was praised by such well-known and diversely-motivated men as William Wordsworth, John Ruskin, William Morris and Sir Robert Baden-Powell.[25] The early part of the century had also brought forth the poetry and novels of Sir Walter Scott and Tennyson's mediaeval romances. It was therefore virtually impossible for Carey to avoid allusion to the chivalric discourse when she created her male characters.[26] Indeed, the plots of at least two novels are partially framed by Arthurian legends, probably as mediated by Tennyson. However, in neither case does Carey simply lift an entire plot or character and re-present a mediaeval drama in Victorian dress.

Michael Burnett, hero of *Lover or Friend?*, appears to have been founded upon the *ideal* of knighthood as deliniated in Tennyson's *Guinevere* rather than upon any particular knight. He embodies all the attitudes and behaviours required by the oath of fealty to King Arthur:

> To reverence the King, as if he were
> Their conscience, and their conscience as their King,
> To break the heathen and uphold the Christ,
> To ride abroad redressing human wrongs,
> To speak no slander, no, nor listen to it,
> To lead sweet lives in purest chastity,
> To love one maiden only, cleave to her,
> And worship her by years of noble deeds,
> Until they won her ... [27]

However, these knightly qualities are brought decidedly up to date. Michael's reverence towards his monarch is proven by his military service; he upholds Christianity (albeit viewed as Protestantism) against the irreligion (which ultimately develops into Roman Catholicism) in another character, Mrs Blake; and yet he will not permit his fictional cousin Geraldine to slander Mrs Blake solely upon hearsay. Redressing human wrongs takes the form of confronting Mrs Blake about the husband she has deserted and the deceit she is practising upon her three children. Perhaps of most importance to the female reader, Michael is constructed as chaste and as having 'love[d] one maiden only',

---

24 Girouard 1981, p. 56.

25 Ibid., pp. 63–4.

26 Carey had certainly read Scott and sometimes used quotations from his novels as chapter headings. See, for example, chapter LI of *The Old, Old Story* [1894].

27 *The Poetical Works of Alfred, Lord Tennyson* (London: Ward Lock, n.d.), p. 361 (hereafter, *Poetical Works*).

worshipping her from afar for many years and desiring not so much fame as the means with which to marry her. From very early on in the novel his knightly devotion to his lady is made explicit:

> Michael was her ally – her faithful, trusty ally. No knight sworn to serve his liege lady had ever been more zealous in his fealty. (*LoF*, pp. 47–8)

However, the strikingly-named Launcelot Chudleigh, a central character in *Only the Governess* [1888], is constructed from two named Arthurian heroes: his namesake, the knight Sir Lancelot, and the more historically-authenticated figure of the Chevalier de Bayard. Each of these earlier sources is utilized in a single phase of the novel. In the opening stages of the narrative, Carey's Launcelot makes advances towards a married woman. However, unlike Tennyson's adulterous couple, this Lancelot and his lady are innocent. Mrs Thorpe, alias Miss Rossiter, certainly masquerades as a single woman; but she does not wish to be unfaithful or bigamously married. She has given Launcelot no encouragement and confesses her married state at the earliest opportunity. The unfortunate Launcelot Chudleigh is even less to blame; he believes that he is paying his addresses to a woman who is free to hear them. It is at this pivotal point in the narrative that the governing paradigm changes. When Carey's Launcelot discovers his (pardonable) mistake, he determines to restore Mrs Thorpe to her husband. Thus, the metaphorical adulterer, Sir Lancelot, becomes King Arthur's ideal knight in his efforts to 'ride abroad addressing human wrongs'. However, because he is both noble-minded and innocent, he can also be ascribed the qualities of the Chevalier de Bayard, who was *sans peur et sans reproche*. Indeed, the chapter in which Launcelot makes his resolve is entitled 'A Modern Bayard'.[28]

Evidently, whilst Carey draws upon literary texts about mediaeval chivalry, the aspects she chooses for repetition are partial and carefully chosen. There are two likely reasons for this selectivity. One is that, although knights in the abstract were brave and courteous and, above all, popular with audiences, knights in the specific tended to be sexually promiscuous, violent and petty. Even Tennyson's ameliorated Geraint is extremely discourteous to his Enid; even Tennyson's Lancelot is guilty of adultery. In short, Carey bowdlerized mediaeval chivalric stories in order to make them suitable for representation in a context of virtuous domesticity. A second likely reason for Carey's selectivity is that she wished to create individualized male characters who were recognizably living in the nineteenth or early twentieth century. It was not sufficient for such characters to be brave, courtly and errant; they were also

28 For details of the original Chevalier de Bayard, see *Brewer's Dictionary of Phrase and Fable*, Tenth revised edition (London: Cassell, 1967), p. 81; see also R.N. Carey, *Only the Governess* (London: Macmillan, 1917 [1888]) (hereafter, *OTG*), chapter 24.

required to play various affectional and hierarchical roles within the family. Above all, they were obliged to be explicitly modern lovers, and to be seen negotiating the social mores surrounding the courtship rituals of their fictional and non-fictional peers.

In the fullness of time, the nineteenth-century chivalric revival gave rise to modern chivalric myths, these gaining wide currency and popularity via media coverage.[29] Such media reports functioned as more than tales of heroic deeds to be read about; they also embodied both desirable and possible behaviours for emulation if the need arose. Few men amongst the general readership could turn their homes into baronial halls or host mock-mediaeval jousts; even fewer could boast noble blood or superior position in society. However, chivalric ideals such as defending the weak and showing deference towards women were available to all men. One of the best-known media myths during Carey's lifetime was that of the wreck of the *Birkenhead*, a troop ship which sank off the coast of West Africa in 1852. According to one account, after the women and children were put into the lifeboats:

> The roll of the drum called the soldiers to arms on the upper deck. The call was promptly obeyed, though every man knew it was his death summons. There they stood, as if on parade, no man showing restlessness or fear, though the ship was every moment going down, down.[30]

A similar version of the story is cited in Samuel Smiles' popular work, *Self Help* [1859], Smiles' version concluding, somewhat sententiously,

> not a heart quailed; no one flinched from his duty in that trying moment … Down went the ship, and down went the heroic band … Glory and honour to the gentle and the brave! The examples of such men never die, but, like their memories, are immortal.[31]

---

29 It is not that incidents detailed in newspapers, periodicals, school-books and so on were untrue, merely that they were constructed within a mythic paradigm. The term 'myth' is used here according to Ninian Smart's definition, though without the overtly religious overtones: '[I]t is convenient to ...include not merely stories about ... the gods.. etc., but also the historical events of a religious significance in a tradition … without prejudice [as] to whether the stories accurately describe what actually occurred in history', Ninian Smart, *The Religious Experience of Mankind* (Glasgow: Collins, 9th impression, May 1979), pp. 18–19.

Thus, the modern chivalric myth may be seen as a story neutral as to truth or falsity, which is based upon an historical event and which is believed to be significant in terms of the (new) chivalric tradition.

30 Girouard 1981, p. 13. Girouard cites a nineteenth-century school history book here. He retails the story in its more probable form on pp. 13–14.

31 S. Smiles, *Self Help*, (London: John Murray, 1902 [1859]), p. 406 (hereafter, *Self Help*). For a similar account, see H.O. Arnold-Foster, *The Citizen Reader* (London: Cassell, 14th edn, ?1889), pp. 113–14.

The accounts are almost formulaic in both content and vocabulary, or, at the very least, reminiscent of a host of similar myths put into straightforward literary form.[32] However, they are represented as unmediated fact.

Carey makes interesting use of both the myth of the *Birkenhead* and a similar modern myth of her own devising when illustrating the behaviour of Michael Burnett, the soldier-hero of *Lover Or Friend?* She appears to have in mind the wreck of the *Birkenhead* when she makes him ponder over 'a story he had once read. Was it the wreck of the *Royal George*, he wondered?' She has him both assert the non-fictional status of the story – 'The name of the vessel escaped him, but he knew the story was a true one; it had really happened' – and phrase his recollection in language remarkably similar to that of Smiles:[33]

> She was a troop ship, and there were hundreds of brave soldiers on board; and when they knew there was no hope, the officers drew up their men on the deck, just as though they were on parade; and the gallant fellows stood there, in rank and file, as they went down to their watery grave.
>
> 'And not a man flinched, you may depend on that', he said, half aloud; 'for they were Englishmen, and Englishmen know how to die.' (*LoF*, p. 254)

Michael's recollection of the story immediately follows his discovery that the woman he loves is about to marry someone else. Thus, his opportunity for emulation of the myth comes, not in this instance because he must face imminent death with equanimity, but because he is in a situation in which he must be gallant and not flinch. The moral he preaches to himself via this story is that he must face the future as those other soldiers faced death: as a man and as a gentleman. The final line of this interpolated story, 'for they were all Englishmen, and Englishmen know how to die', is a reiteration of its purpose, which is to remind Michael of the behaviour and sentiments appropriate to the occasion.

Shortly afterwards, Michael repeats the story of the wreck to sixteen-year-old Kester, the narrator subsequently adding that 'he told it very well, too' (*LoF*, p. 254). From this latter cue, the reader may assume that Michael has already assimilated the prescribed qualities of mind. However, his victory over himself is further endorsed by Kester. Recalling Michael's words the following

32 Tennyson's *The Charge of the Light Brigade* and Cowper's *Loss of the Royal George* express similar sentiments about those who go to their deaths honourably. For Tennyson, see *Poetical Works*, p. 277. For Cowper, see note 33. Accounts of Scott's expedition to the South Pole and the sinking of the *Titanic* are similarly stylized. See Girouard 1981, pp. 2–6.

33 A troop-ship called the *Royal George* was indeed wrecked in 1782, with the loss of 800 lives. William Cowper commemorated the event in a poem in the same year. However, Cowper's *Loss of the Royal George* does not state that the soldiers lined up on deck as the ship went down. See F.T. Palgrave, *The Golden Treasury* (London: Macmillan, 1890), pp. 148–9.

day, Kester works out the contemporary significance of the story, and to the words 'for they were all Englishmen, and Englishmen know how to die,' adds the mental rejoinder, 'Ah, and to live, too.' (*LoF*, p. 256). At this point, the reader is called upon to judge Michael's reaction to his painful situation against the standard of the English soldiers in the story and to decide that he meets the challenge in all respects.

However, this situation, in which continuing to live requires as much courage as facing death, merely parallels an earlier challenge against which Michael has already triumphed. Michael has gained his Victoria Cross for protecting wounded colleagues against enemy attack during the Zulu wars, this distinction being achieved at the expense of permanent disability and the loss of his career. Carey confines the precise details of the skirmish to a single emotive paragraph which fulfils all the requirements of a modern chivalric myth, but she devotes considerably more space to Michael's courage in dealing with the physical and emotional cost of his heroism.[34] Carey thus extrapolates from within these modern myths a brand of 'domestic' courage which is comprehensible to the female reader and which fits plausibly into the female sphere of the home. Facing death by drowning (the example provided in the myth of the Birkenhead) translates into facing a life of shattered hopes. Similarly, facing the enemy in the course of a battle)an albeit fictional account of winning the Victoria Cross) is transmuted into heroically facing the enemies of disability and despair.[35] Michael may thus be viewed as the perfect gentleman, one who is brave under all circumstances, on and off the literal

---

34 The allusion to Tennyson's 'Sir Galahad', 'My strength is as the strength of ten/ Because my heart is pure', in this passage is unlikely to have been missed by nineteenth-century readers. See *Poetical Works*, p. 126.

> [I]n the dim light of the flickering watch-fires, he saw dusky figures moving in the direction of a hut where a few sick and wounded men had been placed. There was not a second to lose; in a moment the poor fellows would have been butchered. Calling out to some of his men to follow him, and not perceiving that he was alone, he ... entered the hut by a hole that served as a window ... the thought of the few helpless wretches writhing in terror on their pallet beds behind him seemed to give him the force of ten men. 'They shall pass only over my body! God save my poor fellows!' was his inward cry, as he blocked up the narrow doorway and struck at his dusky foes like a madman. (*LoF*, p. 31)

35 In his fight with disability, Michael is emulating his own earlier heroism. However, the principle remains the same. An example of 'domestic' courage analogous to the more traditional chivalric myth is to be found in R.N. Carey, *Sir Godfrey's Granddaughters*, (London: Macmillan, 1899 [1892]), p. 393 (hereafter, *SGG*). In this episode, Alick Lyall delays his forthcoming marriage indefinitely so that he can use his entire stock of savings to pay off his brother-in-law's debts. The 'lady' in question is his fiancee:

> No lady of olden times felt her heart swell more proudly, as she watched her knight ride forth to tilt or tourney with her colours floating from his lance ... Was ever a knight more valiant? she thought ... Was he not going forth to ransom the weak and helpless? Would she not wait gladly, thankfully, for half a lifetime for one so leal and faithful?

Figure 4: From *My Lady Frivol* (date unknown), opposite p. 156

battlefield; one who conforms to the ideal, as Carlyle would have it, that 'thou shalt be strong, and not in muscle only, if thou wouldst prevail!'[36]

The Community of the Male

In summary, Carey's fictional gentleman bears the stamp of a public school education though he is unlikely to be especially erudite. He has almost certainly been inculcated with notions of sportsmanship and proper fighting spirit; and he is well versed in myths of chivalry, both ancient and modern. However, in line with the non-fictional world of Carey's time, even when he has been exposed to the appropriate compound of knowledge and experience, this is no guarantee of his consequent gentlemanly behaviour and attitudes.[37] In short, he

36 *Past and Present*, p. 173.

37 In Lyotardian terms, one referent or institution cuts across another, thereby interrupting the connexion between the theoretical deployment of a learnt code and the subject's actual response to it. 'No one ... is entirely powerless over the messages that ... position [them] at the post of sender, addressee or referent.' Yet language-game 'partners' are also 'displaced by the messages that traverse them, in perpetual motion. Each language partner, when a move pertaining to [them] is made, undergoes a 'displacement,' an alteration of some kind that not only affects [them] in [their] capacity as addressee and referent but also as

reflects his counterpart as represented in the non-fictional writings of the real world, whose derelictions and delinquencies may, by a peculiar irony, also be laid at the door of his public school. For, even while the public school as an institution purported to prioritize the dissemination of chivalric referents, it simultaneously permitted its gentlemanly product to evade one of chivalry's essential tenets. That is to say, such establishments encouraged their pupils to circumvent the part of the chivalric code which prescribed an unfailingly courteous and protective attitude towards women. Such a situation came to pass because the public school provided, for those associated with it, an ongoing sense of community and affiliation which had the power to cut across both family ties and alternative value systems. To quote Honey:

> In ... being a community which could exercise an emotional hold not only during schooldays but for life, the public school became an alternative to the Victorian family as a reference group – 'an expression of shared perspectives, value systems, group norms etc.' used by those members who identified themselves with it 'as a standard for self-evaluation and as a source for [their] own personal values and goals'. (Honey 1977, p. 157; punctuation original.)

Honey does not remark on the consequences of such a powerful frame of reference for the rest of society. However, as Eve Kosofsky Sedgwick points out, the public school became 'a crucial link in ruling-class male homosocial formation'.[38] In other words, the 'shared ... value systems' of the public school

---

sender', J.-F. Lyotard, *The Postmodern Condition* (Manchester, Manchester University Press, 1987), p. 16.

Thus, a premise formulated from one conversation (act of communication between individuals) may be modified by another, the effect being to modify an existing state of mind and, by extension, existing modes of behaviour. However, powerful institutions also modify the individual: 'an institution differs from a conversation in that it always requires supplementary constraints for statements to be declared admissible within its bounds. The constraints function to filter discursive potentials, *interrupting possible connections in the communication networks*: there are certain things that should not be said', ibid., p. 17 (my emphasis).

In that there is frequently a gap between desirable modes of male behaviour and their realization, Carey's fictional version of the male subject is as fragmented as his non-fictional counterpart. This is not to say that Carey perceived a fragmented subject, merely that she portrayed what she saw.

38 Sedgwick 1985, p. 176. Sedgwick defines the word 'homosocial' as 'social bonds between persons of the same sex' (Sedgwick 1985, p. 1). In her theoretical opening chapter, she observes that:

> [T]he status of women, and the whole question of arrangements between genders, is deeply ... inscribed in the structure even of relationships that seem to exclude women – even in male homosocial/homosexual relationships ... [I]n any male-dominated society, there is a special relationship between male homosocial (including homosexual) desire and the structures for maintaining and transmitting patriarchal power ... (Ibid., p. 25)

She defines 'desire' as:

promoted a certain freemasonry amongst public school products once they had become full members of the ruling class, and resulted in instances of collusion and exclusion. In particular, women were marginalized for, although the chivalric ideal posited a particular notion of reverence towards women, it had a much stronger orientation towards the cultivation of manly qualities such as toughness and anti-effeminacy. Thus chivalric ideas and practices, as mediated through the more general public school ethos, encouraged those who possessed them to identify with each other in a community of the male rather than with society at large.

The aspect of the chivalric code relating to women was therefore undermined from within the very structure that cultivated it. Chivalric behaviour towards women might have made a man into a gentleman but ultimately a gentleman was responsible to his peers and not to the object of his chivalry. Carey observes this latter phenomenon throughout her novels but perhaps most perceptively in *Sir Godfrey's Granddaughters* [1892]. When the fictional Alick Lyall discovers that his beloved sister Hester has been brought to financial ruin by the debts of her gentlemanly loafer of a husband, he initially judges the miscreant in terms of chivalry and manliness, the values of his education and class: 'to call yourself a man, and to bring the woman you swore to protect to this bitter disgrace!' However, this denunciation is followed by one even more damning, one in which he directly invokes the self-referential community of the male: 'Every honest man will cry shame on you!'[39] At this point in the narrative, Hester herself is virtually forgotten.

In this episode, recourse to the community of the male is benign in its effect upon a woman. The active man in the case draws upon values that not only condemn the unworthy but also aid the victim. However, this is not an invariable outcome in Carey's novels. Nor have such positive outcomes been frequently met with by theorists of homosociality and/or patriarchy *per se*. Eve Kosovsky Sedgwick's major work *Between Men* [1985], is a particularly interesting contribution to research in this field. Citing the work of Rene Girard, she notes that a motif frequently encountered within the European novel-writing tradition is that of the 'erotic triangle', a social grouping consisting of two male 'rivals' and a 'beloved' female in which the male–male relationship is 'even stronger, more heavily determined of actions and choices, than anything in the bond between either of the lovers and the beloved.' Plainly, the desires of the woman in such a situation are subordinated to those

---

analogous to the psychoanalytic use of "libido" – not for a particular affective state or emotion, but for the affective or social force, the glue, even when its manifestation is hostility or hatred or something less emotively charged, that shapes an important relationship. (Ibid., p. 2)

39 *Sir Godfrey's Granddaughters* (London: Macmillan, 1899 [1892]), p. 374 (hereafter, *SGG*).

of both men; her value is that of an object rather than a subject. An understanding of this motif is, in itself, a useful critical tool for analysing certain homosocial relationships in literature and, by implication, for understanding a crucial aspect of society.

However, Sedgwick's project extends beyond an analysis of 'romantic' rivalries. She therefore goes on to overlay the paradigm of the male–male–female triangle with Girard's more general theory that '*any* relation of rivalry is structured by the same play of emulation and identification' (emphasis original). In aligning the parties involved in the erotic triangle with a broader range of 'desire'-based relationships, Sedgwick provides a method for analysing the power relationships underlying all male–male–female triangles whether or not they have a basis in conventional eroticism.[40]

This broader version of the erotic triangle may be profitably used in order to place small sections of the community of the male under the microscope. To do so is valuable because it brings individualized, 'local' power relationships in to sharp focus and thus highlights the androcentrism of day-to-day social transactions. For the critic to utilize the concept of the triangle is for her to confront, at close quarters, a scenario in which two named, or at least individualized, men engage in an exclusionary languagegame that relegates a named or individualized woman from the position of interlocutor to that of a parenthetical remark; it is to view this woman, not as a fully participant sender-addressee-referent (as Lyotard would have it), but as a cipher, a referent only.

It is pertinent, at this point to return to Carey's novel *Sir Godfrey's Granddaughters*, and to the triangle existing between the fictional Alick Lyall, his sister and his brother-in-law. Fortunately for the woman in this particular triangle, the relationship between the two men is, on the whole, supported by mutual contempt bordering on indifference rather than by a stronger emotion such as affection or hatred. It is even more fortunate for her that her brother's beliefs on the subject of debt coincide with her own. For, when Alick asserts the values of the community of the male against his brother-in-law (gentlemen do not behave in this way), the result is that he meets the latter's liabilities (on the grounds that these values must be upheld). That is, he quite accidentally engineers the best possible outcome for Hester. In an alternative scenario, she might have emerged as the victim for a second time as the two closest males in her life made her wretched over either their collusion or their acrimony.

---

40 Sedgwick 1985, p. 21. Sedgwick certainly ascribes to the terms 'erotic' and 'rivals' meanings beyond their dictionary definitions:

> although the triangles that most shape [Girard's] view tend, in the European tradition, to involve bonds of "rivalry" between males "over" a woman, in his view *any* relation of rivalry is structured by the same play of emulation and identification, whether the entities occupying the corners of the triangle be heroines, gods, books, or whatever. (Ibid., p. 23).

The fictional 'triangular' relationship between Philip Worsley, Lord Joslyn and Bonnie Redford in Carey's novel *My Lady Frivol* [1899] is less benign in its effect. In one particular episode Carey ably illustrates that, even if rival males are acknowledged to be gentlemen, a woman's safety and comfort are not guaranteed. At a quiet evening party arranged by Bonnie's uncle, the conceited Philip Worsley is permitted to tease Bonnie with attentions that are manifestly unwelcome whilst Lord Joslyn apparently allows his sporting instincts to overcome the chivalric ideal of protecting a woman from annoyance:

> Bonnie was ... telegraphing for assistance; but he did not appear to understand her signals. Joslyn could be dense when he chose. '*Noblesse Oblige*,' he muttered to himself; 'one can't interfere with another fellow's innings, even if he be a cad; Bonnie must get out of the hole as best she can ... '[41]

It is possible to discern two competing motivations behind Lord Joslyn's use of the term '*Noblesse Oblige*', both of which would be justifiable to his peers in the community of the male though dubious from other perspectives. Either he is privileging the feelings of one of his peers over the feelings of a lady or he is punishing the lady because he feels personally affronted. Perhaps elements of both motivations apply. For Joslyn has, on a previous occasion, seen Bonnie flirting with her tormentor. Thus, when he abandons her in her difficulty, he may be seen to be exercising a form of petty revenge on her and rationalizing his behaviour by reference to sporting fairness. At the same time, even this revenge or punishment is justifiable to the community of the male because Joslyn, as one of their rational/moral number, is accorded the right to judge female behaviour. Yet Lord Joslyn is not the villain of the piece: that role is reserved for the boorish Philip Worsley; and the moral of the story lies not in the conduct of a cad but in the misconduct of a lady. The incident intimates, via Bonnie's unseemly behaviour and consequent discomfort, that a woman is better protected by her own modesty than by her male friends.

However, Sedgwick does not confine the application of triangular theory to commentary on the subordinate position of fictional women in their most significant relationships. Rather, she uses it to build a useful theory about the mechanisms of patriarchy *per se*. Drawing upon Heidi Hartmann's definition of patriarchy, she first posits that the 'erotic triangle' mirrors society itself:

41 *My Lady Frivol* (London: Hutchinson, n.d. [1899]), p. 201. Her tormentor should also have taken the hint. There are few direct allusions to 'pestering' in etiquette books. However, rhetoric suggests that women should have the choice of whether to respond to male overtures. See, for example, Mrs Humphrey, *Manners for Men* (Exeter: Web and Bower, 1979 [1897]), p. 13.

> in making the power relationships between men and women appear to be dependent upon the power relationships between men and men, [Hartmann] suggests that the large-scale social structures are congruent with the male-male-female erotic triangles ... [42]

She then moves on to ally this theory of male-male relationships with Gayle Rubin's notion of woman-as-commodity:

> Gayle Rubin has argued ... that patriarchal heterosexuality can best be discussed in terms of one or other form of the traffic in women: it is the use of women as exchangeable, perhaps symbolic, property for the primary purpose of cementing the bonds of men with men. For example, Levi-Strauss writes, 'The total relationship of exchange which constitutes marriage is not established between a man and a woman, but between two groups of men, and the woman figures only as one of the objects in the exchange, not as one of the partners.' (Sedgwick 1985, pp. 25–6)

Thus, Sedgwick's understanding of the mechanics of patriarchy consists of two closely connected propositions: that solidarity among men enables the domination of women; and that such solidarity is achieved by the use of women as a means of exchangeable property. Put in Levi-Strauss's crude terminology, such transactions appear to be on a par with the slave market. Yet Sedgwick's observations have their counterpart, albeit in fictionalized form, in many of Rosa Carey's novels. The irate brother in *Sir Godfrey's Granddaughters* may be seen to buy the quiescence of a deficient husband and thereby to gain the right, properly a husband's, to regulate the affairs of the entire family. Similarly, regardless of his motivation, when the sporting Joslyn in *My Lady Frivol* refuses to rescue Bonnie, he may be seen to make a gift of her to a fellow male, quite ignoring her own best interests.

However, perhaps the most obvious example of 'traffic in women' is to be met with in Carey's novel, *Lover or Friend?* The situation fits well with Levi-Strauss' interpretation of marriage as a transaction in which 'the woman figures only as one of the objects in the exchange, not as one of the partners', though it is about the prevention of a marital alliance rather than its fulfilment. When it is discovered that the personally impeccable and totally unsuspecting Cyril Blake is possessed of a disreputable mother and a criminal father, the males of his fiancée's family deem it necessary for the engagement to be broken. Notably, his fiancée Audrey is not enlightened about this change in her circumstances until three days after the discovery is made. In the intervening

42 Sedgwick 1985, p. 25. Sedgwick quotes Heidi Hartmann's definition of patriarchy at greater length on p. 3: '[R]elations between men, which have a material base, and which, though hierarchical establish or create interdependence and solidarity among men that enable them to dominate women.'

period, a number of momentous transactions by way of fact-finding, negotiation and decision-making are undertaken by her cousin Michael and her father.[43] However, the novel betrays more than a woman's exclusion from the decision-making process. For, although Audrey is sincerely pitied by both her father and Michael, their own vested interests very evidently take precedence. When talking to Cyril Blake's mother, Michael, who is himself supposed to be in love with Audrey, rushes into an impetuous speech which clearly indicates his priorities:

> you can understand it is not a pleasant business to ask these questions of a lady; but there are many interests involved, and I am like a son to Dr Ross [that is, Audrey's father]. I am bound to look into this matter more closely for his sake and–' he paused … (LoF, p. 300)

Audrey is relegated to the clause that is never spoken; familial relationships, specifically those involving the interests of male kin, are placed first. However, Audrey's father is even more outspoken about the embarrassment that he thinks the disclosure will cause him personally:

> 'Is it likely that a man in my position would allow his family to be allied to a convicted criminal? Would any amount of hushing up render such an alliance tolerable? ... I have never cared much for conventionality, or for the mere show of things; but I suppose that, in some sense, the good opinion of my fellow-men is necessary for my comfort.' (Ibid., pp. 316–17)

Thus, when he says shortly afterwards, 'I must think of my child', the phrase sounds somewhat hollow. Nevertheless, the unfortunate Audrey is not entirely silenced by the community of the male and its own loudly-voiced priorities. She dutifully gives up all hope of marrying Cyril upon her father's command. However, when her father attempts to represent the end of the engagement as a natural consequence of Cyril's fine feelings, she betrays the knowledge that the decision is not entirely in his hands:

> 'If Cyril be the man I think him ... he will be far too proud and honourable to hold you to your engagement.'
>
> 'That may be,' she answered a little wearily. 'I know the strong pressure that will be put on him. You will have no difficulty with him; he will do as you wish. My poor Cyril! how can he do otherwise? (Ibid., p. 349)

The father does indeed have the power to put 'strong pressure' on the lover. The righteous parent has the overwhelming advantage of being the latter's

43 See pp. 290–357.

employer and as such has the power to subject him to ignominious dismissal if he will not do the honourable thing and resign from his post. Thus, with his livelihood taken away from him, Cyril is not only financially unable to marry Audrey but also reliant upon Dr Ross for references. With the additional prejudices of the middle-class community in which he moves working against him and with the implicit appeal to a shared chivalric code on the part of the males in Audrey's family, 'poor Cyril' is indeed unable to 'do otherwise'.

Audrey's exclusion from the decision-making process indicates a great deal about her non-existent position in the community of the male. Moreover, she is, to recall Gayle Rubin's words, 'exchangeable, perhaps symbolic, property for the primary purpose of cementing the bonds of men with men'. She is very visibly an object of exchange; and it is only the unpleasant discovery about Cyril Blake's parentage that arrests the bonding process that has started between Cyril Blake and the males of the Ross family. Initially, the males of Audrey's family are willing to acknowledge Cyril Blake as a 'partner'. Though disappointed with Cyril's comparative poverty, they are even willing to mobilize the mechanisms of the greater community of the male in order to place him on a parity with themselves. Speaking retrospectively, Audrey's father tells Michael of the plans he had made to improve Cyril's lot:

> '"You are certainly not in the position in which I would wish to see my son-in-law," I said to him; "but I will speak to Charrington, and see what is to be done."
>
> 'Well, I have spoken to him, and Charrington only promised the other day that he would push him on. I have no doubt at all that, with my interest and standing in the place, Cyril would have had a house in time, and Audrey's position would have been equal to her sister's.[44]

However, when Cyril's undesirable family connexions become known, his status radically changes. Audrey's male kin no longer wish to '[cement] ... bonds' with him. The gift or 'exchangeable ... property' of a woman is hastily withdrawn and he is told that partnership with him is no longer desired. In this novel, Carey portrays the community of the male in its most self-interested mode. The woman is, by definition, excluded from consideration but even one of its own number is made to experience the extremes of its power of self-regulation: on the one hand, nurturance of its own; on the other, repudiation of the inexpedient.

---

44 *LoF*, p. 317. Dr Ross and Charrington are senior masters at a public school; Cyril Blake is a junior master. The 'house' that the latter might have expected to gain is a boarding house for pupils at the school. This would have been both lucrative and socially desirable. See Honey 1977, p. 301.

Woman as Expert; or, The Gentleman at Home

In her fiction, Carey reproduces the androcentrism of the real world but she observes that androcentrism from a specifically feminine viewpoint. As women are excluded from the community of the male, it is unsurprising that she writes at length about the domestic tastes, habits and vicissitudes of her male characters. Whether or not intentionally, it is in such matters that Carey's novels are tailored to the experience and needs of a female readership. For, in the simple act of representing the domestic servicing of men, she affirms the importance of a time-consuming though potentially undervalued element in the existence of most women. In addition, in depicting her fictional males within the home she depicts them in their least powerful position. Though their womenfolk are dependent upon them financially, they are dependent upon their womenfolk for home comfort.

Yet this is not to say that Carey invariably entertains the reader with images of perfect housewifery and gratified male consumers. In many cases, the reader is led to sympathise with a hard-working breadwinner who, having completed a day's labour, receives neither sympathy nor gratitude from his family when he returns home. For example, the reader can enjoy a safe and smug kind of horror when Mollie gives her schoolmaster brother, Cyril, a cup of cold tea in *Lover Or Friend?* (p. 45). No adverse comment is passed on Mollie but Cyril's tiredness and slight depression are dwelt upon sufficiently for the reader to realize that this is not the homecoming he deserves.

However, the women in Carey's fictional families usually greet their menfolk with better grace and sociability. In *The Household of Peter* [1905], the eponymous hero's sisters always have an inviting tea-table ready for him when he returns home from work, and they always try to provide his favourite foods. Similarly, Anne Frere in *For Lilias* [1885] is always on hand when her brother needs her, though, oddly enough, her consistent good nature and reliability are most strikingly illustrated in a passage which describes a rare rupture in the usual domestic harmony:

> [Capel Frere] expected to find tea-things, a hissing urn, and Anne with a cheerful face – whether she felt cheerful or not – ready to talk to him on any subject he liked to propose … Instead of that, there was that most industrious of women, Anne, keeping blindman's holiday, with a brat of a child sitting comfortably in her lap, toasting its bare feet at the fire, with honest disregard of appearances.[45]

45 R.N. Carey, *For Lilias* (London: Macmillan, 1902 [1885]), p. 22.

Even if Capel Frere's peevishness is like that of a spoilt child who fears that someone else has usurped his place, the rhetoric of the scene suggests that somehow he is being defrauded of something that is his by right.

Yet, throughout her novels, Carey does more than to suggest that women have an obligation to service men. She also argues that the majority of men are incorrigibly helpless with regard to anything domestic, and thus decidedly in need of female assistance. For example, in *Rue With a Difference* [1900], the otherwise intelligent and affectionate Mr Nugent is totally incapable of comprehending the needs of his young daughter. A widower, he feels obliged to leave little Phillipa entirely in the hands of her heartless grandmother and a harsh-mannered nurse even though they both ignore any suggestions he makes for her well-being. He is quite explicit about his ignorance:

> 'Poor little Phil ... if she were only a boy I should know how to deal with her. I am very fond of my little daughter ... but I am obliged to leave her to her grandmother's management.' [46]

Nor does he realize that his daughter is being ill-treated. It takes another woman, Valerie, to undeceive him and to provide a solution. Valerie takes Phillipa into her own home and, by careful nursing, saves the child from a nervous breakdown.[47]

Mr Nugent also requires Valerie's help on more mundane matters. Once he has rid the house of his wicked mother-in-law, he asks for advice on how to turn it into a proper home: 'There are limits to masculine knowledge ... and the drawing-room baffles me' (*RWAD*, pp. 406–7). The reader will not be surprised by the request. Having, earlier in the novel, compared his own substantial but joyless house with Valerie's smaller but cosier cottage, Mr Nugent describes the latter as 'a real home-nest' and, '[sits] in his solitary library in the evening ... [thinking] longingly of [Valerie's] bright little sitting-room' (Ibid., p. 236).

That women should be well versed in the art of creating a home was hardly a radical notion for Carey's time and her novels mirror in fiction what some of her contemporaries were publishing as fact throughout the nineteenth century. For example, the influential Charlotte Yonge, in her oft-reprinted conduct book, *Womankind* [1877], states that:

> Men can seldom, if ever, make a home by themselves, and though they can live their lives without a present one, sometimes rising above the need, sometimes falling below, it is seldom that there is not either in memory or in hope, some precious spot that has been, – nay, that still is the home of their affections, or to which they hope yet to attain. (*Womankind*, p. 264)

46 *Rue With a Difference* (London: Macmillan, 1914 [1900]), p. 125 (hereafter, *RWAD*).
47 Carey uses this term. See p. 230.

And, indeed, Carey even goes so far as to illustrate Yonge's notion that 'men can seldom ... make a home by themselves' by representing in her novels comfortless all-male households.[48] However, Carey goes one stage further than lecturing women about the necessity for creating happy homes. She also obliges at least some of her male characters to be appreciative of the genius inherent in making them. In *Rue With a Difference* the male, excellent in himself, is portrayed as deficient whilst the woman is the expert. Thus, when Valerie kindly lends her expertise to the inept Mr Nugent, and he is appropriately vocal in his thanks.[49] Alas, many passages regarding this kind of female expertise share two inauspicious features: most of the incidents are comparatively trivial and most of the men involved in them are explicitly grateful. The former suggests that Carey was unable to dissemble about female powerlessness in weightier matters; the latter suggests that nineteenth- and early twentieth-century women craved the approval of their menfolk but seldom received it.

It cannot be known with any certainty what Carey's intentions were with regard to her readership. Still less is it possible to recover any knowledge of how (or, indeed, if) her readers employed the novels in relation to their own lives. Nevertheless, Janice Radway's survey of readers of the late twentieth-century mass-produced romance provides, by analogy, a suggestion of how Carey's initial readership might have responded. Radway's research posits a correlation between women who provide a high level of domestic servicing to others and the repetitive consumption of a certain kind of compensatory literature. As Victorian and Edwardian women were also expected to provide this kind of servicing, it may be deduced that they too sought compensation in what they read. Radway's main conclusion is that:

> By immersing themselves in the romantic fantasy, women vicariously fulfil their needs for nurturance by identifying with a heroine whose principal accomplishment ... is her success at drawing the hero's attention to herself, [and] at establishing herself as the object of his concern and the recipient of his care.[50]

---

48 In *Robert Ord's Atonement*, Robert and Garton share a damp house with only one elderly maid-servant; in *Queenie's Whim* Andrew Calcott can afford any number of 'hirelings' but has no one to turn his austere house into a home; and in *Mrs Romney*, Rab Lockhart has a beautiful house but is desperate to marry so that he can share it with someone.

49 Cf. also *ATM*, p. 119. A neighbour of the main male protagonist sets herself the task of making his study habitable. The passage concludes: '"There, doesn't it look nice!" exclaimed Betty, flushed but radiant … And in sheer honesty and gratitude Ned was forced to agree with her.'

50 J.A. Radway, *Reading the Romance* (London: Verso, 1987), p. 83 (hereafter, Radway 1987).

Carey's novels do indeed provide her readers with the opportunity to identify with heroines who are successful in this sense. However, if Radway's theory is extended to include the concept of vicarious approval alongside the concept of vicarious nurturance, it becomes of further relevance to Carey's writing. It permits the notion that Carey's original readers may have immersed themselves in her fiction in order to vicariously fulfil their needs for male approval, by identifying with a heroine whose principal accomplishment is her success at drawing a male protagonist's attention to herself, and at establishing herself as the object of his gratitude.

Conclusion: Compensation, Comedy and Coping Strategies

Although, in her novels, Carey appears to be totally aware of the institutionalised version of masculinity, she constantly undermines it. She does not humiliate men; she merely betrays the knowledge that she has discovered weaknesses in their generally serviceable armour of superiority and rationality. However, she does something more within the temporary space that her novels create for women than simply expose male weakness. She helps the reader come to terms with the 'man's world' in a number of ways, not least by taking the occasional humorous glance at the so-called masters, from the position of omniscient observer rather than that of controlled subject. For example, in *Not Like Other Girls*, Carey makes a fictional contest between three men for the controlling interest in the all-female Challoner family completely absurd.

Archie Drummond is initially complacent about his position. As a clergyman, he has the perfect excuse for visiting the family – a widowed mother and her three marriageable daughters – and for offering advice. However, his assumption that he is without competition soon proves to be unfounded:

> 'They have not a man belonging to them', he had said triumphantly, and then that odious Dick had turned up, and now this extraordinary-looking being who called himself Sir Henry Challoner. Archie took down the 'Peerage' when he got home … He found the name there all right. (*LoF*, pp. 383–4)

He later says of Sir Harry, 'I like quality better than quantity … He is so big, I am sure his brains must suffer by comparison' (ibid., p. 415). Meanwhile, young Dick Mayne, who is engaged to one of the daughters, also resents the competition. The vicar merely inspires his envy – 'such a handsome beggar, too – a prig, one can see that from the cut of his clothes and beard!' – but Sir Harry makes him feel positively violent (ibid., p. 291):

> Mrs Challoner ...was ... heard to say that she almost loved [Sir Harry] like a son – a speech that ... made him excessively angry. 'I should like to kick that fellow', he growled ... But then Dick never liked interlopers. (Ibid., p. 396)

Even the genial Sir Harry is displeased to find that one of his womenfolk is engaged to Dick, whom he deems to be 'somewhat insignificant' (ibid., p. 387; p. 430). Though enmeshed in an androcentric society, the reader can enjoy reading about these fictional clashes precisely because the three men have no rights in the matter and because the Challoners are totally unaware of their petty rivalries. When Carey gives reign to her sence of humour at male expense in novels such as *Not Like Other Girls*, she neither attacks nor alters the fundamental male power-base of Victorian society. However, women are invited to share in the knowledge that a man's sense of his own importance does not necessarily meet his power to act.[51]

In inverting the cultural myth of masculine as normal and rational and in privileging the female perspective, albeit intermittently, Carey is likely to have alienated any male readership. However, in the mid-nineteenth century almost any writing by women could be easily dismissed. J.M. Allan, writing for the *Journal of the Anthropological Society* in 1869, posited that:

> A female novel can generally be detected by the failure in the attempt to draw masculine character, and describe the conversation of men among themselves ... heroes are ... mere caricatures of real living men ... men are more successful in delineating women than women are at delineating men ... There never was a woman who could look into the heart of a man as Shakespeare has looked into the female heart. [52]

Nor was he alone in reaching this kind of verdict. The reviewer for the *Graphic*, in what is a relatively kind review of Carey's *Not Like Other Girls*, writes somewhat similarly. However, the latter at least provides a telling remark about how, and whom, she is supposed to have 'failed'. According to this reviewer, *Not Like Other Girls* is 'essentially a womanly book', and thus it has 'the almost inevitable fault' that 'all the male characters [are] ... more like

---

51 Carey also indulges in humour at expense of Alick Lyall in *Sir Godfrey's Granddaughters* (see pp. 11 168–9 and 230–32); and at the expense of Rab Lockhart in *Mrs Romney* (see pp. 24–103 *passim*).

52 J.M. Allen, 'On the Real Differennces in the Minds of Men and Women', *Journal of the Anthropological Society*, London, 1869, Vol. 7, pp. cxcv–ccxix at p. ccvii. Radway's findings in *Reading the Romance* completely contradict Allen. A bookseller interviewed by Radway is reported as saying: 'I've always thought that women are more insightful into men's psyches than men are into women's. Well, men just don't take the time ...' (Radway 1987, p. 83).

young women than men'.[53] This latter sweeping generalization must be examined more closely if it is to be useful.

It may be concluded that neither all, nor even most, of Carey's male characters fit this description. The fictional experiences and attitudes of most male characters are such that they conform with societal expectation in the real world of Carey's time. Where middle-class male characters are not acceptable to the community of the male, they do not become 'amiable young women' but effeminate or otherwise deficient men and, as such, earn the censure of Carey's various narrators. It must also be borne in mind that all male characters are viewed at all times from a feminine perspective, if only that of the author. The fictional aspects of male personality interrogated by Carey are those that were interesting to her and possibly those that she believed would interest her readers. Therefore the male point of view is neglected.

Perhaps the assertion that 'all the male characters [are] ... more like ... women than men' could be better rendered 'all the male characters will be liked ... more by ... women than men'. This is because Carey's novels contain two types of male characterization that men would have deplored. Some characters are as Carey saw them in reality, their numbers including the mean, the contemptible and the laughable as well as the merely normal; others are portrayed in idealized form, though according to female ideals and acting in roles interesting to women rather than according to male ideals and acting in roles interesting to men. Both the realistic and the idealistic portraits suggest that many men in the real world did not match up to feminine requirements. Perhaps Carey did not portray her male characters badly; perhaps, for their counterparts outside the novels, she sometimes portrayed them a little too well.

53 *Graphic*, 6 July 1884, p. 559.

Chapter 4

Hearth and Home

Representations and Realities

> It is at home that parents and children, brothers and sisters ... mingle in the sweet fellowship of domestic bliss.[1]

> The Vicar still sat by his study fire with his open book before him. Clare always sat opposite to him with her knitting or mending-basket beside her … at times he would lay down his book or push aside his papers, and tell her the day's troubles or the thoughts that were passing through his mind. And then it would seem to the tired, happy wife as though heaven and earth were very near together, and life a great mystery and sacrament of love.[2]

> Few will read [Carey's] work without feeling that the characters have been drawn from life – fortunately for us there are few homes which have not an Aunt Milly ever ready to cheer and comfort …[3]

Many Victorian and Edwardian accounts of home and family life, whether fictional or non-fictional, employ the same small range of referents, represented in fairly predictable configurations. The three accounts of family relationships quoted above may be seen to illustrate this point. The first is from the preface of an admonitory work entitled *The Young Man From Home*, which was published by the Religious Tract Society in about 1890. The book is non-fiction; it would have been deemed by the writer, the publisher and by at least some of the original readership to be representational of an empirical reality. The second passage is truly fictional; it is from Rosa Carey's novel *Sir Godfrey's Grand-Daughters* [1892]. However, in the last of the quotations, a review of one of Carey's novels from 1880, no distinction is made between fiction and reality. The two are regarded as identical in a conceit which praises Carey's work for its realism.

---

1 John Angell James, *The Young Man From Home* (London: Religious Tract Society, n.d. [c. 1890]), p. 7 (hereafter, *The Young Man From Home*).

2 R.N. Carey, *Sir Godfrey's Grand-daughters* (London: Macmillan, 1899 [1892]), p. 148 (hereafter *SGG*).

3 Review of *Heriot's Choice*, *Graphic*, 14 February 1880, p. 182.

Andrew Blake, author of *Reading Victorian Fiction* suggests that such conflations of fiction with reality were common, certainly in the periodical press, during the Victorian era. Having made a study of the *Fortnightly Review* between 1865 and 1875, he concludes that 'Fictions ... were regarded both by the magazine's reviewers and by other contributors as real pictures of society.'[4] However, Blake's own view, that the representation of reality in novels is at best qualified and that fiction has a function beyond that of mere mimesis, is more defensible as well as being more pertinent in the present context. He posits that:

> Fiction is ... an active constituent in society, able to take part in debate and promote change ... Furthermore ... novelists at this time were actually *expected* to preach ... Fiction, then, can be seen not as the passive 'reflector' of an already given society ... Instead, fictional literature can be seen as ... being aimed at specific readerships within it, of presenting, *to that specifically chosen audience*, certain types of information and attitude, and helping to form or change attitudes and behaviour. (Emphasis original)[5]

Blake's suggestion that Victorian texts are both mediated by 'preaching' and designed for specific audiences makes comprehensible the great contrast between the group of nineteenth-century works quoted above and the very different non-fictional representation of reality to be found in some of the social reporting of the age. In the three texts already quoted, the same range of referents regarding the construction of the home are mobilized whether the text purports to be fiction or non-fiction. All three draw upon the basic assumptions that 'home' means rest, comfort, companionship; that the occupants of a home enjoy leisure; that they can afford warm fires. However, these three texts merely produce constructions drawn from a dominant discourse of 'home'. They deal in ideals: an evangelist's prescription of what home *should* be like; a novelist's representation of a less than perfect but *desirable* home; a reviewer's *generalization* about home experience.

By contrast, social reporting in the same period, structured by a commitment to first-hand evidence, case-studies and statistical data, frequently portrays a more fragmented and contradictory picture of home life; one which does not conform so readily to the popular conventions. For example, in an account produced in 1899, the philanthropist and social reformer Seebohm Rowntree

4 Andrew Blake, *Reading Victorian Fiction* (Basingstoke: Macmillan, 1989), p. 120 (hereafter, Blake 1989).

5 Blake 1989, pp. 7–8. Blake had, to an extent, been anticipated by Ian Watt, the latter positing that an feature of the novel was 'a controlling moral intention'. This, too, appears to indicate authorial intervention between the text and the world it purports to describe. See Ian Watt, *The Rise of the Novel* (Harmondsworth: Penguin, 1968), p. 136.

reported that 27.84 per cent of the citizens of York were living in 'poverty'. This he defined as '[having] earnings ... insufficient to obtain the minimum necessities for the maintenance of mere physical efficiency'.[6] Rowntree's report clearly indicates that, however desirable the ideal represented in the previous group of quotations, 'home' defined as a place of comfort, companionship, leisure and warmth hardly denoted a universal experience.

The dominant domestic discourses of the Victorian era and beyond were thus both highly artificial in their construction and almost totally modelled upon the social mores of a complacent middle class. However, as these were the people who controlled the major means of cultural production – everything from ownership of the publishing companies to the making of Parliamentary legislation – they could afford to construct the world from their own point of view. Thus, most writers of non-fiction represented the middle-class home as a norm (as if it were a uniform reality) and most writers of fiction 'preached' a gospel of middle-class social mores (as if it were the only ideal worthy of reader aspiration).

Rosa Carey was undoubtedly a participant in, as well as an observer of, the social mores for her class and age. Her adherence to domesticity as an ideal is evident throughout her writings, her novels suggesting that she believed household harmony to be both the responsibility of the women in the household and the highest form of work to which they could aspire. Marriage, motherhood and more domesticity are seen to be the fitting and desirable rewards for unmarried women who have done their duty well in the parental or familial home.[7] This is not to say that Carey always depicts families living in exact accordance with the dominant; *Sir Godfrey's Grand-daughters*, quoted above, is as much about the difficulties of communal and familial living as about its rewards. Rather, it is to suggest that Carey was not able to represent unchallenged the dominant version of the domestic in a novel with any pretensions to realism. Moreover, in depicting less than ideal homes, she was simply re-presenting an already successful literary paradigm in which the dominant was severely attacked but never seriously undermined. As Rod Edmond, in his study *Affairs of the Hearth*, rightly observes:

> There are very few durable happy families in Victorian literature. General studies of the period depict the Victorian home as a peaceful, even sacred, place, a haven in a heartless world ... [but] Victorian writing

6 Rowntree's report, *Poverty. A Study of Town Life*, was published in 1901. Cited in John Burnett, *Plenty and Want* (London: Methuen, 1985), p. 126.

7 Characters apparently 'rewarded' in this way include Langley in *Queenie's Whim* [1881], the eponymous heroine of *Nellie's Memories* [1868], Judith Hillyard in *But Men Must Work* [1892] and Aunt Milly in *Heriot's Choice* [1877–79]. However, Judith Rowbotham suggests that it might be over-simplistic to view marriage as a reward in such texts. See *Good Girls Make Good Wives* (Oxford: Basil Blackwell, 1989), pp. 43–5.

> is full of unhappy homes, appalling families, and the break-up of happy homes and families ...[8]

Yet the notion of home as a 'peaceful ... sacred ... haven in a heartless world' remains dominant: even if it is only advocated as an ideal, mourned as something lost or, as Andrew Blake suggests, presented to the readership as a subject for debate. For Blake further argues that:

> The novel ... was public property in a way in which family life and letters were not: it gave people a chance to discuss domestic ideology *in public* without touching upon their own domestic secrets. (Blake 1989, p. 72. Emphasis original.)

However, such debates about the domestic were not merely to be found at the level of verbal transaction. For, as with the dominant *per se*, the dominant domestic discourse operated as a fairly homogenous social construction which was constantly under pressure to maintain its own particular hegemony and to resist, so far as possible, the modificatory zeal of any antagonistic forces. As Raymond Williams pertinently observes, a dominant discourse – however well supported by its institutions – cannot simply be thrust upon a quiescent populace:

> [Hegemony] does not just passively exist as a form of dominance. It has continually to be renewed, recreated, defended, and modified. It is also continually resisted, limited, altered, challenged by pressures not all its own ... The reality of any hegemony, in the extended political and cultural sense, is that, while by definition it is always dominant, it is never either total or exclusive ... The reality of cultural process must then always include the efforts and contributions of those who are in one way or another outside or at the edge of the terms of the specific hegemony.[9]

Thus discussion of, and resistance to, the dominant domestic discourses may be seen to have ranged well beyond the realms of fiction and its readership and it is notable that the same discourses and resistances are to be found in works which purport to be factual. For example, Charlotte Yonge predicates her non-fictional work *Womankind* [1877] on the notion that the middle-class women do not need to undertake remunerative employment.[10] However, she is unable to ignore the concrete existence of women of her own social standing who are without financial means. Thus, the book suggests a wry tolerance of their

---

8 Rod Edmond, *Affairs of the Hearth* (London: Routledge, 1988), p. 7.

9 Raymond Williams, *Marxism and Literature* (Oxford: Oxford University Press, 1977), pp. 110–13.

10 C.M. Yonge, *Womankind* (London: Mozley and Smith, 1877) (hereafter, *Womankind*).

deviance from a supposed norm rather than an appreciation of their alternative reality:

> And for the young who need support, it would be well, if they have no special talent, to try to learn to be telegraph clerks, or even dress-making, or *whatever is possible in their station*.
>
> 'The Year Book of Women's Work' will point to the means of getting instruction and employment, and there is *much less* every year of the fear of losing caste by absolute labour. (*Womankind*, pp. 237–8. My emphasis.)

A virtual dismissal of the challenge to the dominant lies in Yonge's qualifiers, 'in their station' with regard to the type of employment and 'much less', added to the phrase 'fear of losing caste'. It seems that, for Yonge at least, the presence of resistance to the dominant ideal does remarkably little to negate or obscure its visibility or power. However, the main purpose of this chapter is to examine the representations of, and the resistances to, the domestic ideal in the novels of Rosa Carey. In order to do this, it is first necessary to look at the individual components of the social construction which the Victorians and Edwardians called home.

Didactic Narratives of Domesticity

The essential features of Victorian and Edwardian bourgeois domesticity are to be found in their purest form in many non-fictional didactic texts of the day, particularly in household manuals and books of advice for women. Although representations of domesticity were based upon middle-class mores, texts were aimed at all levels of society. Charlotte Yonge's definition of a home is representative of dominant thought throughout the period:

> Is it not ... the place where one is always welcome, and above all sure of sympathy and ease? A place ... where, in spite of all love of change or society, one always comes back as the dearest and pleasantest to us, whatever may be its disadvantages. (*Womankind*, p. 264)

However, that Yonge was writing primarily for a middle-class readership becomes evident in passages such as the following:

> the great essential of a home ... is a living room that gives a sense of comfort, cheerfulness and pleasantness. The cottage kitchen ... often fulfils this office to perfection, but among the womankind principally addressed here, it is the drawing-room that generally answers the purpose ... (Ibid., p. 267)

Nevertheless, members of the working classes also received direct attention from the purveyors of the domestic. The barely veiled didacticism of a book entitled *The Two Neighbours: A Tale of Every-day Life* [1887] more than qualifies the work for inclusion here. The protagonists in this book are women who have formerly been domestic servants but who have subsequently married and become full-time housewives. One, Susan, is vain and lazy, the other, Mary, is modest and diligent. The following extract provides, for the reader, a lesson in priorities:

> Mary ... lifted up and examined the wide embroidery ...
> 'I worked it all myself,' said Susan, but she did not add that her house and her husband had been neglected whilst she did so.
> 'How clever you must be,' said Mary innocently, 'to find time for such beautiful fancy work, with all your household duties.'[11]

Susan leaves Mary's house feeling ashamed of her lack of appropriate industry and the next chapter, entitled 'Mary Allen's Rules,' sets out the prescribed behaviour. In this chapter, Mary Allen describes her daily routine in detail and provides a codification of good practice, 'three good old rules which my grandmother taught me':

> 'A place for everything, and everything in its place;' 'A time for everything, and everything in its time;' and 'Never put off till to-morrow what ought to be done to-day.'[12]

There is an obvious similarity between the three maxims quoted above and the three 'Domestic Rules' to be found in a more general reference work called *Enquire Within*:

> i. Do everything at its proper time.
> ii. Keep everything to its proper use.
> iii. Put everything in its proper place.[13]

The work also advises upon more specific matters, these being as diverse as 'Acting Charades' and 'Zinc and Camphor Eye-wash.'[14] However, the *Enquire Within* series appears to have been directed towards a slightly wealthier socio-

---

11 Mrs H.B. Paull, *The Two Neighbours: A Tale of Every-day Life* (London: Frederick Warne, 1887), p. 31 (hereafter, *The Two Neighbours*).

12 *The Two Neighbours*, Chapter 4; quotation from p. 44.

13 *Enquire Within Upon Everything, To Which Is Added Enquire Within Upon Fancy Work*, 42nd edn (London: Houlston and Sons, 1871), p. 93 (hereafter, *Enquire Within* 1871); *Enquire Within Upon Everything*, 96th edn (London: Houlston and Sons, 1899), p. 112 (hereafter, *Enquire Within* 1899).

14 These are listed in *Enquire Within* for both 1871 and 1899.

economic group than that addressed by *The Two Neighbours*. In the 1899 edition, an implicitly female reader is presented with a list of 'Golden Hints for Housewives and Home Comforts' and she is advised to read these 'frequently that their full value may be secured'; but the paragraph continues:

> Let your servants also read them, for nothing conduces more to good housekeeping than for the servant to understand the 'system' which her mistress approves of.[15]

Nor was the gospel of domestic order, as propagated amongst these lesser lights, intended to be shorn of its drawing-room ethos of 'sympathy and ease.' Although there are few references to these requirements in *The Two Neighbours*, much may be deduced from works aimed at middle-class readers. For example, in *Sanitary and Social Essays* [1892], Charles Kingsley exhorts lady district visitors to 'ennoble and purify the *womanhood* of ... poor women; to make them better daughters, sisters, wives, mothers' (emphasis original).[16] The implication is that 'these poor women' are as deficient in 'womanhood' as their district visitors are superior; and that the poor are a class in need of instruction in supposedly normative values.

Looking at the work of writers such as Yonge, Paull and Kingsley, it is clear that the onus for making a home according to this pattern is placed squarely upon the women of a household. Given that the home itself is accorded such high status, one might therefore expect that home-management would be a high-profile and highly-regarded occupation. Yet one receives precisely the opposite impression from the *Manual of Modern Geography*, a textbook for boys which was published in 1861. For, from the section entitled 'National Character' the reader learns that, 'an English*man* ... is unrivalled for good taste in domestic architecture, and his home is always a model of cleanliness, neatness and comfort'(my emphasis).[17] It is strange that a geography textbook should omit all reference to one half of the population of a country. It might be deemed equally strange that the agency behind the much-vaunted 'cleanliness, neatness and comfort' should be unspecified. However, this writer's androcentrism is far from unique. Samuel Smiles also devotes less space to the means of creating a home than he does to the enjoyment a *man* may gain from it, noting that:

15 *Enquire Within* 1899, p. 103. Note the tacit assumption that both servant and domestic manager are female.

16 Charles Kingsley, 'Woman's Work in a Country Parish', in *Sanitary and Social Essays* (London: Macmillan, 1892 [1880]), p. 8.

17 Rev. Alexander Mackay, *Manual of Modern Geography* (Edinburgh: William Blackwood and Sons, 1861), p. 161. Page ix states that the book is addressed to boys.

> The poorest dwelling, presided over by a virtuous, thrifty, cheerful, and cleanly woman, may thus be the abode of comfort, virtue and happiness; it may be the scene of every ennobling relation in family life ... furnishing ... a refuge from the storms of life, *a sweet resting-place after labour*, a consolation in misfortune, a pride in prosperity, and a joy at all times. (My emphasis.)[18]

Note that men labour whilst women merely 'preside'. However, the work of Dale Spender and Nancy Chodorow usefully deconstructs this androcentric view of domestic servicing, rendering it intelligible if not laudible. Spender quotes Marion Glastonbury's trite but pertinent remark that 'men are sincerely ignorant of the processes that supply their comforts', whilst Chodorow provides the following, more detailed, perspective:[19]

> Social reproduction is ... asymmetrical. Women in their domestic rôle reproduce men and children physically, psychologically and emotionally. Women in their domestic rôle as house workers reconstitute themselves physically on a daily basis and reproduce themselves as mothers emotionally and psychologically in the next generation.[20]

Thus Chodorow posits that to be a man or a child is to be a consumer whilst to be a woman is to be a provider; and Spender intimates that to be a provider means to be invisible. The absence of women in Mackay's book for boys may thus be seen to point to this difference of experience between the genders. Men consume domestic labour without seeing its production; women are, of necessity, obliged to see domestic servicing, whether physical or psychological, because they are the ones who provide it.

Yet there was more to the domestic ideal than the middle-class orientated, gender-specific provision of 'sympathy and ease' and 'cleanliness, neatness and comfort'. Home was also the place that shaped the next generation. Yonge says of 'happy homes of peace, and of innocent mirth' that '[t]he women who come from [them] make others' (*Womankind*, p. 271). However, the main purpose of the home, if one believes all that books directed at male audiences have to say on the subject, is to foster 'male genius'. Samuel Smiles was one of the many men to write in these terms, positing that:

> Home is the first and most important school of character. It is there every human being receives his best moral training, or his worst; for it is there

18 Samuel Smiles, *Character* (London: John Murray, 1897 [1878]), p. 40 (hereafter, *Character*).

19 Dale Spender, *Man Made Language* (London: Routledge and Kegan Paul, 1980), p. 221.

20 Nancy Chodorow, *The Reproduction of Mothering* (Berkeley: University of California Press, 1978), p. 209.

> that he imbibes those principles of conduct which endure through manhood, and cease only with life.[21]

The veneer of sheer sentimentalism which he subsequently adds, when he explains the place of women in this nurturant 'school of character', goes some way to obscure the gender inequality inherent in home experience:

> The home is the woman's domain – her kingdom … Her power over the little subjects she rules there is absolute … She is the example and model constantly before their eyes, whom they consciously observe and imitate. (*Character*, p. 37)

It seems that adult men are excluded from her reign. However, there follows on from this effusion a string of anecdotes about great men and the debts they owe to their mothers. Thus:

> De Maistre, in his letters and writings speaks of his ... mother with immense love and reverence. Her noble character made all other women venerable in his eyes. He described her as his 'sublime mother' – 'an angel to whom God had lent a body for a brief season.' To her he attributed the bent of his character, and all his bias towards good; and when he had grown to mature years, while acting as ambassador at the Court of St. Petersburg, he referred to her noble example and precepts as the ruling influence in his life. (*Character*, pp. 42–51).

Similarly, it is said of George Washington's mother that,

> as the richest reward of her solicitude and toil, she had the happiness to see all her children come forward with a fair promise into life, filling the spheres allotted to them in a manner honourable to themselves, and to the parent who had been the only guide of their principles, conduct and habits. (*Character*, pp. 44–5)

Smiles also naively comments that 'We do not often hear of great women, as we do of great men. It is of good women that we mostly hear' (*Character*, p. 43). However, he is not alone in sentimentalising the home as a place where male greatness is fostered. In W.H.D. Adams's *Plain Living and High Thinking* [1883], the first chapter is entitled 'At Home' and it includes a similar section, this being entitled 'A Mother's love illustrated by examples'.[22]

Thus, the domestic ideal, as constructed from overtly didactic sources, may be seen to have entailed the provision, by women, of 'sympathy and ease' and

---

21 *Character*, p. 32. Note that 'human being' means male (women do not attain 'manhood').

22 W.H. Davenport Adams, *Plain Living and High Thinking* (London: John Hogg, 1883), pp. viii, 10.

of ‘cleanliness, neatness and comfort’, to men and children, for the specific purpose of cultivating male genius and morality. The ideal may also be seen to have acquired a veneer of sentimentalism that partially obscured the inherent asymmetry of home experience. The very repetitiveness of these concepts of ethos, order and sentiment appear to give them a normative status against which any other set of behaviours, working patterns or relationships could be adjudged deviant. Together, they imply the existence of a positive stereotype called ‘home’; to imply a standard vocabulary to fit a prescribed experience, regardless of what might have been a far more varied range of experiences in reality. There appears to have been only one kind of vocabulary acknowledged by the dominant about domesticity: that which extolled its virtues and condemned the household that was not run according to its referents.

The Role of Home-maker

In addition to affirming the feminine nature of home-making, both fictional and non-fictional texts from the Victorian and Edwardian period detail a discernible hierarchy for women within a household. The foremost female role within this hierarchy, that of home-maker, was allocated to the closest connexion of the male householder. There was only room for one home-maker per household and it was her duty to administer to all domestic matters, whether practical or psychological.

An unmarried daughter of any age was strictly subordinate to her mother so long as she lived in the parental home. Thus, in the *Girl's Own Paper* for 13 January 1894, a correspondent was told:

> Whether your mother be an invalid or not, your name should be inscribed upon her visiting card, underneath her name, so long as she lives, and you remain – a single woman – under her roof.[23]

However, a widowed mother was herself in constant danger of finding herself set aside if she and her eldest son were members of the same household. A wife always took precedence over a mother and was automatically entitled to take on the home-making role. In her memoirs, Mary Elizabeth Lucy tells of the change in status she experienced when her eldest son married in 1865:

> nor did I realise my position till I went upstairs to take off my things and found my bedroom was prepared for the future Mrs Lucy … So now, on 1st July 1865, I was called upon to give up forever the bedroom I had occupied as wife and widow 41 years … The two days passed at dear

23 *Girl's Own Paper*, 13 January 1894, p. 239.

> Charlecote in preparing for my successor were certainly a trial ... but still I rejoiced that Spencer's marriage was near at hand, and the bright hope of his future happiness dispelled the cloud of my own gloomy thoughts and made me forget 'self' and how changed was my lot ...[24]

Nor was this the full extent of the female hierarchical structure within the family. There was also an acknowledged 'pecking order' amongst cousins and sisters. A correspondent seeking advice from the *Girl's Own Paper* later in 1894 was told:

> On a visiting card for an unmarried lady who has ceased to have her name printed on her mother's card, the name is always preceded by 'Miss'. The Christian name is used when the person is not the daughter of the eldest son, and has not a right to the name.[25]

Thus, the daughter of a younger son would have been obliged to style herself, for example, Miss Anne Smith whilst her cousin, by right, simply called herself Miss Smith. Amongst sisters, a married woman gained her status from her husband's family but the eldest unmarried sister was deemed to have some authority over her younger siblings. In *Womankind* Yonge tells the reader 'the younger ones should remember that the eldest sister at home must always remain the head, and be deferred to' (p. 144).

Any status or power inherent in the home-making role carried with it great responsibility for the well-being of the household. A statement to this effect is to be found in the first chapter of *Everybody's Book of Correct Conduct* [1893]. There, status and responsibility are juxtaposed as if to emphasise their affinity:

---

24 Mary Elizabeth Lucy (ed. Alice Fairfax-Lucy), *Mistress of Charlecote, The Memoirs of Mary Elizabeth Lucy* (London: Victor Gollancz Ltd, 1983), p. 133 (hereafter, *Mistress of Charlecote*). Primogeniture as much as social custom determined her position in the household. (Whilst she retained much of her husband's capital, her eldest son was entitled to the house.) Similarly, an unmarried sister who kept house for her brother lost her central status if he married. When their bachelor brothers both married in 1889, Mary and Katherine Bryce were in their forties and their younger brother was fifty-one so the shock was considerable. Mary, the elder sister, had been the home-maker but she was obliged to make way for her elder brother's wife. The new circumstances were unworkable so the sisters moved out during the same year. See Pat Jalland, *Women, Marriage and Politics 1860–1914* (Oxford: Clarendon Press, 1986), pp. 266–7 (hereafter, Jalland 1986).

25 *Girl's Own Paper*, 18 August 1894, p. 736.The 'Miss' in such a case would have been an older woman and living in her own establishment in order to have her own visiting cards at all. See 'A Member of the Aristocracy', *Manners and Rules of Good Society*, (London: Frederick Warne and Co., 1887), p. 21. Sources other than *Girl's Own Paper* suggest that only the eldest unmarried daughter in the family could appropriate the family name without also appending her christian name. For example, in her memoirs, Mary Elizabeth Lucy cites a letter in which two of her granddaughters (two sisters) are referred to as Miss Lucy and Miss Linda respectively. Lucy was the children's surname. See *Mistress of Charlecote*, p. 139.

> **It is the correct thing**
> To remember that the lady who rules the household must have absolute authority in it and rule as absolute queen. No comfort or order can be obtained without this. If her orders are to be questioned, the correct thing is to do so in private, and never in the presence of the young members of the household, or of the servants.
> [It is also the correct thing f]or the lady who holds this position to remember that the every-day happiness of those in the home circle is in her hands; that she has the greatest power of anyone to make the home a place of peace and happiness, or a place to avoid.[26]

This domestic hierarchy, with its emphasis upon the powerful and responsible home-maker is replicated throughout Carey's novels. For example, she frequently portrays the change of government which occurs when a designated homemaker dies. The notion of precedence by age after a mother's death is made explicit in *Aunt Diana* [1885]:

> 'My dear Alison,' returned the governess solemnly, '... It is true you are young, not much over eighteen; but ... [y]ou are the eldest daughter, and the rightful mistress of the house.'[27]

However, during the more sombre investiture detailed in *Nellie's Memories*, a dying mother imparts more responsibility than authority:

> she took me by the hand and ... solemnly committed my brothers and sisters to my care, bidding me watch over them with a mother's love, and over my father with the tenderness of a wife.[28]

However, Carey's novels do not merely reproduce the dominant version of the female hierarchy; they also interrogate it. Where the etiquette book simply acknowledges the contingent nature of the home-maker's power, the novels further suggest that even this contingent power is far from unassailable. Many novels contain episodes in which the home-maker's legitimate authority is undermined by someone who has absolutely no legitimate reason for doing so.

---

26 'M.C.', *Everybody's Book of Correct Conduct*, (Whitstable: Pryor, 1996 [1893]), pp. 11–12 (hereafter, *Correct Conduct*). However this passage also reveals the limitations of the 'absolute queen['s]' power. On p. 26 the female reader is further reminded that, 'As a Wife ... although you are in authority at home, nevertheless [your husband] is the head of the house'. For a didactic narrative about the power and responsibility of the home-maker see 'The Contrast' in *The Mother's Friend,* Vol. 4, 1863, pp. 4–7,.

27 R.N. Carey, *Aunt Diana* (London: Office of 'The Girl's Own Paper', n.d. [1885]), p. 121 (hereafter, *AD*).

28 R.N. Carey, *Nellie's Memories* (London: Richard Bentley and Son, 1892 [1868]), p. 2 (hereafter, *NM*).

In *Only the Governess* [1888], problems arise when Ivan Thorpe, a middle-aged bachelor, unexpectedly marries. Though the young wife formally becomes mistress of the household in place of his unmarried sister, Miss Thorpe does not give up the reins of government easily.[29] She yields up the household keys and her seat at the head of the table, but she constantly criticizes the inexperienced young wife's attempts at household management and magnifies the least of her faults to her husband. The long-suffering wife tells another character in the novel:

> 'She had been everything to him once and she could not forgive me for taking her place; from the first she misunderstood and disliked me.'[30]

Similarly, Etta, the poor relation in *Uncle Max* [1887], undermines, and finally usurps, the position of the rightful home-maker, Gladys. She then proceeds to make the lives of Gladys and her younger sister very miserable. Etta is merely a distant cousin of the householder; Gladys is his elder sister. In fictional terms at least, a woman who seizes power not her own cannot possibly wield that power for the good of others.

Yet, in spite of the centrality and exclusivity of the home-maker, other females had their legitimate role to play.[31] According to Yonge, the 'eldest home sister' had her responsibilities in the nursery but, as Carey's tales such as *Averil* [1890–91], *Cousin Mona* [1895] and *Our Bessie* [1888–89] convincingly suggest, all young women could play their part in bringing 'sunshine' into the home.[32] These didactic novels, published by the Religious Tract Society and aimed at a 'teen-aged' audience, are especially rich in characters ripe for emulation.

In the first, orphaned poor relations Lottie and Annette try to make life happier for the sorely-tried home-maker, Averil. Besides running errands and sharing the household mending, they supply Averil with the affection and sympathy that is otherwise lacking in her home life. Meanwhile, Averil herself only undertakes the home-maker role because her stepmother is too indolent and too extravagant to do her rightful duty. Thus Averil not only manages the finances and builds up good working relationships with the servants but also

29 For a sister with a pleasanter attitude towards a prospective sister-in-law, see R.N. Carey, *At The Moorings* (London: Macmillan, 1914 [1904]), p. 286. (Hereafter, *ATM*.) For a sister distraught at having her sense of usefulness taken away from her when her widowed brother re-marries, see R.N. Carey, *Life's Trivial Round*, 2nd edn (London: Hutchinson, n.d. [1899–1900]), Chapter 13 (hereafter, *LTR*).

30 R.N. Carey, *Only the Governess* (London: Macmillan, 1917 [1888]), p. 192 (hereafter, *OTG*).

31 **'It is the correct thing** ... For the women of the household to make it pleasant and attractive, and for the men to show their appreciation of these efforts', *Correct Conduct*, p. 9.

32 *Womankind*, p. 136.

bears the complaints and ill temper of her stepmother and stepsisters whilst she does so. Each of the three women who attempt to create a home in this novel offer a paradigm or partial paradigm for emulation by the young reader. Though Averil's financial independence and worldly wisdom are only within reach of the few, all are capable of cultivating her even temper. More easily acquired by the young are Lottie's sunny and optimistic nature and Annette's intuitiveness and restfulness.

In *Cousin Mona* another orphan finds her role of assistant home-maker equally difficult. For Rufa, who lives with the eponymous cousin Mona and her brother, Everhard, the impediment to domestic happiness is the decline of Mona's brother into premature senility. Yet even here the establishment of a happy home is accomplished as Rufa slowly attempts to make herself both pleasant and useful around the home. The lesson to the young reader is that even the most uncongenial of home circumstances can be improved, whatever the status of the woman willing to attempt the task. By comparison, the eponymous heroine of *Our Bessie* has a much easier task; from the start, she is represented as a much-loved eldest sister and her mother's right hand.

However, such heroines are not only to be found in Carey's overtly didactic fiction. Other young women who provide household 'sunshine' without formally taking on the home-maker role include Joan in *The Key of the Unknown* and the eponymous *Mrs Romney*, who lives with her parents-in-law. Other novels suggest an even greater degree of usefulness. Grace in *Not Like Other Girls* [1884] acts as governess to her younger sisters as well as taking on her share of the household chores, whilst Irene in *The Sunny Side of the Hill* [1908] practically runs the house – she has 'a genius for it' – and thus enables her mother to take on 'parochial work'.[33]

Conversely, where Carey portrays female characters who detract from household harmony, these receive marked narratorial criticism. For example, an only daughter, Muriel, in *The Mistress of Brae Farm* [1896], is censured for following her own pursuits and neglecting her mother who is both lonely and seriously ill. In essence, Carey is normative in her presentation of the home-maker and her female hierarchies are clearly defined. Either the right or the wrong person takes on the home-making role; and the remaining women either contribute to the well-being of the household or they do not. Yet even successful home-makers in the novels are represented in such a way as to suggest that, in life, home-making work was difficult and, at times, distinctly unsentimental.

When portraying the home-maker at work, Carey addresses both the ethos and physical maintenance of the household, though the emphasis is usually upon the former. In keeping with the norms of the servant-employing classes of

33 R.N. Carey, *The Sunny Side of the Hill* (London: Macmillan, 1908), p. 12.

Carey's time, home-makers decide upon the tasteful arrangement of the furniture though they seldom actually move it, make the coffee at breakfast time though they seldom boil the water or lay the table, and make and mend household linen and clothing though they seldom wash or iron anything.[34] However, it is quality of mind rather than delimitation of tasks which distinguishes the home-maker from her servants; and it is the ability to sympathize with the joys and sorrows of others within the household that makes her a good home-maker rather than a bad one. Thus, in *At The Moorings*, Sheila tenderly encourages her brother to talk about the woman he loves even though his marriage will displace her from her current position of authority within the household (*ATM*, pp. 282–5). Similarly, in *Queenie's Whim*, it is said of a home-maker, 'Langley's opinion, Langley's sympathy, were always claimed, and never in vain.'[35]

Efficient though uncongenial home-makers are to be found in Carey's novels – for example the lachrymose Joanna Chaytor in *Mollie's Prince* [1898] and the endlessly occupied Mrs Herrick in *Herb of Grace* [1901] – but they are usually fairly minor characters and are usually censured for their lack of sensitivity. The preferred personal qualities in a home-maker, a good temper, willingness to serve others and the possession of an innately refined nature, are discussed at greater length. In obliging her home-making heroines to be of benign temperament, Carey concurs with that prodigy of domestic virtue, Mrs Isabella Beeton:

> GOOD TEMPER SHOULD BE CULTIVATED by every mistress, as upon it the welfare of the household may be said to turn; indeed, its influence can hardly be over-estimated, as it has the effect of moulding the characters of those around her, and of acting most beneficially on the happiness of the domestic circle. Every head of household should strive to be cheerful ... Gentleness, not partial and temporary, but universal and regular, should pervade her conduct ...[36]

Correspondingly, Carey does not permit her approved fictional home-makers to be even righteously angry with other members of their households. In *Aunt*

---

34 Furniture: in *At The Moorings*, Betty actually moves furniture, but enlists help with heavier pieces (pp. 118–9); in *Sir Godfrey's Grand-daughters*, Gerda suggests moving a cabinet and her fiancé says 'I'll have it moved tomorrow' (p. 368). Coffee: *Aunt Diana*, p. 116. R.N. Carey, *Heriot's Choice* (London: Macmillan, 1899 [1877–9]) (hereafter, *HC*), p. 45 illustrates dissatisfaction if the coffee is not good. Sewing: see R.N. Carey, *Robert Ord's Atonement* (London: Richard Bentley and Son, 1898 [1873]) (hereafter, *ROA*), p. 122 for making garments; p. 191 for mending.

35 R.N. Carey, *Queenie's Whim* (London: Macmillan, 1914 [1881]), p. 96 (hereafter, *QW*).

36 Mrs Isabella Beeton, *Beeton's Book of Household Management*, an illustrated facsimile of the 1st edn (London: Chancellor Press, 1994 [1861]), p. 4.

Diana, the much-tried Alison has just cause to remonstrate with her younger sister but ultimately refrains from doing so:

> 'Mabel, how can you be so disagreeable?' began Alison hotly. But she cooled down on remembering Aunt Diana's advice – 'Never get warm over an argument, Ailie. When you begin to feel angry, it is time to hold your tongue.' And Alison held hers. (*AD*, p. 202)

Along with many authors of non-fictional works, Carey lays a particular injunction against displays of ill-temper by wives towards their husbands. J.W. Kirton, author of *Happy Homes and How to Make Them* [c. 1871] advises wives to be pleasant even when their spouses provoke them:

> If he should be inclined to dispute with you, abstain from a long argument with him. Let it be a standing motto, 'never to irritate.' Gentleness is the best way to carry a point, and to keep a husband in a good temper is one of the duties of a wife.[37]

Similarly, Charlotte Yonge, whilst aware that men could be at the root of much ill temper, ultimately deemed the general happiness of the household to rest on female effort alone:

> To make a really happy home the father must co-operate with her. If he is thought of with terror for his temper, or if he cannot or will not tolerate his children's interruptions, there will be less peace and gladness, but still the mother can keep up the home element if she gather the children round her, keeping him and his requirements foremost in her own estimation and the children's with the dutifulness of love. (*Womankind*, p. 265)

Such admonitions render normative the fictional situation in which Carey makes a wife apologize for upbraiding the husband whose extravagance has ruined them:

> 'I was not good to you tonight, Julius. I had no right to be so angry with my husband.'
>
> 'I forgive you, my dear child!' he returned magnanimously.'

37 J.W. Kirton, *Happy Homes and How to Make Them* (Birmingham: Educational Trading Co., n.d. [c.1879]), p. 132 (hereafter, *Happy Homes*). See also *Correct Conduct*, p. 25:

> As a Wife
>
> **It is not correct** …
>
> To allow [your husband] to see you worried, or crying over trifles. It will weary him of you sooner than anything else. It is the correct thing for you to make the sunshine of life for him, as he has all the responsibility, and must of necessity have many trials heavier than you can know of.

> 'Yes, but I'm not sure I forgive myself. It is a wife's duty to bear everything ...' (*SGG*, p. 384)

Yet a peaceable nature is insufficient in itself. Carey's novels suggest that a home can only be created by a woman whose interest in the household is affectional rather than pecuniary and she often posits that hired servants have neither the ability nor the incentive to create a home on behalf of their employers. For example, in the following passage from *Queenie's Whim*, the eponymous heroine, even though formally estranged from her uncle, willingly renders him the service that the paid nurse has forgotten:

> 'Why do you look towards that door? do you want anything?
>
> 'That woman has forgotten my medicine,' he muttered, 'and I have that strange sinking again. Hirelings are not worth the price of the bread they eat.'
>
> 'Let me give it to you,' returned Queenie, rising, and mixing the draught ... Queenie skilfully raised the invalid and put the glass to his lips ... (*QW*, pp. 71–2)

By using the word 'hireling', Carey permits biblical resonances to add depth to the distinction between loving service and financial transaction.[38] Herself no hireling, Queenie is indeed willing to look after her own; but having the care of her incapacitated young sister means she is unable to respond to her uncle's plea that she come to nurse him. Though desperately poor, she reluctantly turns down his offer of a good salary for the work, telling him:

> 'It goes to my heart to refuse you. If I were free I would come and serve you, not only for the sake of the money, but because mamma loved you so dearly.' (*QW*, p. 74)

However, the fictional Andrew Calcott's desire to have Queenie living with him is not limited to a wish for reliable nursing. He also craves the presence of someone from the same social background as himself; someone to whom he can entrust his domestic happiness as well as his physical comfort. As he tells Queenie, 'Mrs Morton is a very capable person, but I should like someone who would read to me and amuse me' (*QW*, p. 72). In short, he wants someone who, in taking on this familial position, can provide his luxurious but empty house with the ethos of a home. Another man who requires more of his domestic circumstances than a housekeeper can provide is the fictional Doctor Stewart,

---

38 According to St John's gospel, 'he that is an hireling ... whose own the sheep are not ... careth not for the sheep', John 10:12–13. See The Holy Bible, Authorised King James Version (Glasgow: Collins, n.d. [1611]). This was the only version of the Bible used by the Church of England for most of the Victorian era.

who is to be found in the same novel. He begins by observing to himself that his housekeeper makes him extremely comfortable:

> Jean, excellent woman, knowing his ways, had lighted the fire and brought his slippers down to warm. 'I am not so badly off as a bachelor that I need be in such a hurry to change my state ...' (*QW*, p. 344)

Yet he concludes that he does not regret his forthcoming marriage:

> Well, she is a dear woman, and I don't repent of what I have done; for, in spite of Jean's excellent management, one feels a trifle dull sometimes now that the old mother's gone and Edie is married.' (Ibid.)

The fictional doctor is portrayed as being somewhat unromantic about his bride but Carey at least permits her reader to see that she will be something more than a privileged servant. To quote the narrator of Carey's later novel *Sir Godfrey's Grand-daughters*, those 'little graceful finishes that bespeak cultured taste' are vitally important.[39] Yet, one further point is to be made on this account: such 'graceful finishes' and 'cultured taste' are not the automatic result of either middle-class or amateur status. They need to be cultivated assiduously if they are not innate. Thus, the character who has the role of home-maker in the household under discussion here is unfavourably contrasted with the woman who will take on the role in the future. Pamela is the householder's sister; Gerda his prospective wife:

> Pamela evidently had no domestic capabilities; those little graceful finishes that bespeak cultured taste were totally wanting at Roadside. The drawing-room was large but somewhat bare-looking; two or three easy-chairs had been dragged to the edge of the hearth-rug, leaving an empty space; books and work and papers were thrown on the big, roomy couch. 'It could be made so much better,' thought Gerda, with the irritated feeling of seeing good material wasted. Her fingers longed to unloop and readjust the stiff draperies that hung over the window; she would have pushed the big couch into that snug corner by the fire, and the cabinet of old china should have been moved to the other end of the room. Gerda amused herself that night settling a thousand fanciful details; she put herself in Pamela's place. With a few pounds, a very few indeed, the room should look lovely. One of those Oriental nondescript stuffs should be fashioned into a portiere; a dozen or two yards of cretonne, a little Madras muslin, a big jar, and a palm would do wonders. (Ibid.)

At this point in the narrative, Gerda is not specifically thinking of the drawing-room as her own. Rather, she is instinctively exercising her more general

39 *Sir Godfrey's Grand-daughters*, p. 227.

faculty of home-making over the material that presents itself. It is only incidentally that, by so doing, she demonstrates her suitability to be a wife.

The Homemaker's Rewards, Punishment and Training

In Carey's novels, the immediate reward for domestic competence, good temper, willing service and innate refinement is usually a contented household and male approval for the home-maker. Thus, when the fictional Aunt Milly takes over the stricken Lambert household in *Heriot's Choice*, the local doctor is soon made to name her 'a mother in Israel', this being an allusion to the biblical Deborah, who, in an important sense, mothered an oppressed nation.[40] This compliment to Aunt Milly's judicious management of the household appears to be Carey's highest praise for a home-maker. It is Carey's acknowledgement that home-making is no easy task; that it is potentially an embattled position. In addition, because a 'mother in Israel' is someone to whom all will come for advice, the title also describes Aunt Milly's centrality in the family and her availability as one who will dispense both wisdom and solace. Langley Clayton in *Queenie's Whim* also receives this kind of accolade:

> That she was a woman infinitely loved and respected was plainly evident. Langley's opinion, Langley's sympathy were always claimed, and never in vain; the same patient attention, the same ready help, were given to all. (*QW*, p. 96)

This centrality within the family home is very often succeeded by a suitable marriage and a similar role within the marital home. Thus, both the 'mother in Israel,' Aunt Milly, and the 'loved and respected' Langley Clayton marry, though not until they are in their thirties. It is notable that each marries a widower whose first marriage was unsatisfactory and that each attracts a partner on account of personal qualities rather than physical beauty. In each case the husband is intimate with her entire family and thus knows of her domestic virtues; in each case the husband knows that he will be gaining a home of the kind he has not known since childhood.[41]

Yet there are occasions upon which Carey varies this pattern of domestic virtue rewarded. The eponymous heroine of *Averil* is not appreciated by her stepfamily in spite of her efforts, both domestic and financial, on their behalf. Nor does she eventually marry as do many other of Carey's older, poorer and

40 See Judges 4:4; 5:7.

41 However, Carey does not make these stories especially romantic. Aunt Milly only gets her man after he has proposed to his eighteen-year-old ward and subsequently broken the engagement. Langley Clayton marries the lover she rejected in a fit of pique in her youth but only after she has nursed the woman he married subsequently through her last illness.

disabled female characters. However, she is ultimately able to arrange her life more to her liking when the ungrateful stepfamily emigrates to Canada. Similarly, Ellison in *The Mistress of Brae Farm* is poorly rewarded for taking in a destitute cousin and her child. Her fiancé and the cousin fall in love and eventually marry, rendering Ellison's portion that of single blessedness.

However, for heroines who do not marry, another kind of reward is possible: that of pseudo-maternity. The eponymous Averil enjoys an affectionate, almost maternal, relationship with the two young cousins who live with her as well as a familial relationship with a number of poor 'pensioners' for whom she provides a village home. Similarly, Ellison in *The Mistress of Brae Farm* experiences motherhood at one remove through her relationship with her ex-fiancé's children. Other characters are made to take on a mother's role in its entirety. Thus, Anne in *For Lilias* [1885] brings up her adopted daughter from the age of two and Miss Jem in *The Highway of Fate* [1902] becomes 'mother' to a child of six. However, there are a variety of 'maternal' roles to be had. That of Sister Frances in *No Friend Like a Sister* [1906] is threefold: caring for her patients, studying the welfare of her nurses and enjoying her role as aunt to the children of her married brother and sister.

That single women should bring up children was a far from unusual notion for Carey's time but, whilst the fictional Anne's brother is made to paraphrase the proverb 'Old maids' children and bachelors' wives are always paragons,' Carey's 'maiden' mothers are not subject to the ridicule frequently to be found in fiction.[42] Rather, their 'maternity' is constructed in terms similar to those describing a birth-mother. Anne's 'daughter', Marjory,

> seemed to fill the void in Anne's life, and lend to it a little of the importance and joy of maternity; the interest that is often missing in a single woman's life was hers by adoption and choice.[43]

In expanding the conventional perception of the maternal role, Carey places the rewards of the unmarried domestic woman virtually on a par with those who marry.

However, when the home is not well run, the indignant cries of offended males fill the pages. In this respect, Carey's fiction accords very much with the

42 *Brewer's Dictionary of Phrase and Fable*, Tenth revised edition, (London: Cassell, 1967), p. 62 (hereafter, *Brewer*). For another reference to 'old maids' children see *Aunt Diana*, p. 38. For the kind of ambivalence with which old maids are regarded in fiction, see also Mrs J.H. Ewing, *Jackanapes* [1879] in *Jackanapes and Other Tales*, (London: J.M. Dent and Sons, 1931), pp. 5–52. Carey herself had the sole care of four nieces and nephews for several years. See H.C. Black, *Notable Women Authors of the Day* (London: Maclaren, 1906 [1893]), p. 151 (hereafter, Black 1906).

43 R.N. Carey, *For Lilias* (London: Macmillan, 1902 [1885]), p. 36. See also *Aunt Diana*, p. 259: 'there are some unmarried women whose large natures can embrace a whole world of little ones, and such a one was Aunt Diana'.

dominant. Carey may forgive a female character for being unmarried but she does not afford the same kind of immunity to those who are inefficient in the performance of their domestic duties. Although she may portray the failed home-maker sympathetically, she seldom strongly censures the obstreperous male. Any sympathy with the female character is on account of her failure, not because she has been upbraided.

Hence, when Richard in *Heriot's Choice* makes cutting remarks to his fifteen-year-old sister on account of her poor housekeeping, he remains unreproved. Even his father remarks that he is 'too hard at times' but no one appears to tell the culprit that he must curtail his contemptuous speeches (*HC*, p. 56). In the following extract, Olive, the disorganised and hard-pressed home-maker, is attempting to do her German homework and, at the same time, serve coffee:

> 'There, you have done it again,' [said Richard] 'The second clean cloth this week disfigured by these unsightly brown patches.'
>
> 'Something must be the matter with the urn,' exclaimed Olive ...
>
> 'Nonsense, the only fault is that you will do two things at a time. You have eaten no breakfast ... and made us all uncomfortable. And pray how much German have you done?'
>
> 'I can't help it, Cardie; I have so much to do, and there seems no time for things ... I am sorry ...'
>
> 'Actions are better than words,' was the curt reply. (*HC*, pp. 45–6)

The authoritarian and censorious brother is himself only nineteen years old and is neither the breadwinner nor the head of the family. Yet, ostensibly, his right to complain is upheld. Carey has their aunt, who observes the scene, consider him to be, at least in part, justified. In the space of a single page, sympathy for the young home-maker becomes admixed with sympathy for her tormentor:

> 'I am half inclined to find fault with Richard myself ... he does not make sufficient allowance for a very young housekeeper ... No wonder Richard's fastidiousness is so often offended; but his continual fault-finding makes her worse ...'[44]

Women who suffer under the auspices of a poor home-maker are not usually permitted to be so vocal. Thus, characters such as Mollie in *Lover Or Friend* [1890], Gladys in *Uncle Max* and Philippa in *Rue With A Difference* [1900] have to wait for outsiders to recognize their plight before their lot can be improved.

---

44 *HC*, p. 52. Similar complaints from brothers towards their sister (though with more justification) are found in *Aunt Diana*.

If the narratorial voice in the novels applauds the home-maker who has domestic expertise and a benign temperament, conversely approval is withheld from women who wilfully fail to provide the appropriate ethos and servicing. Such 'failures' are also rewarded according to their perceived deserts. A number are specifically 'punished', in a kind of 'poetic justice', for the misery they inflict upon others. For example, Etta in *Uncle Max* wrongfully usurps the home-making role and wrongfully uses her power once she is in control. Her reward for this non-nurturant behaviour is permanent banishment from the luxurious home to which she is accustomed. Placed in an isolated area, beyond the bounds of the family and her own class, there is little chance of her being able to take any kind of even pseudo-maternal role. However, this is the nature of her punishment. Similarly, Augusta in *No Friend Like A Sister* makes life so unbearable for her sisters and her sister-in-law that they all move out of the family home. Her fictional 'punishment' is threefold: having driven her family away, she is lonely; for most of the narrative she is made to experience unrequited love; and, when she finally marries, it is because the man in question needs a nurse rather than a wife. Thus, her maternal role comes to her very late and when it does it is an inversion or perversion of the usual reward for domestic duty well done. Her 'baby' is a querulous adult.

However, to have maternity or pseudo-maternity withheld is not the fate of all unsuccessful home-makers. If the person in the role is merely young, or sincere but incompetent, Carey permits her to learn and to improve. Thus, in *Heriot's Choice*, the burden of housekeeping is removed from fifteen-year-old Olive's shoulders by an aunt who comes to live with the family. This permits Olive a period of training for future usefulness. Similarly, an even younger homemaker, Dossie, is relieved of the job of trying to create a home for her father in *Only the Governess*. Nor is age the only deciding factor; a woman is also judged on the opportunities she has had in order to gain domestic experience. For Huldah, the eponymous heroine of the same novel, there are mitigating circumstances. She 'had no mother to guide [her]' in early life and had no good example to follow thereafter (*OTG*, p. 192). Thus, she is permitted to not only run a home badly but also to leave her husband without losing her ultimate earthly reward, maternity. Olive and Dossie eventually marry happily; Huldah, who is already married, returns to an appreciative husband and is eventually portrayed as the mother of three children.

In short, Carey does not always perfectly assimilate the hegemonic discourse of the home-maker, or rather, she is not so closely bound by this particular reality that she cannot see alternative readings. She subverts the dominant by making visible the potential brutality of the male; she sympathizes with the woman who cannot produce the appropriate qualities of the home-maker on demand, for what ever reason; and she broadens the range of potential rewards available to home-makers, by expanding the usual interpretation of the maternal role. Either she has, in her role as addressee, absorbed referents from outside of the hegemonic, or she has exercised her power to alter the discourses of the hegemonic before re-presenting them to her readers. Yet in spite of these manipulations of the stereotype, Carey's homemakers tend to conform to, or are compared unfavourably with, the stereotype presented by the etiquette book and the household manual.

The Parental Ethos

The ethos in approved households is, in virtually all cases, parental: even in households occupied entirely by adults; even in households where the parents in question are, for some reason, absent. However, the strong paterfamilias figure is not found at all. A brief survey of Carey's forty-one novels produces a list of thirty-two in which a major female character has no father living or whose father dies early on in the narrative.[45] Of the major households with which the heroine in question associates (through kinship, employment or friendship), in only sixteen out of forty-one cases is the householder's primary relationship within the household that of husband or father. In seven novels it is that of elder brother; in four more, that of some other male relative.[46] In the remaining thirteen novels no husband, father, or father substitute is present at all. These latter households are either all-female or have a female householder.[47] According to this reckoning, most heroines both *live* in households that are not headed by husbands or fathers and associate with households that are not headed by husbands or fathers.

Amongst the few fathers that are to be found in Carey's novels, a number of them tend to be weak and ineffectual; whilst in the few cases where a father

45 Heroines whose fathers are alive throughout the narrative: Barbara in *Barbara Heathcote's Trial*; Audrey in *Lover or Friend?*; Catherine in *Mrs Romney*; Waveney in *Mollie's Prince*; Githa in *The Angel of Forgiveness*; Maureen in *The Sunny Side of the Hill*; Alison in *Aunt Diana*; Bessie in *Our Bessie*. (*Other People's Lives*, being a collection of short stories, is impossible to classify.)

46 See Appendix to this chapter for table of 'Paucity of Husbands and Fathers in the Heroine's Most Significant Household'.

47 The following heroines are householders in their own right: Ellison in *The Mistress of Brae Farm*, Valerie in *Rue With a Difference*, Dinah and Elizabeth in *Herb of Grace*, Miss Jem in *The Highway of Fate*, Christian in *A Passage Perilous*, Elinor in *No Friend Like a Sister*.

Significant households in the following novels have a female householder who is not a heroine: *Not Like Other Girls* (Mrs Challenor), *But Men Must Work* (Miss Hillyard), *Averil* (Mrs Willmot), *Little Miss Muffet* (Mrs Foster), *Cousin Mona* (Miss Gordon), *The Sunny Side of the Hill* (Miss Brydon), *The Key of the Unknown* (Lady Mary).

fulfils an appropriate role, authority tends to be visibly lacking.[48] For example, Audrey, heroine of *Lover Or Friend*, is hardly in awe of her parent:

> 'If you want to do a thing, do it quickly, and without telling anyone, that is my motto. Father is no one. If I were going to run away from home, or do anything equally ridiculous, I should be sure to tell father first; he would only recommend me to go first class, and be sure to take a cab at the other end, bless him!'[49]

Nevertheless, these non-authoritarian fathers tend to be endearing, or at least much loved, even on occasions when the narrator perceives there to be actual deficiency. For example, of Ned's long-dead spendthrift father in *At The Moorings* it said that, 'With all [his] sins, never had a father been so tenderly loved' (*ATM*, p. 29). Similarly well loved, though with rather more cause, is the impecunious art-teacher and painter Everhard Ward, to be found in *Mollie's Prince* [1898].

The bias against normative fathers and towards other relations as heads of families is perhaps a reflection of Carey's own life.[50] Her father died in 1868, and her mother in 1871. Thus, she wrote about eight of her novels whilst living in her elder brother's household, about sixteen whilst living with her elder widowed sister and her children, and the remaining fourteen or so after moving to her own all-female establishment in 1897 or 1898.[51] Carey's work also reflects an age in which many parents died before their children reached maturity, in which a greater age range amongst siblings enabled some brothers to take on the role of head of household, and in which powerful social and economic factors encouraged siblings to remain living together after the demise of their parents.[52]

---

48 Of the eight fathers of heroines still alive, five are satisfactory. See: *Barbara Heathcote's Trial*, *Our Bessie*, *The Sunny Side of the Hill*, *Lover or Friend?*, *The Angel of Forgiveness* [1907]. Father not an active constituent in the household: *Aunt Diana*. Father providing poorly for children financially: *Molly's Prince*, *Mrs Romney* [1894].

49 R.N. Carey, *Lover or Friend?* (London: Macmillan, 1915 [1890]), p. 13.

50 It is certainly against the grain of etiquette books such as *Correct Conduct*, which take the home headed by a married male householder to be the norm.

51 This chronology is based upon Helen Black's interview with Carey, which probably took place in 1891, upon the evidence of her will and upon the addresses on her later publishing contracts. (See Black 1906, pp. 145–56, *passim*). Carey appears to have lived in the parental home until 1871, in her brother's home until 1885 and with her sister until 1897 or 1898. At this time, she moved to her own establishment, where she died in 1909.

52 Life expectancy was about 40 years in the mid-nineteenth century and had only improved to 52 years for males and 55 years for females by 1911–12. See Pat Jalland, *Death in the Victorian Family* (Oxford: Oxford University Press, 1996), pp. 5–6 (hereafter, Jalland 1996). Family size declined from the 1870s (marriages of the 1860s lasting more than twenty years produced an average of 6.16 live births but those of the 1880s produced only 5.3) whilst the death-rate for infants under a year old remained fairly constant throughout the nineteenth century, at around 154 per thousand life births (Jalland 1986, p. 175; Jalland 1996, p. 120).

Nevertheless, the ethos in approved households is, in virtually all cases, parental, the word 'mother' in particular functioning as an emotive metonym for the home itself. However, Carey was far from being the only Victorian writer to make use of this kind of metonymy. For example Mrs Craik takes the notion to its extreme in *John Halifax Gentleman* [1856]. Throughout the latter half of the novel the narrator, Phineas, consistently describes Ursula and John Halifax as 'the mother' and 'the father.' Carey does not go to these lengths but a good example of how she uses the word 'mother' to mean 'home' with all its permitted resonances is to be found in *Robert Ord's Atonement*:

> The mother's room was suited for tête-à-têtes, for quiet droppings-in of two or three; a place for the vicar to sit before the fire ... and read his letters. It had a great crimson couch appropriated by invalids. Here sick bodies and sick hearts were nursed by the mother herself.[53]

Effectively, the room which constitutes the physical fabric of the home, the uses to which the room is put, and which manifest the ethos of the home, and the home-maker/mother, the major occupant of the room, are undifferentiated. One reason for Carey's constant references to the mother as a signifier of the home is that the homemaker's role was perceived by the dominant discourse as maternal rather than sexual; nurturant and self-abnegating rather than assertive and individualistic. The approved home-maker or potential home-maker in Carey's novels is therefore made to utilise 'motherly' referents. The character is framed in one of three ways: she is a mother, acts like a mother or quotes her mother. In the first two cases it means she can be relied upon to be self-sacrificing for the good of the household; in the third, she is indicating that the home she creates will be religious by keeping the commandment to 'Honour thy father and thy mother' (Exodus 20:12). She will also be humble about her own merits because she is giving credit to the mother who taught her rather than claiming any originality. In Carey's novels, if a mother is quotable then she must be good; if a daughter quotes her, the daughter must also be good.

Notably, some of the most oft-quoted mothers in Carey's novels are those who have long since died.[54] Even more touchingly, some daughters are made to

---

However, family size ultimately depended upon material circumstances. In 1874, amongst the professional and upper classes the mortality rate for infants under one year was a relatively low 8 per cent (Jalland 1996, pp. 121). Thus, a fictional 'average middle-class family from the 1880s', comprising a group of five doubly-orphaned siblings, the eldest male of whom was the legal guardian of the remainder, would have been quite plausible.

53 *ROA*, p. 57. Carey does not consistently – or even extensively – refer to Mrs Ord as 'the mother' throughout the novel. After this passage, the conflation of Mary Ord as mother with the home becomes implicit.

54 *Queenie's Whim*, p. 73; *Uncle Max*, p. 12; *Heriot's Choice*, p. 79; *At The Moorings*, p. 38.

draw comfort from their departed mothers in other ways than by simply quoting their wisdom. Olive in *Heriot's Choice* likes to sing her mother's favourite hymn. She tells her aunt on one occasion, 'I had forgotten everything. I thought mamma was singing it with us, and it seemed so beautiful' (*HC*, p. 79). Olive also spends some time beside her mother's grave each Sunday afternoon. She explains:

> 'I ... pour out all my trouble to her, just as I used to ... [S]ometimes I fancy she answers me, not in speaking, you know, but in the thoughts that come as I sit here … Others may laugh at it ... but it is impossible to believe mamma can help loving us where she is; and she always liked us to come and tell her everything … '[55]

By this act of faith, to Olive, the family home is still complete even though her mother is no longer physically with her.

However, mothers in Carey's novels are not simply important in terms of providing the home-makers of the next generation with role-models. Potential husbands for heroines – especially the more distant or taciturn – indicate their suitability for the married state by their relationship with their mothers. For many of these heroes, too, the mother in question has long since died. The intimation is very much that the son seeks to re-create the home of his early youth by finding a wife who is just like his mother. However, there is an added dimension to this quest. A man who has appreciated his childhood home and who loves and misses his mother can be relied upon to do his part in establishing such a home; a man who reveres his mother's memory can be relied upon to treat all women well. Both Reginald Lorimer in *The Old, Old Story* [1894] and Garth Clayton in *Queenie's Whim* are sentimentally attached to paintings of their mothers. In the former case, the mother is smiling down at her son 'from the wall by his own fireside'; in the latter the picture of the mother with the 'sweet gentle face' is in her son's special 'den' or study.[56] It is as though the mother still keeps the home together even though she cannot personally supervise its management.

In other cases, the hero will only speak about his mother to one whom he deems to be in some way like her. This is an indicator that he will eventually propose marriage to, and be accepted by, the woman favoured with the confidence. That such confidences are a privilege is made explicit in *At The Moorings*:

---

55 *HC*, p. 70. See also *Basil Lyndhurst*, p. 467. For a daughter communing with her parents through music, see *Robert Ord's Atonement*, pp. 113–14. Perhaps more unusually, a son is made to say 'One never loses one's mother' in *At The Moorings*. See p. 242.

56 R.N. Carey, *The Old, Old Story* (London: Macmillan, 1900 [1894]), p. 6; *Queenie's Whim*, p. 153.

> as though some overpowering impulse moved him, Luke began to speak of his mother, first hesitatingly, and then as though it were a joy to him to talk of her …
>
> Sheila was much touched. She understood clearly that this reserved, self-contained man was paying her a rare compliment; but she had no idea that she was the only woman, with the exception of his aunt, to whom he had ever spoken to of his mother.[57]

Even the phrasing of the passage is similar to that of a Victorian proposal of marriage: he speaks 'hesitatingly'; she is 'touched' at the 'compliment' and she is described by the invisible narrator as 'the only woman' to have his confidence outside his family.[58]

A similar correlation between a man's mother and his potential bride is to be found in *Sir Godfrey's Grand-daughters*. In this case, a direct comparison is made between the two, though no displaced declaration or proposal occurs. The infatuated hero of the novel, Alec Lyall, is to be found sitting up late one night, pondering over his accounts:

> [I]t was evident that some important decision was weighing in the balance … [S]ome abstruse calculation seemed to trouble him; then his brow cleared …
>
> 'It is not so bad, after all,' he muttered, 'and things will improve. One would have to be careful, and work hard for some years; but my father began on less.' Then he paused, and his eyes glistened as he thought of his mother. She had always been a hallowed memory to him; her fair face and calm, gentle ways would never be forgotten … Something in Gerda's voice and expression had reminded him of his mother.
>
> 'Why should I not feel my way with her?' he said to himself …' (*SGG*, p. 241)

The correlation Carey makes between mothers of saintly memory and prospective wives is interesting in its own right. It bespeaks a commitment to an explicit range of domestic values, including that of family continuity. However, the presence of displaced courtship narratives is even more interesting. It suggests that, through the agency of motherly referents, Carey elevates and romanticizes the often tedious role of household management without sexualizing it.

---

57 *ATM*, p. 241; see also *OB*, p. 119

58 See *The Ladies' and Gentlemen's Letter Writer* [1862], Letter LXXXI, 'From a Young Lady to a Young Clergyman who has offered marriage'. This includes the line 'I feel both honoured and pleased by your preference.' Similarly, in *Correct Conduct*, the wife is reminded that 'your husband has paid you the compliment of selecting you out of the world of women' (p. 21).

Conclusion

Although Rosa Carey was far from being an iconoclast, the resistances to the dominant version of domesticity to be found within her novels are many and varied. She does not appear to question the domestic ideal itself but she betrays an awareness that the role of the woman in the home was far from being a sinecure. She does not speak of the labour and neglect to mention the labourer, as does the Reverend Mackay in his description of the Englishman's model home. Nor does she depict gainful employment solely as something undertaken by men and the home as somewhere without 'toils and troubles' analogous to 'the outer world', as does Samuel Smiles. Household tasks, for example the ever-present mending, are deemed to require genuine exertion and women who work in the home are seen to tire towards the end of the day. In addition, where the tensions inherent within the female hierarchy might be as invisible to men as domestic servicing is itself, Carey treats such tensions as being of the utmost importance to the women involved.

Carey's novels also appear to question the conventional wisdom of her time, that the only worthwhile occupation for women is marriage. They convey the message that whilst a wife can indeed take on the role of home-maker and render all other women in the household lower in status, it does not mean that these women are thereby superfluous. Carey's novels set out an important and dignified position for each woman within the household because they indicate that each woman can make a positive addition to the household ethos. In addition, Carey plays with the convention that marriage and maternity are the reward for duty well-performed in the familial home. Some narratorially-approved spinsters are rewarded with pseudo-maternity. That is, they receive sole charge of a child. However, such fictional women are constructed in much the same way as are birth-mothers rather than receiving the ridicule more generally directed at single women with child-care responsibilities. Thus the rewards of spinsters are on a par with those of women who marry.

Finally, Carey has certain of her male characters take more than a consumer's interest in the domestic sphere by making them both revere their mothers and utilize this devotion in the building of their future domestic circumstances. This devotion goes beyond W.H.D. Adams' glib description of 'A Mother's love illustrated by examples', for narratorially-approved bachelors only tend to speak of their mothers when they are near to proposing marriage. In their intention to reproduce the home of their childhood, specifically through the work of someone who takes the place of the revered mother, such characters give validity to the domestic world itself.

Appendix

Paucity of Husbands and Fathers in the Heroine's Most Significant Household (Male Heads of Household Only)

Title of Novel	Name of Heroine	Heroine's Relationship with Householder in her Most Significant Household	Householder's Relationship with Family Residing in Household
Nellie's Memories	Nellie	sister	brother
Wee Wifie	Fay	wife	husband
Robert Ord's Atonement	Rotha	friend	husband
Barbara Heathcote's Trial	Barbara	daughter	father
Wooed and Married	Dympha	employee	son
Heriot's Choice	Milly	sister	father
Queenie's Whim	Queenie	friend	brother
Mary St John	Mary	sister	husband
For Lilias	Marjory	'daughter'	brother
Uncle Max	Ursula	friend	brother
Only the Governess	Huldah	employee	step-son
Basil Lyndhurst	Olga	sister	husband/father
Lover or Friend?	Audrey	daughter	husband/father
Sir Godfrey's Grand-daughters	Gerda	niece	husband/father
Mrs Romney	Catherine	daughter-in-law	husband/father
The Old, Old Story	Gloden	niece	husband
Dr Luttrell's First Patient	Olivia	wife	father
My Lady Frivol	Eden/Bonnie	employee/niece	uncle
Life's Trivial Round	Berrie	housekeeper	father
At The Moorings	Sheila	sister	brother
The Household of Peter	Ranee/Vera/Sallie	sisters	brother
The Angel of Forgiveness	Githa	daughter	father
Esther Cameron's Story	Esther	niece	uncle/brother-in-law
Aunt Diana	Alison	daughter	father
Merle's Crusade	Merle	employee	husband
Our Bessie	Bessie	daughter	father

In Carey's novels there are vast casts of characters and these characters frequently move from place to place. This has made it difficult to produce statistics that are both meaningful and succinct. Many novels contain more than one heroine and many contain a heroine who lives in more than one significant household in the course of the novel. Thus, the table above claims to give nothing more than an impressionistic view of family construction in Carey's novels. With these limitations in mind, the heroine of each novel is listed in column [1]. Column [2] lists the relationship of the heroine to the householder in her most significant household. Column [3] lists the householder's status or title in relation to his closest family ties within the household. (The heroine does not necessarily participate in this set of relations.) Thus, in *Uncle Max*, Ursula's relationship to the householder is that of friend but his primary relationship within the household is that of brother to his two sisters. Similarly, in *Basil Lyndhurst*, Olga is sister to the householder. However, his primary relationships within the household are those of husband and father.

Chapter 5

Sentimental Heresies

There's No Place Like 'Home'

In a nineteenth-century conduct book called *Happy Homes and How to Make Them*, the reader is given the following admonition:

> HAVE A FAMILY ALTAR OF YOUR OWN.–
> 'Wherever the family appears in its beauty, wherever moral health is fortified ... wherever we find united progress, manly effort, tenderness, vigour, harmless mirth, [and] deep sorrows, accompanied by genuine consolations ... you will find that those who love and support each other, together bend the knee.'
>
> If such be the case, then let us recommend the practice of daily reading the Bible ... and also of seeking God's blessing by prayer. By this means you will best secure a virtuous, moral, happy, and godly home ...[1]

Although it is impossible to gauge the level of religious adherence in the homes of Victorian and Edwardian England, the message itself was a commonplace. The proposition, that a happy home is a religiously-motivated home, may be found in literature ranging from the hearty 'self-help' books of Samuel Smiles to the fulsome novels of Marie Corelli.[2] However, it may also be seen that Victorian and Edwardian society had domesticated Christianity. The opening of the chapter entitled 'Home' in Charlotte Yonge's non-fictional work, *Womankind* [1877], may be taken as an indication of this tendency. Yonge writes:

> The Altar and the hearth! Well may they be coupled together, and well does Wordsworth in his 'Lark' describe the faithful heart as –
> 'True to the kindred points of Heaven and Home!'[3]

1 J.W. Kirton, *Happy Homes and How to Make Them* (Birmingham: The Educational Trading Company, n.d. [inscribed 1871]), p. 79 (hereafter, *Happy Homes*).

2 See Samuel Smiles, *Thrift* (London: John Murray, 1876) p. 326; Marie Corelli, *The Sorrows of Satan* (London: Methuen, 1899 [1895]), p. 203.

3 C.M. Yonge, *Womankind* (London: Mozley and Smith, 1877), p. 264. Wordsworth's poem is actually called 'To A Skylark' and does not mention the human heart at all. Written in 1825 when Wordsworth was anything but a conventional Christian, it, too, has been appropriated by the establishment here. For the full text of the poem, see William Wordsworth,

Popular religious texts of the Victorian and Edwardian eras often posited, and indeed generated, links between what the society of the time circulated by way of discourses on the home and what they believed to be the biblical authority underlying them. Yet, whilst the word 'home' is found in the Bible in both the Old and the New Testaments, in no instance does it have the resonances to be found in Victorian and Edwardian writing. The domestication of Christianity depended upon not only the opportunity for commentary and glossary that popular secondary texts on the Bible provided but also the arrival of a particular moment in the history of domesticity itself. These conditions did not obtain in biblical times and even the translators of the King James Bible and the compilers of the *Book of Common Prayer* did not add the kind of gloss needed to produce the 'domestic' religion of the late nineteenth and early twentieth centuries.[4]

In the Bible, of the fifty-one references to the word 'home', the vast majority refer to the actual location of a person's dwelling-place, as is one of the meanings of the word today. Other references simply make 'home' the opposite of 'abroad' (Lamentations 1:20; Leviticus 18:9). A few of the latter superficially appear to permit additional meanings but ultimately any perceived similarity to the nineteenth-century home may soon be proved to be Victorian accretion. For example, the notion of women as 'discreet, chaste, keepers at home' (Titus 2:5) suggests both a physical location and a foreshadowing of the

---

'To a Skylark' [1827], l.12, in *The Works of William Wordsworth* (Ware: Wordsworth Editions Ltd., 1994), p. 209 (hereafter, *Works*).

4 The King James Bible was first published in 1611 and the *Book of Common Prayer* in 1662. At this time there was little concept of the nuclear family, companionable marriage or childhood as a distinct phase of development. Arguably, the nurturant home on the modern model only arrived with Rousseau's *Emile* (1762) and the sentimental version of the home only with the non-fictional narratives from the late 1830s onwards, for example those in the conduct books of Sarah Stickney Ellis. It only arose in the fiction in the 1850s, with the advent of Patmore's *The Angel in the House* and Yonge's *The Heir of Redclyffe*, both published in 1854. This view differs in detail from that expressed in Nancy Armstrong, *Desire and Domestic Fiction* (Oxford: Oxford University Press, 1987), p. 5. Armstrong argues that notions of the sentimental domestic are to be found in fiction as early as Samuel Richardson's *Pamela* (1740–41). Admittedly, the heroine of *Pamela* operates through 'psychological motives' and is thus 'sentimental'. It is also admitted that the book has a domestic setting. However, it is posited here that neither the home itself nor the woman in relation to the home were sentimentalized until later in the century.

Something may be deduced about the meanings that the translators of the Bible attached to the word 'home' from *The Shorter Oxford English Dictionary*, 2 vols (Oxford: Clarendon Press, 1991), p. 976. Of the eight substantive meanings listed, the term was used to denote the household 'occasionally' in Old English and the grave or future state in Middle English. However, the popular twentieth-century understanding of the word only began to emerge later. These later meanings are attributive rather than substantive: 'of, relating to or connected with home ... domestic, family', 1552; 'treating of domestic affairs' does not appear until 1797; whilst the appearance of 'family or home life' as an expression is attributed to Samuel Smiles (1812–1904).

Victorian division of society into public and private spheres, the woman's place being designated as 'at home'. J.W. Kirton, author of *Happy Homes and How to Make Them*, certainly utilizes the verse from Titus as if this meaning were easily discoverable in it. His chapter on the duties of a wife contains as a heading the very words 'A Wife Should be a Keeper-At-Home'. The section begins:

> Some women are everlastingly gadding about like butterflies from flower to flower; of such it is said, 'Whose feet abide not in her own house.' ...
>
> While it is the man's place to be *out*, it is the woman's place to be at HOME. An inspired writer says, 'Teach the young women to be discreet, keeping at home, good, obedient,' etc.
>
> Yes, 'The sphere of women is home – the asylum of love, the nursery of virtue ... the circle of all tender relationships ...'[5]

However, taken solely in its biblical context, this reference to 'discreet, chaste, keepers at home' is about the virtue of the individual rather than the private sphere of the family. Besides, this apparent reference to 'housekeeping' in the domestic sense is immediately set at nought when compared with the Old Testament passage, 'neither keepeth [he] at home, who enlargeth his desire ... and cannot be satisfied', in which the subject is emphatically male.[6] The implication here is that the temperate man should also be a keeper at home. Nevertheless, it is easy to see how the passage from Paul's epistle to Titus could be appropriated and used as a justification for the establishment of public and private spheres.[7]

An example of the extent to which the biblical notion of home had been overwritten by the domestic ideal as it arose in the mid-nineteenth century is to be found in the Rev. H.C. Lees's devotional work, *The Divine Master in Home Life* [1915]. Early in the first chapter the author notes that:

> By derivation 'home' means the same as 'village.' But how far the word has advanced since then! And it is affection which has created an

5 *Happy Homes*, pp. 120–21. Punctuation and capital letters original. The words 'Whose feet abide not in her own house' are to be found in Proverbs 7:11 and they apply to a woman who behaves like a harlot. Where explicit biblical endorcement of the notion of public and private spheres is lacking, Kirton fashions the two available quotations into a rhetorical choice for women: will you be a wife or a whore?

6 Habakkuk 2:5.

7 The only other biblical passages even remotely suggestive of home on the Victorian and Edwardian model are those in which the word home is preceded by a possessive pronoun (John 19:27, John 16:32 and John 20:10); of these only the first is suggestive of nurture. The two remaining instances which appear not to be purely references to location are Ecclesiastes 12:3–7 which speaks of man's 'long home', the grave, and 2 Corinthians 5:6. The latter is discussed below.

> atmosphere in which the idea of mere dwelling has given way to thought of the most restful of life's realities.[8]

In this passage the author appears to be aware that the word 'home' meant one thing in biblical times and another in the twentieth century. However, by page 160, Lees writes of the 'exquisite domestic picture' of Christ's childhood as if it was of the same nature as the 'advanced' home of the affections. It is also notable that, when he describes the ideal twentieth-century home as a place of comfort and beauty, Lees alludes to the allegorical Palace Beautiful in *The Pilgrim's Progress* rather than to any passage in the Bible.[9] It seems that there is no equally potent biblical equivalent.

'... on earth as it is in Heaven'

However, the most important appropriation of a biblical text for domestic purposes entails a decontextualised reading of 2 Corinthians 5. Here, the basis for another facet of the Victorian discourse of home may be found. In it, there are two orders of location, effectively two kinds of home: the home on earth and the home in Heaven. The chapter opens with the comforting notion that

> we know that if our earthly house of this tabernacle were dissolved, we have a building of God, an house not made with hands, eternal in the heavens.[10]

---

8 Rev. Harrington C. Lees, *The Divine Master in Home Life* (London: Religious Tract Society, 1915) (hereafter, Lees 1915). Although published six years after Carey's death, it indicates that the discourse had not greatly changed over many years.

9 Lees 1915, p. 11. John Bunyan's religious allegory, *The Pilgrim's Progress*, was initially published in two parts, the first in 1678 and the second in 1684. The Palace Beautiful is alluded to in both. It was still widely read in the nineteenth century and Rosa Carey has characters discuss it in *Merle's Crusade* [1886–87] and *Our Bessie* [1888–89].

10 The actual context of this phrase, from 2 Corinthians, is as follows:

> *16* ... though our outward man perish, yet the inward *man* is renewed day by day ...
>
> *18* ... we look not at the things which are seen, but at the things which are not seen: for the things which are seen *are* temporal; but the things which are not seen *are* eternal. (2 Corinthians 4:16–18[Emphasis original])
>
> *1* For we know that if our earthly house of *this* tabernacle were dissolved, we have a building of God, an house not made with hands, eternal in the heavens ...
>
> *2* For this we groan, earnestly desiring to be clothed upon with our house which is in heaven ...
>
> *4* ... not for that we would be unclothed, but clothed upon, that mortality might be swallowed up of life. (2 Corinthians 5:1–4. [Emphasis original])

Given that the passage speaks of physical decay and of being clothed with 'life', it seems that the 'house not made with hands' is the body rather than a physical building or set of familial relationships.

Although, in context, the 'earthly house' refers to the human body, the phrase is often taken to mean a literal house, or even a family home. According to this interpretation, the home has a spiritual as well as a temporal basis. The successful home is thus permeated with the essence of the heavenly home, the eternal aspect surviving the inevitable dissolution of the temporal. In a sense, the temporal and the eternal are seen to occupy the same space. David Lyall's domestic novel, called *The House Not Made With Hands* [1912], certainly carries this resonance.[11]

However, the sixth verse in this same chapter from 2 Corinthians gives the opposite impression, stating that 'whilst we are at home in the body, we are absent from the Lord'. This proposition sets up a choice of mutually exclusive psychological 'locations' for the individual: a choice of either a spiritual or a temporal 'home'. Given that being with the Lord is the desired object, the verse implies that it is impossible for the Christian to be 'at home' in any temporal sense; 'the body' must be rejected in favour of 'the Lord'. Novels written from this perspective are frequently intrusively religious, given that they are, effectively, world-denying. For example, an anonymous tale published by the Religious Tract Society, entitled *Uncle Jabez; or The Teachings of Adversity* [c. 1871], is largely composed of the articulated worries of an ideally religious and poverty-stricken family that the miserly uncle of the title is, in the religious sense, 'not prepared to die'.[12]

Thus, if the Victorians and Edwardians deemed it desirable to draw a parallel between earthly and heavenly homes, there was some kind of biblical basis. However, the message gleaned from scripture was at best ambiguous. There were two basic positions that could be taken by the domestic-religious Victorian or Edwardian: a hierarchy of the two types of home or an identification of the two. In strictly theological terms, earthly homes were at best a poor shadow of the heavenly home and at worst a snare rather than a support. In this analysis, hierarchically, the heavenly home and the earthly home are completely separate and share nothing of each other's nature. However, popularly, the two orders of home were the subject of identification,

---

11 David Lyall [Mrs Burnett Smith, generally known by her maiden name, Annie S. Swan], *The House Not Made With Hands* (London: Hodder and Stoughton, n.d. [1912]). The main plot follows the fortunes of a second wife, Alison Crewe, whose task is to turn her new family's opulent but uncentred and irreligious household into an earthly home which reflects its heavenly counterpart. Although this novel was published three years after Rosa Carey's death, the two women were contemporaries. Annie S. Swan was in print at least as early as 1883 and Carey remained in print until at least 1924.

12 'By the author of "Margaret Browning," etc.', *Uncle Jabez; or The Teachings of Adversity* (London: Religious Tract Society, n.d. [inscribed 1871]), p. 36. However, even this story does not sustain an otherworldly discourse continuously. The family comes out of adversity with all reasonable middle-class aspirations satisfied. The three boys become a minister, a doctor and the owner of a profitable business respectively and the mother and daughter become leisured women.

whereby the home on earth and the home above were somehow linked, the earthly partaking of the heavenly nature and preparing its inhabitants for the call to the final home. The Rev. Lees straightforwardly utilizes the identificatory model:

> If home be the dearest place in the world, and Christ be the 'joy of heaven to earth come down,' then to have Christ in the home is to anticipate Paradise at once.[13]

This same chapter concludes with an exhortation to the reader to pray that '"Christ may make His home in our hearts," and His heaven in our homes.' The book concludes with an even more explicit parallel:

> For He Who has gone, and they who have followed Him have left us something behind. And we who have known Him standing, walking, sitting with us in our homes, shall not count it strange to enter into His home, palace though it be, and find Him standing there with our loved ones, to welcome us in. (Lees 1915, p. 213)

Notably, Lees's book was published by the Religious Tract Society. The organization evidently deemed there to be nothing indecorous in his writing.[14]

However, the Victorians and Edwardians often played with the concept linguistically, shifting from one stance to the other. In another Religious Tract Society publication, *The Young Man From Home* [c. 1890], there appears to be an ambivalence about which model of earthly and heavenly homes should be adopted.[15] For more than three-quarters of the book, James uses the word 'home' to describe in glowing terms the temporal household that the young male reader has supposedly recently left.[16] However, in the penultimate

---

13 Lees 1915, p. 1. Lees quotes from the first verse of Charles Wesley's hymn 'Love Divine, All Loves Excelling'. For the full text of the hymn see hymn 520 in H.W. Baker (ed.), *Hymns Ancient and Modern*, Standard Edition (London: Printed for the Proprietors by William Clowes and Sons, 1916 [1861]), p. 152.

14 Whilst the use of a number of R.T.S. publications in this chapter was initially an accidental bias, this balance has not been changed as the views expressed in the texts are known to have been acceptable to a broad range of opinion within the Christian churches. The R.T.S. agenda was to provide non-sectarian, non-doctrinal material that was conducive to the promotion of the Christian life. Whilst virulently anti-Romanist, its policy-making bodies included representatives from all shades of mainstream Protestant thought. The distribution of these texts indicates an even broader acceptability amongst 'consumers'. For details of the composition of the R.T.S. Executive Committee and of the variety of bodies applying for grants of books and tracts, see the Minutes of the Executive Committee, held amongst the Records of the United Society for Christian Literature at the School of Oriental and African Studies, London University. See USCL/RTS fiche boxes 1–24 (1799–March 1953).

15 John Angell James, *The Young Man From Home* (London: Religious Tract Society, n.d. [inscribed 1892]) (hereafter, *The Young Man From Home*).

16 See, for some examples, *The Young Man From Home*, pp. 7, 37, 39, 80, 83.

chapter, the author proclaims that 'This world is *not* our home, and unhappy is the man who makes it such. HEAVEN IS THE HOME OF IMMORTAL MAN' (italics and capitals original). From this page onwards, the references to temporal homes become fewer and, except for the title of chapter 7, 'Religion Considered as a Preparation for Super-Intending a Home of your Own Upon Earth, and for Going to an Eternal Home in Heaven', he usually substitutes the word 'household' (*The Young Man From Home*, p. 128). It appears to be the author's intention to eclipse the temporal meaning of the word 'home' with the more spiritual meaning, for the book concludes with a dire warning:

> There is a home for all truly penitent prodigals IN HEAVEN; and there is a home for all impenitent ones, but it is – IN HELL.[17]

Yet, taken overall, the object of the book is manifestly twofold: to train young men to be effective on earth as well as to prepare them for heaven. Although 'This world is *not* our home,' there is a chapter entitled 'Religion Viewed as a Means of Promoting the Temporal Interests of its Possessor', in which the reader is asked, 'Do you wish to prosper and get on in the world?' and is told 'it is quite lawful for you to wish it, you *ought* indeed to wish it' (italics original; quotations from p. 119). According to James, if there was no home on earth worth having, there was apparently something very like one.

In her capacity as a novelist, Rosa Carey makes good use of both models. Yet, even though she was overtly and sincerely religious, her writings tend to be fictions permeated with religion rather than tracts thinly veiled by fictions. Thus many of her allusions to the heavenly home are merely euphemisms for the process of dying. For example, in *Heriot's Choice*, Aunt Milly says of her niece who is desperately ill, 'I think she wishes to know if God means to take her home', and in *Cousin Mona* [1895], the eponymous heroine says of her brother, 'God has ... taken him home first'.[18]

However, Carey can, like James, shift between identifying the heavenly with the earthly home and ranking them hierarchically. For example, in *Our Bessie* [1888–89], Carey begins on the identificatory model. In this instance, a concrete location within the family home becomes, by association, a point of contact with Heaven itself. For the reader is told that, following the death of her younger sister, the eponymous Bessie 'would creep softly into a certain empty room' to say her prayers and:

---

17 Capitals and emphasis original. See *The Young Man From Home*, p. 159.

18 R.N. Carey, *Heriot's Choice* (London: Macmillan, 1899 [1877–9]), p. 183 (hereafter, *HC*); *Cousin Mona* (London: RTS, 1897 [1895]), p. 242.

> Sometimes as she prayed the sense of her sister's presence would come over her strongly; she could almost feel the touch of the thin little hands ...[19]

As she prays in the room where her sister has lived and died, Bessie can feel the presence of one who has 'gone home'. The reader is then directly addressed with the assurance that:

> Somewhere, not here, but in the larger room of a purified existence, your beloved one lives, breathes, nay, thinks of thee.[20]

The creation of a parallel between 'a certain empty room' and 'the larger room' surely indicates that the spiritual and the temporal are very close, even if they do not occupy the same space. However, this comforting identification is eclipsed by two later images, which then establish the more scripturally sound hierarchy. First of all, the direct narratorial intervention concludes with the words, 'Be comforted; one day we shall meet [those who have died], and the friendship of time will become the love of eternity' (*OB*, p. 186). In this passage, the spiritual and the temporal are firmly restored to a hierarchical order. The temporal is not disparaged, merely placed in an eternal context.[21] In a passage some two pages later, the unsatisfactory nature of this life is spelt out far more emphatically. For Bessie is made to quote the philosopher Henri-Frederic Amiel to her fictional sister, Christine, who feels she had been unkind to the now departed Hatty:

> Life is short, and we never have too much time for gladdening the hearts of those who are travelling the dark journey with us.[22]

Thus, it would seem, at the last, that the earth is a not a home but the site of a pilgrimage during which there is nothing but suffering.[23] Only at the end of the

19 R.N. Carey, *Our Bessie* (London: Office of the *Girl's Own Paper*, 1914 [1888–9]), p. 186 (hereafter, *OB*).

20 That people 'live' after death is biblically verifiable. See Matthew 22:32. Luke 16:22–32 (the story of Dives and Lazarus) indicates that it is possible for the dead to think of the living. However, the same passage would indicate that the dead are not permitted to return in any way in order to edify the living. Carey treads on the very outskirts of orthodoxy here.

21 Cf. the relativism of the biblical quotation, 'For now we see through a glass darkly; but then face to face' (1 Corinthians 13:12).

22 *Our Bessie*, p. 189. Carey quotes this same passage in R.N. Carey, *Basil Lyndhurst* (London: Macmillan, 1904 [1889]), pp. 5–6 (hereafter, *BL*). See Henri-Frederic Amiel, *Amiel's Journal, The Journey Intime*, ed. and trans. Mrs Humphrey Ward (London: Macmillan, 1901 [1895]), p. 146 (hereafter, *Amiel's Journal*). The first volume of the journal was initially published in French in 1882. *Amiel's Journal* is on record as being one of Rosa Carey's favourite books. See Helen C. Black, *Notable Women Authors of the Day* (London: Maclaren, 1906), p. 155.

23 Cf. Job 5:7; 14:1.

'dark journey' of life on earth is there a real home. Yet Carey probably selected the latter passage as much for its social message about kindness as for its religious overtones. A more typical Evangelical message is contained in the paragraph sited above the quotation from Amiel:

> '... think ... of how, by your waywardness, you have wounded the loving heart of Jesus ... Let the sense of Hatty's loss send you to Him in penitence for pardon.'

For both practical and compassionate reasons Carey most often uses the identificatory model. If earthly homes can be made to resemble in some faint way the Heavenly Home, this increases the dignity of domestic work and gives it additional meaning; housework becomes Heaven-work. However, even more importantly, such an identification tempers the starkness of death and the austerity of the established religion. Certainly Carey's characters who see a connexion between the home on earth and the home above are better comforted in cases of bereavement than their more theologically-correct counterparts. Thus, when Olive in *Heriot's Choice* sings her dead mother's favourite hymn – 'I had forgotten everything. I thought mamma was singing it with us, and it seemed so beautiful.' – she feels that the family, divided by death, has become reconstituted (*HC*, p. 79). By this act of faith, the family home is still complete even though her mother is no longer physically with her.[24] She is better consoled than her brothers, who can only view this reminder of their mother as a reminder of their great loss:

> 'One's most sacred feelings trampled upon mercilessly,– it is unpardonable ... Such cruel heedlessness deserves reproof, but it is all lost on Livy; she will never understand how we feel about these things. (*HC*, pp. 77–8)

Mr Brett, the clergyman in *At The Moorings* [1904], also believes that his mother is still with him:

---

24 Cf. also Felicia Hemans, *The Faith of Love*, lines 37–48:

'Nor shut mine ear to the song of old,
Though its notes my pangs renew,
– Such memories deep in my heart I hold,
To keep it pure and true ...

'By the presence that about me seems
Through night and day to dwell,
Voice of vain bodings and fearful dreams!
– I have breathed no *last* farewell!

See *The Poetical Works of Felicia Dorothea Hemans* (London: Humphrey Milford, Oxford University Press, 1914), p. 532.

> 'One never loses one's mother ... I do not know that I am fanciful or superstitious, but I have an odd belief in my mother's nearness. One cannot argue on such matters, but love teaches us many things. I should not care to part with my special creed, I am not so enamoured of loneliness.'[25]

The recipient of these confidences agrees with him but notes that '[t]here is too little faith in this world' and that '[p]eople are far too ready to bury their dead and to forget' (ibid.).

Yet an impressive feature of Rosa Carey's writing is her sense of proportion. Carey, like James, wrote with one eye on heaven but the other very firmly on earth. Possibly the best example of this balance of priorities is to be found at the conclusion to *Doctor Luttrell's First Patient* [1897]. The elderly widow, Madge Broderick, whilst looking heavenward, counts her temporal blessings. She sometimes tells her niece:

> 'I have two lovely homes ... One here with you and Marcus and the darling children, and one in the "many mansions" where Fergus and baby boy wait for me.'

Nor is Madge unwilling for this state of affairs to remain. The sentence which follows, the last in the novel, reads: 'And as she said this a radiant smile would light up her features like sunshine.'[26] Carey manages to balance the necessity for a home on earth, in both its physical and its spiritual manifestations, with the scriptural assertion that life is a pilgrimage and that death could come at any time. She does this, not by denying the presence of death but by domesticating it. By small acts of faith, some characters in her novels retain their family circles unbroken even though death has intervened.

Intimations of Immortality

However, Carey also appears to subvert the austerity of the established religion by filling out more orthodox pieties with allusions to the early work of William Wordsworth. This entails another range of sentimental heresies though these do

25 R.N. Carey, *At The Moorings* (London: Macmillan, 1914 [1904]), p. 242 (hereafter, *ATM*).

26 R.N. Carey, *Doctor Luttrell's First Patient*, initially serialised in the *Girl's Own Paper* 3 October 1896 – 20 March 1897. Quotation from 20 March 1897, p. 397. Madge's reference to 'many mansions' is an allusion to John 14:2. Whilst noting Carey's unorthodox theology, it might be added that 'baby boy' does not have a name. If this is because he died before he was baptised then, theologically speaking, Madge could not meet him in Heaven. The *Book of Common Prayer* states that, 'None can enter the Kingdom of God, except that he be regenerate and born anew of Water and of the Holy Ghost' (p. 181).

not, in themselves, have even the semblance of biblical authority. In keeping with her interest in maintaining the family circle even when family members die, she seems to show particular sympathy with Wordsworth's contention that without a sense of immortality there could be no love. In the first of his *Essays Upon Epitaphs* [1810], Wordsworth writes that:

> the sense of immortality, if not co-existent and twin birth with Reason, is amongst the earliest of her offspring ... *it is to me inconceivable, that the sympathies of love towards each other, which grow with our growth, could ever attain new strength, or even preserve the old, after we had received from the outward senses the impression of death ... if the same were not counteracted by those communications with our internal Being, which are anterior to all these experiences* ... [I]f the impression and sense of death were not thus counterbalanced, such a hollowness would pervade the whole system of things ... that there could be no repose, no joy. Were we to grow up unfostered by this genial warmth, a frost would chill the spirit, so penetrating and powerful, that there could be no motions of the life of love; and infinitely less could we have any wish to be remembered after we had passed away from a world in which each man had moved about like a shadow. (My emphasis.)[27]

Wordsworth thereby asserts that the ability to love is based upon the intuitive knowledge that loving others is a safe investment of feeling. The human soul is immortal so the object of the affections is never lost.

With more feeling than theological accuracy, Carey, too, describes the advent of the spiritual into the temporal and the promise of a specific kind of immortality. In *The Old, Old Story* [1894], a temporal love made possible because of a guarantee of the eternal is the experience of a long-married couple, Clemency and Reuben Garrick. For part of the story, Clemency is away from home and Reuben can only visit her for a few minutes each day. Yet, on his departure:

> Clemency would watch him until he was out of sight, and then go back to her work with the love-light still in her eyes – that strange, mysterious radiance, God-given and divine in its origin, and which is as lovely in aged eyes as in the eyes of youth.
>
> [The much younger] Reginald's quick, ardent love [for his fiancée, Gloden,] was only a flickering torch as yet, compared to the steady lamp lighted in Clemency's quiet eyes. It takes a lifetime of proving and bearing before the full mellow glow can be reached, that light that comes from God, and burns to all eternity.[28]

---

27 William Wordsworth, *Selected Prose*, ed. John O. Hayden (Harmondsworth: Penguin, 1988), p. 325 (hereafter, *Selected Prose*).

28 R.N. Carey, *The Old, Old Story* (London: Macmillan, 1900 [1894]), p. 328 (hereafter, *The Old, Old Story*). Here, Carey steps dangerously near to heresy, for the Bible states three

The 'proving and bearing' that Clemency has undergone suggests Wordsworth's notion of 'the sympathies of love ... towards each other, which grow with our growth', whilst the light which will burn 'to all eternity' bespeaks 'the impression and sense of death counter-balanced' by 'those communications with [the] internal Being, which are anterior to ... experiences [of death]'.[29]

Given her staunch Anglicanism, it seems unlikely that Carey sympathized deeply with the notion that immortality could be intuited through the 'internal Being' or self rather than through the person of Jesus.[30] It would thus seem even less likely that she could countenance the non-Trinitarian theism of Wordsworth's Ode, *Intimations of Immortality*.[31] Nevertheless, her novel *Heriot's Choice* appears to be predicated upon this particular poem and, in this novel, Carey's young heroine, Olive, has an unusually direct intimation of the hereafter. Close to death, Olive feels as though she is substantially reunited with her dead mother. However, she does not actually die because her father and brother recall her to temporal life. The experience is related twice, first to her Aunt Milly:

> '... it was only Cardie's voice that brought me back ... I was falling – falling into dark, starry depths, full of living creatures, wheels of light and flame seemed everywhere, and then darkness. I thought mamma had

---

times that 'in the resurrection they neither marry, nor are given in marriage' (Matthew 22:30; Mark 12:25; Luke 20:35.) Carey could probably escape the charge on the grounds that they will love each other through eternity rather than remain married in the earthly sense. The notion that marriage might continue after death is suggestive of Swedenborg. See Emanuel Swedenborg, *A Compendium of the Theological Writings*, ed. Rev. S.M. Warren (London: Swedenborg Society, 1909), pp. 444–58, especially p. 455: 'They who are in love that is truly conjugial look to what is eternal.'

29 Cf. also Wordsworth's Ode, *Intimations of Immortality From Recollections of Early Childhood* [first published 1807] (hereafter called *Intimations of Immortality* or 'the *Ode*'), stanza 9:

> Hence in a season of calm weather
> Though inland far we be,
> Our Souls have sight of that immortal sea
> Which brought us hither
> Can in a moment travel thither ...

For the full text of the poem see *Works*, pp. 587–90.

30 Cf. John 14:6.

31 Late twentieth-century scholars are divided as to whether the *Ode* is about literal or figurative immortality. J.A. Hodgson discusses the two major schools of thought, humanist interpretations and transcendental interpretations (basically Christian), before going on to make his own analysis. I take Hodgson's stance of non-Christian theism. See J.A. Hodgson, *Wordsworth's Philosophical Poetry 1797–1814* (Lincoln: University of Nebraska Press, 1980), pp. 104–9. However, of most importance here is Rosa Carey's response. This cannot be known in any absolute sense. Any estimate of her belief in the matter can only be based upon a knowledge of her own Christian adherence and upon the reception of Wordsworth's poetry in the late nineteenth century.

> got me in her arms, she seemed by me through it all, and then I heard Cardie say I should break his heart, and then he sobbed, and papa blessed me. I heard some gate close after that, and mamma's arms seemed to loosen from me, and then I knew I was not dying.' (*HC*, pp. 190–91)

Up until this point, Olive articulates her experience in terms reconcilable with the Christian tradition, the gate representing the entrance to heaven and her mother's presence being a pretty conceit in keeping with the notion of going to the eternal home.[32] It is when she relates her experience a second time that her narrative runs against the grain of normative Christianity. She tells a family friend, 'I know what death means now. When I come to die, I shall feel I know it all before' (*HC*, p. 193). This, predictably, brings about an orthodox Christian response:

> 'But you did not die, dear Olive!' exclaimed Ethel, in a startled voice. 'No one can know but Lazarus and the widow's son; and they have told us nothing.'[33]

Yet Olive's reply is an assertive 'all the same I shall always feel that I know what dying means'. She continues, occasionally interrupted by an awed audience:

> 'When I close my eyes I can bring it all back ... the deadly shuddering cold creeping over my limbs, everyone weeping round me, and yet beyond a great silence and darkness; we begin to understand what silence means then.'
>
> 'A great writer once spoke of "voices at the other end of silence,"' returned Ethel ...
>
> 'But silence itself – what is silence? – One sometimes stops to think about it, and then its grandeur seems to crush one. What if silence be the voice of God!' (Ibid.)

Olive's experience of a 'great silence' beyond the noisy temporal weeping around her is strongly suggestive of Wordsworth's contention that it is possible to view the temporal and the eternal simultaneously. For, in his *Ode*, Wordsworth writes of the shadowy recollections of immortality which make 'Our noisy years seem moments in the being/Of the eternal Silence.'[34]

32 The idea of a heavenly gate has a biblical basis. See Matthew 16.19, in which Jesus says to Peter: 'And I will give unto thee the keys of the kingdom of heaven'. Thus, (Saint) Peter is envisaged as being the keeper of a literal door or gate.

33 Ibid., Lazarus – John 11: 1–46; the widow's son – Luke 7:11–16.

34 Cf. also *Amiel's Journal*: p. 21, 'O silence, thou art terrible! ... Thou showest us within ourselves depths which make us giddy, inextinguishable needs, treasures of suffering'; p. 130, 'The divine state *par excellence* is that of silence and repose, because all speech and all action are in themselves limited and fugitive.'

Moreover, as if to emphasize the Wordsworthian nature of her intimation of immortality, Carey has the fictional Olive – who is herself a poet – look out of the window on to a landscape located only about thirty miles from Grasmere.[35] There,

> she could see the dark violet fells, the soft restful billows of green, [and] silver splashes of light through the trees. How peaceful and quiet it all looked. (*HC*, p. 193)

Olive's dispirited appraisal of the landscape recalls the worthy rather than ecstatic determination on Wordsworth's part to make the best of Nature's 'habitual sway', that is, of the temporal world, rather than to mourn the 'delight' of immortality. The final stanza of his *Ode* begins:

> And O, ye Fountains, Meadows, Hills and Groves ...
> Forbid not any severing of our loves!
> Yet in my heart of hearts I feel your might;
> I only have relinquished one delight
> To live beneath your more habitual sway.[36]

That living under the 'more habitual sway' is not Olive's choice is indicated by the explicitly Christianized passage which immediately follows the description of the fells:

> Ah! if it had only been given to her to walk in those green pastures and 'beside the still waters of the Paradise of God;' if that day which shall be known to the Lord 'had come to her when "at eventide it shall be light;"'– eventide! – alas! for her there must still remain the burden and heat of the day – sultry youth, weariness of premature age, 'light that shall be neither clear nor dark,' before that blessed eventide should come, 'and she should pass through the silence and into the rest beyond.'[37]

However, this overtly Christian conclusion to the episode does not satisfactorily contain Olive's communicable experience of dying. Olive

---

35 Poems purported to be by Olive are to be found on pp. 178–9. These were actually written by Carey's long-time friend and house-mate, Helen Marion Burnside. The novel is set primarily in Kirkby Stephen, a village Carey knew well. Her brother-in-law, Canon Simpson, was the clergyman there for a number of years.

36 *Intimations of Immortality*, stanza 11 (ll. 191–5). In chapter 5. of the same novel, Olive's sister, who also misses her dead mother, has a fit of crying and finally falls into a healthy sleep; 'that kindly foster-nurse Nature often taking restorative remedies of forcible narcotics into her own hands'. Cf. Wordsworth's *Ode*, stanza 6: 'The homely nurse doth all she can / To make her Foster-child, her Inmate man, / Forget the glories he hath known …'

37 *HC*, pp. 193–4. See also Psalms 23:2, Zechariah 14:7, Matthew 20:12.

remains a female Wordsworth who both has and shares intimations of immortality.

It is unlikely that Carey deliberately introduced these allusions into her writing in order to provide a non-Christian element; and, indeed, had she been deemed heretical by either her readers or her reviewers, comment would certainly have been made. For *Heriot's Choice* was initially serialized in the *Monthly Packet*, a publication with an extremely High Church bias, which had as its editor the pro-Oxford Movement novelist, Charlotte Yonge.[38] Nor can it be said that Carey was unique in alluding to Wordsworth's early poetry in conventional religious contexts. The Rev. H.C. Lees is once again a good case in point. The latter describes Jesus as having come from Heaven to earth,

> 'not in utter nakedness' even along the valley-road of incarnation, but 'trailing clouds of glory' from God Who is His Home.[39]

The more likely explanation is that such writers permitted themselves a great deal of literary licence. They made their allusions safely, if not unthinkingly. When Wordsworth wrote his *Ode*, he was still far from being religious in the conventional sense but, by the time of his death in 1850, he was the poet of the Establishment; a friend to both the Church of England and the Oxford Movement.[40] Seamus Heaney goes so far as to suggest that, 'As the years

---

38 *Heriot's Choice* was serialized in *The Monthly Packet* between July 1877 and October 1879.

39 Lees 1915, p. 2. Wordsworth writes:

> Our birth is but a sleep and a forgetting:
> The Soul that rises in us, our life's Star
> Hath had elsewhere its setting,
> And cometh from afar:
> Not in entire forgetfulness,
> And not in utter nakedness,
> But trailing clouds of glory do we come
> From God, who is our home …

See *Ode*, stanza 5. Notably Lees does not claim that ordinary human souls arrive on earth in the same way. See also Lees 1915, p. 98: 'the child is the father of the man' (*Works*, p. 79).

40 William Blake described Wordsworth as a 'Heathen Philosopher' (see *Critics on Wordsworth*, ed. Raymond Cowell [London: George Allen and Unwin, 1973], p. 14). However, school-books make no note of this. J. Logie Robertson, *A History Of English Literature*, 3rd edn, revised (Edinburgh: William Blackwood and Sons, 1900), notes of Wordsworth that, 'Nature to him was a living thing, the expression of a universal spirit, which communicated its own thoughts in direct impulses to man through the medium of hills and valleys, starry skies and flowing streams [etc.]' (p. 257). J.M.D. Meiklejohn, *The English Language: Its Grammar, History and Literature*, 28th edn enlarged (London: Meiklejohn and Holden, 1907) speaks merely of Wordsworth's unaffected style and suggests that '[h]e drew aside poetry from questions and interest of mere society and the town to the scenes of Nature and the deepest feelings of man as man.' (p. 416). Whilst in each case the word 'Nature' is capitalised, the concept does not appear to be treated in any religious sense.

proceeded, Wordsworth became more an institution than an individual.'[41] He was also Poet Laureate, an honour later denied to the more obviously heretical Swinburne. These credentials would probably have been sufficient for Carey and, indeed, for Lees; they would have needed to look no further.

'Their graves are green, they may be seen'

Whatever the theological differences between Carey's religious beliefs and the original conception of Wordsworth's *Ode*, the two writers certainly shared an interest in the physical presence of graves. In particular, parallels may be drawn between Carey's characters who visit the graves of their loved ones and the little girl in Wordsworth's popular poem, *We Are Seven* [published 1800]. In *We Are Seven*, Wordsworth has his little cottage girl insist that her dead brother and sister are still part of her life whilst the narrator vainly tries to convince her otherwise. The narrator suggests that 'If two are in the church-yard laid,/Then ye are only five', but the little girl lists her evidence to the contrary:

> 'Their graves are green, they may be seen,'
> The little maid replied.
> 'Twelve steps or more from my mother's door,
> And they are side by side
>
> 'My stockings there I often knit,
> My kerchief there I hem;
> And there upon the ground I sit,
> And sing a song to them.
>
> 'And often after sun-set, Sir,
> When it is light and fair,
> I take my little porringer,
> And eat my supper there.
> (*Works*, pp. 83–4)

Given the variety of tasks performed at the graveside, the little cottage girl effectively still lives with her siblings. She sings to them, eats with them and performs her domestic duties by their side. She even lives with them in a literal sense: her home is 'the church-yard cottage' (l. 23). As Alan Gardiner succinctly explains:

> The adult is capable of mathematical calculation but lacks the child's intuitive awareness of eternal nature. Interestingly, it is the narrator who

41 *The Essential Wordsworth*, selected and with an Introduction by Seamus Heaney (New York: Ecco Press, 1988), p. 7.

> holds the conventional religious notion of life after death, telling the child that her brother and sister are 'in Heaven' (l. 62). But to the child Heaven is an irrelevance; the living and the dead are inseparable. She has not lost her brother and sister but continues to enjoy with them a shared existence.[42]

Carey once again appears to have found a visual image satisfying without considering the theological implications. As a Christian, she certainly would not have considered Heaven to be 'an irrelevance'. However, as has also been demonstrated, she did not consider that family members were lost in death. Thus, in *Heriot's Choice*, the visionary Olive describes her weekly visits to her mother's grave in terms very little different to those used in *We Are Seven*:

> 'I can come and pour out all my trouble to her, just as I used to ...[S]ometimes I fancy she answers me, not in speaking, you know, but in the thoughts that come as I sit here … Others may laugh at it ... but it is impossible to believe mamma can help loving us where she is; and she always liked us to come and tell her everything … '[43]

Nor is this the only instance where Carey emphasizes the visiting of a loved one rather than simply the visiting of a grave. In *Basil Lyndhurst,* the first-person narrator describes in detail how she takes her brother's children to where their mother is buried:

> It seemed a sort of weekly treat to the children; even Willie would plead to go. 'It is my turn to go to mother!' he would say. 'And mine, too,' Girlie would chime in; 'I'm mother's dirl, too!'. It was wonderful how much we found to do, how busy the children would be. Sometimes they brought their little watering pots, or planned what flowers they would plant for the summer; they would hush their little voices as they talked, as though they feared to wake that tender mother.[44]

Whatever the theological implications, this particular picture of children working and playing around the grave of their mother is a soothing and

---

42 Alan Gardiner, *The Poetry of William Wordsworth* (London: Penguin, 1990), p. 40.

43 *HC*, p. 70. Cf. also Felicia Hemans, *The Message to the Dead*, ll. 41–4:

And tell our gentle mother,
That on her grave I pour
The sorrows of my spirit forth,
As on her breast of yore.

See *The Poetical Works of Felicia Dorothea Hemans* (London: Humphrey Milford, Oxford University Press, 1914), p. 305.

44 *BL*, p. 467. A less concrete echo of Wordsworth's poem is found in R.N. Carey, *A Passage Perilous* (London: Macmillan, 1906 [1903]), p. 136. The vicar's wife tells her new neighbour, 'We have lost three children, Mrs John, – two baby boys and May; but we always speak of our six children.'

attractive one. A possible explanation as to why Carey portrays death in this way is to be found in another of her novels, *At the Moorings*. Here, two characters, Sheila (Miss Lassiter) and Betty examine the 'truth' value of euphemistic statements about death:

> 'So many of us have died, our "green gardens" fill fast' ...
>
> 'I like that idea "green gardens",' observed Miss Lassiter thoughtfully; 'it seems to veil so prettily the bald grim fact of death. I have had more than one argument with my brother on that very subject ... he once said that you might as well ... plant flowers on a rock as to disguise that one stupendous reality "by mere meretricious word-embroidery".'
>
> 'Your brother must be a pessimist,' [Betty] said ...
>
> 'Perhaps you are right; but his pessimism harms no-one but himself. And after all ... men look at things from such a different standpoint. "Word-embroidery", as he calls it, is dear to the feminine mind.'
>
> 'Yes, I suppose so; but all the same I like things to be true ... I never had time for pretty conceits that had no real meaning. It was [my sister] Martha who used to talk about the "green gardens" when we were children; and when Rosie and Drummond and Willie died, we used to go every week to plant flowers and tidy our gardens. When I was a tiny mite, I used to say that they were buried flowers, which would sprout into angels one day, and I really believed it.'
>
> A sweet expression crossed Miss Lassiter's face, but she kept her thoughts to herself ...[45]

Here, Carey suggests that it is legitimate to use 'word-embroidery', so long as it has a basis in truth. Moreover, such 'word-embroidery' tastefully veils that which would otherwise be devastating to live with. Miss Lassiter's 'sweet expression' indicates to the reader that 'green gardens' and 'buried flowers ... sprout[ing] into angels' are as near to the 'true' as is the 'the bald grim fact of death' itself. Where both versions represent the truth, Carey chooses the more positive of the two. Here is another kind of sentimental heresy in which those

---

45 *ATM*, pp 6–7. (See *The Old, Old Story*, p. 423 for another reference to a 'green garden'.) Similarly, in *Heriot's choice*, Ethel imagines that her little sister who has died is growing up in Heaven, taught by angels (see p. 131). On this occasion, Carey quotes some apt lines from Longfellow's poem, *Resignation*:

> Not as a child shall we again behold her;
> For when with raptures wild
> In our embraces we again enfold her,
> She will not be a child;
>
> But a fair maiden, in her Father's mansion ...

For the full text, see *The Poetical Works of Longfellow* (London: Ward Locke, 1882), pp. 149–50. This particular sentimental belief actually has some biblical basis. See 1 Corinthians 13:11–12, in which there is an analogy between a child growing to adulthood on earth and the partial earthly knowledge to be exchanged for perfect knowledge at some stage after death.

who are bereaved never lose the person who has died. Something tangible as well as something immortal remains. This borders on the heretical because, within the Christian tradition, the soul should be regarded as in Heaven and hence far away, whilst the body should be seen as a mere shell. Yet, because Carey provides an obviously orthodox religious basis to her novels, this heresy, like any others she uses to provide comfort for her readers, is rendered invisible.

Carey also appears to have shared Wordsworth's belief in the greater social utility of graves. According to the latter, a gravestone is erected 'for a satisfaction to the sorrowing hearts of the survivors' but, even if it only bears the deceased person's name and dates of birth and death, it also contributes to the preservation of the extended family and to the stability of the community (*Selected Prose*, p. 327). In the third of his *Essays on Epitaphs*, Wordsworth argues that:

> As ... the name is mostly associated with others of the same family, this is a prolonged companionship, however shadowy; even a tomb like this is a shrine to which the fancies of a scattered family may repair in pilgrimage; the thoughts of the individuals, without any communication with each other, must oftentimes meet here. – Such a frail memorial then is not without its tendency to keep families together; it feeds also local attachment, which is the tap-root of the tree of Patriotism. (*Selected Prose*, pp. 370–71)

Given Carey's preoccupation with the home and the family, it is easy to see why the image of 'a frail memorial ... not without its tendency to keep families together' might have appealed. However, Wordsworth's notion of 'local attachment' may also have interested her. Wordsworth explores the sense of belonging which graves can inspire in a little more detail in the first of the *Essays Upon Epitaphs*. In this essay, his generic description of worship in a country parish church has a comforting, domestic quality about it which makes the regular juxtaposition of the quick and the dead appear truly desirable. To Wordsworth, the people buried in the country churchyard are yet a part of the society; they provide the living with a sense of history, a sense of community and a lesson about the future:

> The sensations of pious cheerfulness, which attend the celebration of the sabbath-day in rural places, are profitably chastised by the sight of the graves of kindred and friends, gathered together in that general home towards which the thoughtful yet happy spectators themselves are journeying. Hence a parish-church, in the stillness of the country, is a visible centre of community of the living and the dead; a point to which are habitually referred the nearest concerns of both. (*Selected Prose*, p. 330)

It is possible that Carey looked to this concrete view of the graveyard as representing past, present and future when she wrote the description of the ruined Croft Church in her novel *No Friend Like a Sister* [1906]:

> Centuries ago, the Croft Church had been the parish church, until Cromwell's Roundheads had destroyed it. Later on, a little graveyard had been made in the ruins. One arch and the font were still in good preservation, but so many bricks had been removed that only the foundation of the walls remained. The graves were few and quite uncared for but ... Elinor had been surprised to hear that now and then there were baptisms in the old ruins, and that not many years before the marriage service had been read over an elderly pair … Neither of them had been any further than [the two nearest villages], and Dan Winter had stoutly refused to be wedded 'unless th'ould parson would tie him and Liza up in the Croft Church.'[46]

The passage contains everything that one would expect from someone who was influenced by Wordsworth: centuries of unwritten rural history; contented (or at least placid) rural people; graves from the past but pointing the living towards the 'general home'; and baptisms representing the temporal future.

Yet whilst the churchyard seen in this light is an object lesson for the community at large, Carey utilizes its concrete presence to make statements about the home and the private sphere. If one of her fictional homes overlooks a churchyard and the inhabitants are comfortable with its proximity, then this is a sign that such characters have narratorial and, implicitly, authorial approval. On many occasions, a family is to be found living next to the churchyard simply because the home is a vicarage. This is the case in novels such as *Heriot's Choice*, *Robert Ord's Atonement* [1873] and *Mary St John* [1882]. However, in other cases the location appears to be less accidental. In *The Household of Peter* [1905], the eponymous hero and his sisters live close to the churchyard in which departed members of their own family are buried:

> The Red House was nearly opposite St Andrew's [church]. Across the wide boulevard was ... a row of low white cottages abutting on the church-yard. The outlook was singularly quiet and peaceful, and hallowed by the thought of dear ones laid to rest in the shady corner behind St Andrew's.[47]

The 'peaceful' and 'hallowed' outlook of The Red House indicates a restful and religiously-motivated home and is suggestive of the 'local attachment' favoured by Wordsworth. Yet, in *Queenie's Whim* [1881], as much may be

46 R.N. Carey, *No Friend Like A Sister* (London: Macmillan, 1906), p. 157 (hereafter, *NFLAS*).

47 R.N. Carey, *The Household of Peter* (London: Macmillan, n.d. [1905]), p. 7.

deduced about the inhabitants of Church-Stile House even though the adjoining churchyard contains no family graves. Discussion of the churchyard highlights the differences in character between the various members of the Clayton family but, simultaneously, it emphasizes their attachment both to each other and to the family home. Significantly, the only truly dissenting voice, the eponymous Queenie, is, at this point, an outsider:

> Within a few feet were tall palings, and a granite obelisk; then some sparsely scattered tombstones ...
>
> 'I am afraid it strikes you as very dismal,' said Langley softly, as they stood together at the windows ...'
>
> 'I suppose one would get used to it in time,' replied Queenie, somewhat evasively. Her healthy young vitality shivered a little at the incongruity between the warm cosiness of the life inside and the gleaming tombstones without, within a few feet of the fireside round which the family circle gathered.
>
> 'But you think we ought always to be reading Hervey's *Meditations* and considering our latter end,' broke in Cathy gaily. 'Nothing of the kind, I assure you; Garth grumbles and declares that he will build a new house for himself higher up the hill, and Ted agrees with him; but I don't mind it in the least, and Langley likes it.'
>
> 'Do you?' asked Queenie ... curiously.
>
> 'I love it,' was the quiet answer.[48]

In this extract, only the outsider is depressed by the churchyard. All the permanent occupants of the home simply respond, in good-humoured fashion, according to their roles within the household. Garth and Ted, the men of the house, merely take advantage of the Englishman's supposed right to grumble, though they have no real objection. Cathy, the flippant child, delights in shocking her audience but it is evident that she loves her home. However, Langley, as a successful home-maker, who takes seriously her role as creator and sustainer of the household ethos, is completely open about her ability to see something positive in the presence of graves. Her 'quiet answer', based upon the confidence that comes from a proper understanding of graves, indicates that she will produce a tranquil, religiously-motivated and securely-rooted home environment for everyone else. The other members of the household can afford to grumble or be flippant: none of them seriously object to the graveyard and what it stands for, and they have the home-maker, Langley, there to transmute death into religion on their behalf.[49]

---

48 R.N. Carey, *Queenie's Whim* (London: Macmillan, 1898 [1881]), p. 94 (hereafter, *QW*).

49 Cf. also Martha in *At The Moorings* who transmutes graves into 'green gardens' (already quoted).

Queenie, the outsider, provides the only negative response: she mentally shivers. This is perhaps because, at this stage, she has no home of her own, no graves of her own, no 'local attachment' and no one to provide her with a more positive view of death. Similarly, in *No Friend Like A Sister*, the loving sisters-in-law who live near the ruined Croft Church enjoy walking around the graveyard but their less happily-circumstanced friend Agnes finds the view depressing (p. 165).

Thus Carey and Wordsworth share two concepts relating to the physical presence of graves. The resting places of the dead provide a meeting place (whether psychological or physical) for the family who has lost a much loved member, and they express the history and stability of the community. However, Carey has one further use for them as a device in her fiction. She uses the graveyard as an indicator of positive home ethos. Where close physical proximity with the dead is positively rated, this indicates that members of the family are at peace with themselves and with each other.

Conclusion

As an author who emphasized affectional familial relationships, Carey evidently found it necessary to euphemize the constant presence of death. For, although the united family was the ideal, she was compelled to acknowledge that all families had to cope with the partings wrought by death. This recourse to euphemism resulted in what she called 'word embroidery' and what has, in this chapter, been called sentimental heresy. Such conceits suggest an awareness on her part that even the most devout and resigned survivor needs more support and encouragement than that supplied by the unmediated pages of the Bible. Thus, although the ostensible religious content of Carey's writing is biblical in emphasis, her approach is far from being fundamentalist.

However, Carey's recourse to sentimental heresy seems to indicate more than a desire to comfort the bereaved who might find the religion of the Book insufficient in itself. The presence of such non-canonical matter additionally suggests that she was perturbed by the inability of many official mediators of the Book, that is, the clergy of the established church, to meet the spiritual needs of their parishioners. Credence is given to this interpretation by the presence in the novels of a number of ingenuous and obviously untaught characters who are in need of religious instruction. Characters displaying wildly unorthodox religious beliefs or expressing personal discomfort about biblical teachings tend to be children or uneducated country people. However, they may be seen as the outspoken – because uninhibited – portion of the community: those who are permitted to speak out whilst others, equally unlearned in religious terms, feel obliged to remain silent. Both implicitly and explicitly, they represent the failure of their clergymen to make the tenets of their religion either comprehensible or relevant.

A number of the episodes in which these characters appear are amusing, though not without poignancy. The 'Sister' referred to in this passage from *Wee Wifie* [1869] is a sister of charity:

> little Tim, dying of his broken bones, whispered as 'Our Sister' kissed him, 'I am wishing you could die first, Sister, and then it would be first-rate, seeing you along with the gentry at the Gate;' for, to Tim's ignorant mind, the gentry of heaven were somewhat formidable. 'And what am I to say to them, plase your honour? when they come up and says "Good morning, Tim;" but if sister were along of them she would say, "It is only Tim, and he never learnt manners nohow."'[50]

Clearly, this fictional child does not lack belief in heaven. Yet he seems to have a totally unbiblical belief that there are certain social qualifications for being accepted there.[51] However, speeches by uneducated adults even more clearly imply a deflected or diffused criticism of an establishment which is failing them; an establishment that countenances clergymen who cannot relate to their congregations or provide any kind of personal example. Gale Warburton in *No Friend Like A Sister* is particularly subject to this kind of comment:

> Sunday after Sunday the little flock gathered in Tylcote Church, listened with cold respect and reverence to their vicar's carefully delivered discourse, and, after browsing on the scanty pasturage provided for their nourishment, went home with perhaps the text still lingering in their memory.
>
> 'That was a grand text the vicar gave out this morning,' observed Caleb Strong, the little deformed bootmaker; 'I can't call to mind that I ever heard these words before – "Curse ye Meroz, said the angel of the Lord, curse ye bitterly the inhabitants thereof; because they came not to the help of the Lord, to the help of the Lord against the mighty." My word, Liz, how he rolled out the words – it was like the swell of the organ or a poem; but the queer part is, I haven't a notion what he meant by it ... Caleb ... spen[t] his Sunday evening hunting vainly through his mother's old brown Bible for the text that had so fired his imagination ... (*NFLAS*, pp. 174–5)

Thus, for all his erudition, the vicar leaves even the most earnest seeker of spiritual enlightenment to flounder helplessly. Moreover:

---

50 R.N. Carey, *Wee Wifie* (London: Macmillan, 1894 [1869]), p. 419.

51 In the New Testament, wealth is actually viewed as an impediment to attaining heaven. See Matthew 19:16–21. Jesus Himself was a 'friend of publicans and sinners', see Matthew 11:19. Thus, lack of status in the community was no barrier to Heaven either.

> Rev. Gale Warburton never visited his people; he had so little to say to them that it was embarrassing on both sides; he was not sufficiently in touch with them to make such visits either pleasant or profitable. He could decipher hieroglyphics and even converse in Hindustani, but the hearts of his parishioners were a sealed book to him. When they ... asked for help, he was never known to refuse it; and when they sent for him, he would ... go to the sick and dying; but it may be doubted whether those few beautifully read prayers yielded much comfort.
>
> 'The vicar's a gradley sort of chap, but he don't have much to say to a mon,' observed old Richard Fawcett ... he was speaking to his best friend Anna Keith, who was ministering to him, as she ministered to all the ailing bodies and minds in the neighbourhood of Crow Farm. 'He is turribly fine and learned, nae doubt, but the words seem more stone than grit, and fairly chokes me.' (*NFLAS*, pp. 175–6)

However, Carey's fictional clergy are criticized for a number of reasons.[52] For example, one vicar in *Mary St John* has such a soporific effect on his Sunday-school scholars that:

> During the sermon most of the younger children fell asleep and dropped off their forms; some were picked up and shaken by the pale-faced teacher; others were propping their heavy heads against Mary. The vicar went droning on, excellent man, with his secondly and thirdly, and his slow summing-up of practical points.[53]

Though preaching a 'practical' sermon, he cannot make it lively enough to be memorable.

As if for contrast, a successful clergyman is often to be found paired with an unsuccessful one. Thus, the aristocratic and erudite Gale Warburton may be compared with a visiting preacher, Forbes Rutherford, at whose sermon 'every soul seemed stirred to new emotion' (*NFLAS*, p. 350). However, many much shorter sketches are to be found in the novels, in which the measuring of one man against another is made more explicit. In *The Old, Old Story*, the contrast is made between a vicar, Rev. Carrick, and his curate, Ewen Logan:

---

52 Cool, lifeless or overly erudite sermons: Mr Clive in R.N. Carey, *Nellie's Memories* (London: Richard Bentley and Son, 1892 [1868]), pp. 101–2; Mr Heath in *Heriot's Choice*, p. 67; Mr Charrington in R.N. Carey, *Herb of Grace* (London: Macmillan, 1903 [1901]), p. 169; Archie Drummond in R.N. Carey, *Not Like Other Girls* (London: Macmillan, 1905 [1884]) p. 160. Ascetic clergymen who are critical towards their parishioners: Horace Glyn in R.N. Carey, *Sir Godfrey's Granddaughters* (London: Macmillan, 1899 [1892]), p. 138; Ewen Logan in *The Old, Old Story*, p. 31.

53 R.N. Carey, *Mary St John* (London: Macmillan, 1909 [1882]), pp. 261–2 (hereafter *Mary St John*).

> it must be owned that a little more of that charity that thinketh no evil would have added to Mr Logan's popularity and usefulness in his dealings with his flock.
>
> 'I don't hold with snipping talk myself,' observed one godly old woman; 'it converts no-one, and only makes ill-feelings. There's Nannie Stubbs gone clean against Mr Logan, in spite of his powerful sermons, and all because he tackled her too sharply about pleasuring on a Sunday evening. The vicar – God bless him! – would just have said, "Nannie, I have missed you the last Sunday or two; how's that, my woman?" in a friendly sort of way that would have given no offence.'[54]

The ardent Mr Logan speaks with painful accuracy of 'sabbath-breaking' but the pleasing and conciliatory fiction that her clergyman had missed her would have been more effective.

In addition, in cases where clergymen have zeal without warmth, erudition without enthusiasm or a basic lack of sympathy with their parishioners, Carey generally puts such conciliation as is possible into the hands of the laity rather than into the hands of other clergy. These characters are usually women of only moderate learning or average intellectual powers, 'word-embroider[ers]' rather than academics, who win others over to faith as much by love as by reason. Thus, in *No Friend Like a Sister*, the puzzling text from the Bible is found and explained to Caleb Strong by Rev. Warburton's much-slighted sister, Agnes; prayers and spiritual comfort for the dying Richard Fawcett are supplied by the lower-class Mrs Keith. Similarly, in *The Old, Old Story*, Mr Logan's mother dispenses 'goodies' to the elderly women of her son's new parish whereas he dispenses little but wholesome admonitions (*The Old, Old Story*, p. 436).

However, notwithstanding the implied criticism of the formal earthly medium, it is clear that Carey yet believed in the message. There seems to be no reason to doubt either her adherence to the Church of England or her sincerity or orthodoxy as a Christian. She herself taught a Sunday-school class for many years. It would appear that she merely attempted to bring the ideals of the church to the hearth and the bond of affection associated with the family to the service of the church by whatever means were at her disposal. Thus, in spite of her sentimental heresies, the establishment religion was never seriously undermined. Rather, compensatory strategies of an unorthodox kind were brought to the aid of orthodoxy.

---

54 *The Old, Old Story*, p. 31. A similar contrast is provided by the vicar and the curate in *Mary St. John*. On p. 261 the vicar sends the children to sleep during the sermon; on p. 266 the curate asks his wife, 'am I not bound to my people by a tie as holy and as binding as my marriage vows?' Cf. also *Heriot's Choice*, pp. 67 and 72.

Conclusion

It is pertinent to conclude this study of Rosa Carey's fictional responses to the themes of insanity, 'spare' women, male dominance, the home and religion with some reference to how her work was regarded during her life-time. After all, she was writing for her contemporaries rather than for unknown posterity, even though value and meaning may still be attached to her writing today. However, in looking at Carey's work from any perspective, a major problem to be overcome is that of the paucity of secondary sources. Carey gave few formal interviews to the journalists of her day and there is very little dedicated criticism, past or present.[1] Thus, it is necessary to turn to the reviews of her work that appeared in journals and newspapers during her lifetime.[2] Of course reviews, like any other texts, are subject to both personal idiosyncrasy and vested interest. Nevertheless, as readers themselves, reviewers at least manage to highlight some of the issues that interested the reading public of the late-nineteenth and early twentieth centuries.

---

1 Most useful critical work to date is Jane Crisp, *Rosa Nouchette Carey*, Victorian Fiction Research Guides 16 (Queensland: Victorian Fiction Research Unit, 1989). It also lists a number of interviews with Carey. Articles about Carey not included by Crisp are one by Helen Black in the *Girl's Own Paper*, 16 September 1897, pp. 801–2 and one by Helen Marion Burnside in the *Girl's Realm Annual* for 1902, pp. 313–17. However, each of these contains wording identical to Helen Black, *Notable Women Authors of the Day* (London: Maclaren, 1893 [1906]), pp. 145–56. As the 1893 material used in the articles of 1902 and 1906 is only partially revised and updated, the chronologies of these later articles (and that of Black 1906) may not be accurate.

2 As Carey's reviews cannot provide a full picture if taken in isolation, they are placed within a broader context of novel-reviewing activity. Thus, reviews studied, where not directly quoted and thus individually sourced, are from the following American and English journals and dated between 1868 and 1909.

Academy	*Liverpool Daily Post*
Athenaeum	*Manchester Guardian*
Bookman	*Nation*
Graphic	*Pall Mall Gazette*
Leeds Mercury	*San Francisco Chronicle*
Literary World	*Spectator*
Literature	*Woman's Signal*

All reviews of novels appearing on the same page as a Carey review were scrutinized in order to gain an overall impression of reviewing criteria. The majority of these reviews for Carey's novels are listed individually in Jane Crisp's monograph. (See note 1.)

The reviews of Carey's novels and those of her peers contain little by way of consensus as to what is desirable in the novel genre. Thus, in the early 1880s, one reviewer complains that a novel by Carey is marred by an 'undue obtrusion of the religious element' whilst another tartly remarks that a Mrs Lovett Cameron possesses 'descriptive power ... higher than her moral teaching'.[3] Similarly, in the early years of this century, one reviewer deems Carey's novel of the moment to be 'old-fashioned' because 'no attempt at epigrammatic dialogue is made' whilst another takes exception to Ellen Thorneycroft Fowler's work because her characters' 'continued crackling of epigram' is 'almost overpowering'.[4] And, of course, reviewers have differing ideas about the same book. Thus, Capel Frere, a character in Carey's novel *For Lilias* (1885), is both a 'finished male portrait' and 'more than a bit of a bore'.[5] Yet, even allowing for the lack of consensus, it is possible to identify three broad areas relating to the novel to which the reviewers addressed themselves throughout the period: analysis of technique; discussion of moral content; and classification according to genre and supposed readership.

Analysis of technique often amounts to discussion of characterization and dialogue with regard to their credibility as representations of the real world. Carey comes in for a good deal of adverse comment under this heading. In 1897 a reviewer for the *Literary World* suggests that her stories are 'so pure and high in their moral tone that we must not condemn then for their lack of reality', whilst in 1902 a reviewer for the *Athenaeum* comments that 'Miss Carey's puppets and their manner of play are known and admired by many'.[6] Even perfect verisimilitude is cause for complaint on one occasion. When *Rue With A Difference* is reviewed by the *Academy* in 1900, an innocuous piece of dialogue brings forth a tirade of indignation out of all proportion to the supposed offence:

> the point is, not that the hostess should have so spoken, but that Miss Carey should have set the words down. The book is full of nothings – mild, inoffensive, and inexpressibly tedious. It is so negligible that in the very act of perusal you scarcely know whether you are reading it or not.[7]

Yet other reviewers acknowledge the appeal of a novel containing more truth than excitement, one writing of *At The Moorings* (1905) that

3 Review of *Mary St John* in *Academy*, 9 December 1882, p. 411; review of *In a Grass Country* in *Athenaeum*, 26 September 1885, p. 398.

4 Review of *At The Moorings* in *Athenaeum*, 24 December 1904, p. 869; review of *Fuel of Fire* in *Athenaeum*, 11 October 1902, p. 482.

5 *Athenaeum*, 26 September 1885, p. 398; *Academy*, 26 September 1885, p. 200.

6 Review of *Dr Luttrell's First Patient* in *Literary World*, 6 November 1897, p. 279; review of *Herb of Grace* in *Athenaeum*, 11 January 1902, p. 45.

7 *Academy*, 'Fiction Supplement', 3 November 1900, p. 413.

> its happenings are always within the limits of probability, and its men and women are delineated faithfully, sympathetically, and with knowledge of the gentler sides of humanity. The story is very skilfully handled ...[8]

However, to twentieth century eyes at least, the reviewers' major obsession throughout the period seems to have been not with realism or its alternatives, but with matters of novel length and the constraints occasioned by the standard three-volume format. Dissatisfaction with the format is evinced as early as 1869, a dispirited reviewer for the *Athenaeum* telling readers that '[i]f three-volume novels are a necessity of life, we should try to make the best of them'.[9] However, by 1880 the murmurs are considerably louder. In the *Graphic* for 14 February a reviewer announces that 'the days of three-volume novels are over, and a little judicious "boiling down" will, as a rule, make most books more attractive'.[10] Carey's novels escape criticism in this particular set of reviews but the length of her novels is commented upon frequently throughout her career. There are complaints that *Robert Ord's Atonement* (1873) is of 'unwieldy length' and (with more than a touch of exaggeration), that *The Mistress of Brae Farm* (1896) 'would make about six of the ordinary volumes that we used to have in the novel of the past'.[11]

Three specific length-related criticisms are levelled at the three-volume novel. The first is that it tends to have a weak plot but strong individual episodes. As a result the shape of the narrative is obscured or plot development is hindered. Thus, Carey's *Barbara Heathcote's Trial* (1871) is deemed to be marred by 'a want of concentration in the story' and Mrs Humphrey Ward's *Robert Elsmere* (1888) to suffer from 'diffuseness'.[12] A second criticism is that some authors 'pad out' their novels with material not essential to the plot in order to reach the length required by publishing contracts; and a third is that such long novels can be unnecessarily complicated by the introduction of too many events or characters.[13] Carey is never accused of padding her novels with non-essential material but she is certainly accused of other kinds of excess. The most amusing version of this latter complaint is to be found in a review of *Mary St John* (1882):

> [There is] altogether too much in her three volumes. The critic feels inclined to say to her what he says to his hair-cutter, 'If you please, I

8 *Bookman*, April 1905, p. 31.

9 Review of Mrs A.D.T. Whitney, *Hitherto: a Story of Yesterdays* in *Athenaeum*, 11 December 1869, p. 776.

10 Review of *Mrs Lancaster's Rival* (anon.) in *Graphic*, 11 February 1880, p. 182.

11 *Athenaeum*, 17 May 1873, p. 627; Supplement to *Spectator*, 26 June 1897, p. 896.

12 *Graphic*, 11 November 1871, p. 463; *Academy*, 17 March 1888, p. 184.

13 Padding: see review of *Mrs Lancaster's Rival* in *Graphic*, 14 February 1880. Over-complication: see review of Miss Beale, *Idonea* in *Academy*, 12 March 1881, p. 186

> want it thinned.' There is too much talking, too many insignificant events, too long 'waits' between the acts of the drama.[14]

Evidently, Carey wrote ideal novels from a publisher's point of view but the form in which she excelled was far from popular with some critics. In making judgements about novel length and structure, reviewers seem to be moving towards a kind of literary formalism based upon the male-orientated classical education that was *de rigueur* throughout the period. Such judgements appear to be informed by scholarly notions of satire, tragedy and epic, and by an appreciation of epigram, perhaps acquired from the non-fictional realm of *belles-lettres*.

Aristotle's *Poetics* seems to be in particular requisition. The charge that Carey's *Lover or Friend?* (1890) is 'over long for the solution of its plot' appears to be closely allied to Aristotle's dictum on 'limit of magnitude'.[15] Similarly, the description of a novel called *A Family Likeness*, as 'a really workmanlike performance, with a beginning, a middle, and an end, all in their places and in due proportion', is straight from the *Poetics*.[16] Yet Aristotle's notion that tragedy is the highest form of art comes across more strongly than any dictum regarding structure. The reviewer who writes that one of Carey's novels contains 'plenty of conversation ... but not many incidents or striking reflections' is bound to be dissatisfied if the Aristotelian standard requires that the text take for its guiding principles the 'imitation of a noble and complete action', and the notion that 'the most important ... [part] is the arrangement of the incidents'.[17]

Given the 'domestic' content of most of Carey's novels, one would not expect recurrent discussions of classical themes to appear in reviews of her work at all. Indeed, of all the reviews in the sample, in only one instance is she charged with writing 'a rather melodramatic episode' in a manner that is both 'tedious' and 'a little tragi-comic'; and in only one case does a reviewer note with favour that 'the second and third volumes of a novel 'are not without their element of tragedy'.[18] However, this is not surprising: in Aristotelian terms, the

14 *Academy*, 9 December 1882, p. 411.

15 *Athenaeum*, 27 September 1890, p. 414. '[W]hatever length is required for a change to occur from bad fortune to good or from good fortune to bad ... is sufficient limit of magnitude' (*Poetics* 7, Golden 1974, p. 116). All quotations from Aristotle, the *Poetics*, are taken from *Classical Literary Criticism: Translations and Interpretations*, edited with commentaries by Alex Preminger, Leon Golden et al. (New York: Frederick Ungar, 1974), pp. 108–39. This translation of the *Poetics* was actually made by Golden so the text is hereafter referred to as Golden 1974.

16 *Academy*, 24 December 1892, p. 586; *Poetics* 7 (Golden 1974, pp. 115–16).

17 Review of *Uncle Max* in *Athenaeum*, 5 February 1887, p. 189; *Poetics* 6 (Golden 1974, p. 114).

18 Review of *Not Like Other Girls* in *Academy*, 22 March 1884, p. 199; review of *Lover or Friend?* in *Academy*, 11 October 1890, p. 315.

place allocated to 'domestic' fiction such as that written by Carey – and one it fills quite well on account of its dissimilarity to classical tragedy – is that of classical comedy. The domestic novel details 'probable incidents' and happy endings rather than 'human action and life' typically 'end[ing] in misfortune'; it utilizes 'mean' or conversational language rather than 'language that has been artistically enhanced'; and its major characters are 'baser men' rather than great ones, if, indeed, they are men at all.[19] The classically-minded reviewer appears to depreciate the genre accordingly.

When reviewers discuss the moral content of novels, a key term in the general debate is that of Sensation. The *Shorter Oxford English Dictionary* succinctly defines Sensation as 'the production of violent emotion as an aim in works of literature or art'.[20] However, a more graphic description of the term, and one related specifically to the genre of the Sensation novel, is provided by a reviewer for the *Athenaeum* in 1868:

> it tells a story which from beginning to end abounds in incidents and coincidences inconceivable to ninety-nine out of every hundred of its readers, and to the solitary unhappy odd one only barely conceivable with wonderment ... fond lovers who suddenly discover themselves to be nearly related to one another, and gallant officers who find themselves in a ball-room *vis a vis* to a forgotten victim to culpable gallantry ten years back, are not pictures that appeal to anything but imagination ...[21]

Carey was seldom accused of writing novels of this kind; rather, her work was described by the reviewers as being in antithesis to it. The following critique of her novel *Other People's Lives* (1897) could have come from any review of her work – positive or negative – over the entirety of her writing career:

> When one is exhausted with hairbreadth escapes, or irritated by literary brilliance, or unnerved by the poser of social questions, one may safely turn to Miss Carey, for her books will help one to forget these things. Yet she can tell a story well and in good English, and her characters are singularly like the people we meet at a garden party.[22]

---

19 The *Poetics* on comedy: 'Probable incidents' (ch. 9; p. 117); happy endings (ch. 13, p. 121); 'mean' or conversational language (the iambic metre as 'conversational' and associated with the development of comedy, also, writers of comedy 'less dignified,' ch. 4, pp. 111–12; 'standard words' as 'mean' (ch. 22, pp. 130–31); 'baser men' as the subject of comedy (ch. 4, p. 111; ch. 5, p. 112). The *Poetics* on tragedy: 'human action and life' (ch. 6, p. 114); plots 'end[ing] in misfortune' (ch. 13, p. 120); 'language that has been artistically enhanced' (ch. 6, p. 113); tragedy about 'noble subjects presented in an elevated metre' (ch. 5, p. 112).

20 *The Shorter Oxford English Dictionary*, 3rd edn (2 vols), revised and edited by C.T. Onions (Oxford: Clarendon Press, 1991), p. 1939.

21 The novel alluded to, *Nature's Nobleman*, 'By the Author of "Rachel's Secret"', is reviewed in *Athenaeum*, 5 December 1868, p. 750.

22 *Literature*, 16 April 1898, p. 449. Yet even Carey was adversely criticized on moral grounds earlier in her career. Her lapses from grace include: allowing the eponymous heroine

Indeed, reviewers represent Carey's novels as being moral almost to a fault. For example, a review in the *Graphic* describes *Only the Governess* as

> an exceedingly pleasant novel, and likely to be deservedly popular. The virtue is extremely welcome, if only by way of a change; and the small beer of incident is bright and refreshing, as well as wholesome and sound.[23]

However, adverse remarks about excessive or outdated morality multiply as the nineteenth century progresses, even her advocates perceiving that large numbers of readers would find her work old-fashioned and lacking in excitement. Thus the critic of *Other People's Lives*, who admires Carey's work despite a lack of 'hairbreadth escapes ... literary brilliance, or ... social questions', writes kindly if somewhat sadly:

> We are glad to see that a new and cheaper issue of Miss ... Carey's stories is announced by Messrs. Bentley, for the fact shows the existence among us of a taste too likely to be extinguished by the varied and piquant items in the menu now offered to readers of fiction. A generation or two ago she would naturally have been in vogue; nowadays one might have questioned whether there were room for so simple and unaffected a chronicle of commonplace people as is contained in her latest publication.[24]

However, these fears, articulated in 1898, were only to be fully realised after another three decades. For, whilst the literary world changed around her, Carey continued to produce well-written fiction that was as out of date as marriage, maternity and household management could ever be. Meanwhile, the supposedly well-informed were reading – or writing – novels about the 'New Woman'.

The third major topic discussed by reviewers is that of the classification of works of fiction, either in terms of content or in terms of supposed readership. Classificatory reviews range from those about novels with a purpose – a novel advocating the Married Woman's Sister's Bill, a 'total abstinence' tract – to novels dedicated to specific aspects of society – a novel of theatrical life, a

of *Queenie's Whim* (1881) to fall in love with a man who is about to engage himself to someone else; placing the heroine of *Basil Lyndhurst* (1889) in the position of waiting for the hero's first wife to die so that she can step into her shoes; and 'adopting the ugly American habit of making all girls wiser than their mothers' in *Not Like Other Girls* (1884). See *Academy*, 12 March 1881, p. 186; *Academy*, 20 July 1889, p. 36; *Academy*, 22 March 1884, p. 199.

23 *Graphic*, 24 March 1888, p. 319.

24 *Literature*, 16 April 1898, p. 449.

hunting novel.[25] In addition, there are to be found the kinds of genre classification which would be exploited in later years by the larger publishing corporations. Thus, there are references to 'a police novel' and to 'Indian novels'.[26] This obsession with classification grows rather than diminishes over the years. Reviews of Carey's novels become littered with judgements such as 'quite suitable for the school-room' and 'fairly passes muster in its class'; and the author herself becomes 'warrant for expecting a pretty love-story'.[27] The merchandising of Carey's books largely on her name becomes possible because she is both long-lived and prolific in output. There is the material with which to create a market for a predictable product; she becomes a known quantity. Neither reviewer nor review-reader is obliged to enjoy the product on offer but at least it is knowable and thus unproblematic.

However, the ultimate stage in the classification of novels appears to be reached when some journals make classification integral to journal structure. The single general review section is, on occasions, made to yield to a policy of reviewing all novels of a particular genre together. Hence, purchasers of the *Literary World* in June 1896 are presented with the option of reading (or avoiding) a selection of reviews solely on 'Novels of English life' and those reading the Fiction Supplement to the *Academy* in November 1900 are presented with a section of reviews entitled 'The Novel of Domesticity.'[28] For better or worse, a book by Carey is reviewed under each of these headings. It seems that the commodification of the book, whether as author-product or as genre-product, had come to pass long before the sophisticated distribution networks and multi-media advertising had come into existence.

An exploration of Carey's reviews and those of her peers thus reveals an increasing polarization between 'academic' types of evaluation on the one hand and classification according to genre and supposed readership on the other. Discussion of technique tends, in places, towards a qualitative assessment typical of the later academic literary establishment. This drive towards the intellectualizing and academicizing of English literature as a subject and discipline dealing in established theoretical texts is suggested by the reviewers' recourse to Aristotle's *Poetics*. Leon Golden posits that this revision in critical practice did not occur until the twentieth century:

---

25 Mrs Craik, *Hannah*, reviewed in *Graphic*, 11 November 1871, p. 463; Major R.D. Gibney, *Earnest Madement*, reviewed in *Athenaeum*, 23 December 1882, p. 845; Mr John Coleman, *The Rival Queens*, reviewed in *Graphic*, 26 March 1887, p. 334 ; Mrs Lovett Cameron, *In a Grass Country*, reviewed in *Graphic*, 7 November 1885, p. 523.

26 M. Malot, *Conscience*, reviewed in *Athenaeum*, 17 March 1888, p. 338; Mrs Croker, *A Family Likeness*, reviewed in *Academy*, 24 December 1892, p. 586.

27 *Rue With a Difference*, reviewed in *Athenaeum*, 24 November 1900, p. 680; *Uncle Max*, reviewed in *Academy*, 5 February 1887, p. 90; *Rue With A Difference*, reviewed in *Academy*, 13 October 1900, p. 310.

28 See *Literary World*, 27 June 1896, p. 202; *Academy*, 3 November 1900, p. 413.

> The nineteenth century was a period of eclipse for the *Poetics*: romantic critics, operating under new premises – a theory of the imagination rather than a theory based on the materials of poetry – reacted sharply against Aristotle, or at least against the Aristotle of neoclassicism. Their doctrines are often antithetical to the *Poetics*: the exaltation of lyric over drama, of character over plot, of 'genius' over 'rules' and, most importantly, of expression over imitation.[29]

And, indeed, the domestic novel itself seems to fit Golden's paradigm of the romantic in terms of its individualized characterization and of its loose-knit and multifaceted plot. However, evidence of something beyond personal opinion and an enthusiasm for lyricism is to be found in reviews of domestic novels more than a decade before the end of the nineteenth century. Even a review from 1900, which reproduces Aristotelian concepts in an almost jocular fashion, points to a history of usage. The reviewer writes:

> If we had to criticize ... [this novel] in Aristotelian terms, we should say that we were sensible of the pity and the fear, but missed the cathartic effect.[30]

This writer is familiar with the notion that classical criticism can be applied to nineteenth-century literature. The existence of the review suggests that formal critical influences were present amongst academic institutions and their products from a time earlier in the century; it implies both a reviewer who has previously studied the *Poetics* and a readership capable of understanding the allusion. This is suggestive of a fairly widely disseminated culture of literary theory, or at least the widespread use of a classical text which has been meaningfully discussed in English. The demise of the domestic novel as a universally topical genre may thus be seen as partially due to a revival in classically based criticism.

Meanwhile, the continuing publication and sale of novels such as those written by Rosa Carey points to the existence of an alternative readership which had different expectations from its reading matter; one which cannot have cared greatly whether or not the novels were erudite according to a male academic tradition. A glimpse of this alternative – and largely silent – audience, along with its preoccupations and requirements, may nevertheless be encountered in the reviews of Carey's novels. Reviewers believed this readership to be overwhelmingly feminine. Thus, for example, the review of *Sir Godfrey's Granddaughters* in the *Athenaeum* concludes with the assertion that

29 Golden 1974, p. 107.

30 The novel, Robert Hichens, *Tongues of Conscience*, was reviewed in *Literature*, 3 November 1900, p. 349; cf. *Poetics* 7 (Golden 1974, p. 115).

> the reader who likes Miss Carey's bright and mercurial style of telling a domestic romance will understand that he (or, a little more probably, she) has a treat in prospect.[31]

That Carey's reviewers had a poor opinion of the intellect and general level of education of this feminine readership is evident. Perhaps the most damning of all the reviews is the one of *Queenie's Whim* to be found in the *Graphic* in 1881. Having begun by referring to the novel as 'sweetly pretty', the reviewer goes on to say that:

> It is not to be accounted a fault, under all the circumstances, that the novel contains too much talk, and reports in over-minute detail how everybody looks and what everybody wears. For these little matters, though faults in themselves, are the very things for which so many people thoroughly enjoy stories like 'Queenie's Whim.' Such novels are like good long gossips about one's acquaintances among a set of good-natured and innocent-minded, if not very intellectual people, who find it refreshing to cry over the sorrows of their neighbours, and infinitely comforting to know for certain what their neighbours wore.[32]

The construction of the female reader herself as one of the 'innocent-minded, if not very intellectual' participants in the 'gossips' about 'little' matters is strongly indicative of a belief on the part of the reviewer that women were incapable of taking an interest in more weighty matters. It is indeed unlikely that many of Carey's readers were familiar with Aristotle's *Poetics* or had enjoyed any of the benefits of a Classical education. Nor were many women able to broaden their horizons by taking up public-sphere employment of the kind available to men. Thus, of those with the most leisure to read, many were confined to the domestic world of the home and family and to household routine. Their priorities were bound to be different from those of their male peers. Yet one must be careful not to underestimate their powers of discrimination. For, by the later decades of the nineteenth century, private secondary education and some opportunities for higher education had become available to the women of the middle classes and the Education Act of 1870 had brought basic literacy to a much higher proportion of the population than ever before.[33] Whatever the opinion of the reviewers, at least a portion of Carey's readership is likely to have selected her novels in response to reasoned choice.

---

31 *Athenaeum*, 5 November 1892, p. 626. See also review of *Not Like Other Girls* in *Graphic*, 7 June 1884, p. 559.

32 *Graphic*, 19 March 1881, p. 275.

33 That the effect of the Act was instantaneous is questionable. However, literacy was acknowledged to be on the increase throughout the nineteenth century. See Peter Keating, *The Haunted Study* (London: Secker and Warburg, 1989), pp. 400–401.

Reviewers occasionally gave this preoccupation with detail a more positive emphasis, commenting on the novels' 'essentially feminine' focus. Thus, the reviewer for the *Athenaeum* notes of *The Household of Peter* that:

> Like Miss Carey's other novels, this is an essentially feminine book, and, like them, it is not lacking in charm for the sex to which it especially appeals. Woman's joy in afternoon tea with hot sweet cakes and cream, and woman's anxiety over the waning freshness of a blouse, are herein developed with the author's accustomed sympathetic insight.[34]

The reviewer has selected a few items as a synecdoche of the whole novel, thus in certain respects trivializing its overall scheme. However, she or he does not give the impression of dismissing it completely. The reference to Carey's 'sympathetic insight' into the day-to-day incidents that make up most women's lives does not appear to be entirely ironic. Though the reviewer does not appear to subscribe to the values and priorities that dictated Carey's subject matter, there does appear to be an acknowledgement that these matters are of interest to others.

The exact composition of Carey's readership is by no means obvious from the reviews alone. However, one feature of it that is fairly consistent is the reviewers' insistence that her books are suitable for the young girl. For example, a review in the *Literary World* in 1896 notes that she 'can always be depended upon to write good, wholesome novels for girls, with reasonably unobtrusive morals'.[35] Nor would Carey herself have argued with this assessment. She is on record as saying '[m]y ambition has been to do good and not harm by my works, and to write books which any mother can give a girl to read'.[36] This single factor would not have endeared her to many readers of her day. For, not only was the standard of 'books any mother can give a girl' deemed to be remote from contemporary life, it also carried a painful reminder of the limitations placed upon artistic expression by nineteenth-century institutions such as Mudie's Select Library. Such restrictions led Charles Reade to demand that he be allowed to write – and publish – fiction 'not adapted to the narrow minds of bread-and-butter misses' and George Moore to state that '[l]iterature and young girls are irreconcilable elements, and the sooner we leave off trying to reconcile them the better'.[37]

---

34 Review of *The Household of Peter* in *Athenaeum*, 21 October 1905, p. 539.

35 Review of *The Mistress of Brae Farm* in *Literary World*, 12 December 1896, p. 456. See also review of *Life's Trivial Round* in *Athenaeum*, 16 June 1900, p. 745; review of *The Key of the Unknown* in *Athenaeum*, 2 October 1909, p. 389.

36 See Helen C. Black, *Notable Women Authors of the Day* (London: Maclaren, 1906 [1893]), p. 154.

37 Cited in Guinivere Griest, *Mudie's Circulating Library* (Newton Abbot: David and Charles, 1970), pp. 137–40.

Figure 5: From *Nellie's Memories* (1922), opposite p. 200

Figure 6: From *Nellie's Memories* (1922), opposite p. 52

With regard to readers other than the young girl, it is necessary to return to what reviewers say about the content of the novels. The material more easily lends itself to conjecture about psychological profiles than class status, though the majority of heroines in the novels fall into the middle classes. Yet, though the readers themselves are shadowy, their perceived needs are very clearly stated. For example, reviews in the *Woman's Signal* and *Literature* suggest that, then as now, women simply enjoyed reading love stories. One might conjecture that a certain portion of readers bought the novels precisely because 'Miss Carey has a perfect belief in lasting and faithful love.'[38] Similarly, it is likely that many readers relied upon the 'warrant for a pretty love-story' that Carey's name guaranteed, another reviewer opining that:

> *My Lady Frivol* ... belongs to that class of romance which will always find grateful readers. The most timid need never fear that the love story of the governess-heroine will have untimely ending.[39]

In her survey of late twentieth-century romance-readers, *Reading the Romance* (1987), Janice Radway notes that her respondents deemed a happy ending to the book to be essential to their enjoyment and we may conjecture that the same was true of female romance-readers a hundred years ago.[40] So keen were Radway's respondents to avoid disappointment that many of them actually read the endings to their romances before purchasing them, 'to insure [sic] that they will not be saddened by emotionally investing in the tale of a heroine only to discover that events do not resolve themselves as they should'.[41] The review of *My Lady Frivol* from *Literature* suggests that, metaphorically at least, nineteenth-century romance-readers did the same. According to the reviewer, such 'timid' readers elected to ensure that their forthcoming '[emotional] investment' was secure, not by reading the last few pages of the book, but by making sure that the right author's name was written on the cover.

The novels also appeared to attract those who wished to enter wholeheartedly into Carey's fictional worlds and to empathize with the joys and sorrows of her characters. Thus, the reviewer for the *Academy* notes of *The Old, Old Story* that 'at the end [the reader] will sincerely rejoice that all goes well. This he must do because Miss Carey is herself wrapped up in her people.'[42] Similarly, a reviewer for the *Leeds Mercury* notes that 'the story will recommend itself to all those who like prosperity and happiness to be the

38 Review of *Other People's Lives* in *Woman's Signal*, 23 December 1896, p. 403.

39 *Rue With A Difference*, reviewed in *Academy*, 13 October 1900, p. 310; review of *My Lady Frivol* in *Literature*, 6 January 1900, p. 23.

40 Janice Radway, *Reading the Romance* (London, Verso, 1987) (hereafter, Radway 1987).

41 Radway 1987, p. 99.

42 *Academy*, 3 November 1894, p. 348.

portion of any characters in a book in whom they are interested'.[43] However, the potential for emotional investment did not stop at the level of the mere observer who rejoiced in the happiness of others. There was also, apparently, a readership which enjoyed the purely emotive sentimentalism to be found in some of Carey's works:

> the author of *For Lilias* has now a public of her own, who are no doubt very grateful to her for creating so many really good people, that spend the bulk of their time in saying 'loving words' and telegraphing 'loving glances' to each other.[44]

Yet not all reviewers despised the notions of a sentimental plot or a (romantically-conceived) happy ending. The same review of *My Lady Frivol* from *Literature* sums up what might well have been the philosophy of many a reader:

> after all, a simple romance told without affectation is more welcome and better art than a gloomy novel with a purpose.[45]

To summarize, it seems that Carey's readership, as sketched by the reviewers, has a number of definite requirements and that Carey's novels in some measure fulfil them. First, her readers need fiction that is optimistic and that concludes happily. Next, this fiction has to provide opportunities for reader input (enthusiasm or sympathy) and to supply various kinds of vicarious experience (a share in the fictional sentimental and emotional experiences of key characters). Finally, it has to be congruent with the reader's everyday experience and to valorize the reader's actual existence outside the novel. It is thus apt that in the *Bookman* for January 1901, a reviewer suggests that, ultimately, Carey's readership enjoys not so much a 'literary' experience as a psychological one:

> Miss Carey may be said to suffer from her own excellence. Her books are so uniformly straight, and true, and tranquil, and charming, that we have learned to depend on her, and know she will give us no surprises. One is tempted to compare the mental fare of her providing with dinner in a well-ordered household; it is pleasant, wholesome, restful; but it will never stir one to that excitement which would be inseparable from dinner in a Dora Copperfieldian establishment. Miss Carey must take comfort from the certainty that the well-ordered household is the one in which the

43 Review of *My Lady Frivol* in *Leeds Mercury*, 4 October 1899, p. 3.
44 *Academy*, 26 September 1885, p. 200.
45 *Literature*, 6 January 1900, p. 23.

> majority of us would choose to live; the other establishment is more suitable for smiling at from the outside.[46]

Carey's implied reader, as constructed by this review, requires a predictable product and one which yields a positive psychological effect. She prefers to participate in the 'well-ordered household' of Carey's novels rather than to simply read about some other kind of establishment; she wants to enjoy vicariously the tranquillity, charm and pleasure of an ordered and benign universe rather than to endure the discomforts and uncertainties depicted in more 'artistic' fiction.[47]

Regardless of how this restful quality is valued, the novels do indeed appear to leave the reader in a buoyant frame of mind. However, in this book it has been argued that Carey's novels go beyond merely tranquillizing the reader. Though reviews suggest that the novels reinforce dominant ideologies about gender roles, it has been argued that Carey's novels do more than replicate a position of oppression for women. Rather, through the articulation of common concerns and interests, the valorization of certain values and the invitation to the woman reader to participate in a feminine community, Carey may be regarded as feminist or, at any rate proto-feminist. It has been suggested that Carey's novels are, in several important ways, nurturant of women and endorse women's lived experience. Thus, those who fail to fit in with normative society are permitted to see themselves reflected sympathetically in Carey's attractive miscreants, potential heroines and wretched victims; single women see their position treated positively; home-making, with its attendant joys and sorrows is dramatized and thus acknowledged as real work; the reader is helped to come to terms with living in a 'man's world'; and religion is mediated through the home, thus domesticating the unbearable fact of death. Far from radical in outlook, Carey may yet be termed a proto-feminist as she writes positively and sympathetically about all matters concerning women.

This first in-depth study of Rosa Carey's forty-one novels has been an attempt to 'rediscover' a significant nineteenth-century writer. For, hitherto, she has been doubly marginalized: initially by her contemporaries, preoccupied as they were with the growth of a restrictive literary formalism; and latterly by the

46 Review of *Rue With a Difference* in the *Bookman*, January 1901, p. 131.

47 The 'product' does not sound especially inviting when described in these terms but many reviewers, both positive and negative, display an awareness that Carey has a large and enthusiastic readership. As a reviewer notes of *Uncle Max* [1887],

> The interest is sober, and for the most part domestic; and the number of novel-readers who prefer well-written narratives of this class is probably quite as large as the number of those who crave abundant sensation.

Other reviewers are more scathing about the value of Carey's optimistic and comforting outlook on life. For example, the word 'soothing' is used in an apparently derogatory sense on three separate occasions (*Academy*, 24 December 1892, p. 586; *Athenaeum*, 21 October 1905, p. 539; *Athenaeum*, 17 October 1908, p. 469).

present-day academic establishment, preoccupied as it is with a small range of canonical and 'feminist-canonical' texts. Yet Carey's novels of domesticity, for all their concern with everyday events and minor morals, are arguably as discursive as many other genres currently popular with critics. To employ the rhetoric of Lyn Pykett's critique of Sensation fiction, Carey's writings may be viewed as more than expressions of the 'contained, conservative domain of the proper feminine'. They may be explored as 'sites in which many of the contradictions, anxieties and opposing ideologies of Victorian culture converge and are put into play'.[48]

48 See Lyn Pykett, *The Improper Feminine* (London: Routledge, 1992), pp. 50–51: We need to see [the sensation novel] not simply as either the transgressive or subversive field of the improper feminine, or the contained, conservative domain of the proper feminine. Instead we should explore [it] as a site in which the contradictions, anxieties and opposing ideologies of Victorian culture converge and are put into play …

Bibliography

'A Medical Man', *Cassell's Family Doctor* (London: Cassell, 1897)

'A Member of the Aristocracy', *Manners and Rules of Good Society* (London: Frederick Warne, 1887)

'An Old Boy' [Thomas Hughes], *Tom Brown's Schooldays* (London: Macmillan, 1898 [1857])

'By the author of *Margaret Browning*', *Uncle Jabez; or The Teachings of Adversity* (London: Religious Tract Society, n.d. [inscribed 1871])

'M.C.', *Everybody's Book of Correct Conduct, Being the Etiquette of Every-day Life* (Whitstable: Pryor Publications, 1996 [1893])

'Medicus', *The Pocket Doctor* (London: Cassell, n.d. [c. 1914])

Adams, W.H. Davenport, *Plain Living and High Thinking* (London: John Hogg, 1883)

Allen, J.M., 'On the Real Differences in the Minds of Men and Women', *Journal of the Anthropological Society*, Vol. 7, 1869, pp. cxcv–ccxix.

Althusser, Louis, 'Ideology and Ideological State Apparatuses' in *Essays on Ideology* (London: Verso, 1987 [1970])

Amiel, Henri-Frederic, *Amiel's Journal, The Journey Intime*, ed. and trans. Mrs Humphrey Ward (London: Macmillan, 1901 [1895])

Armstrong, Nancy, *Desire and Domestic Fiction* (Oxford: Oxford University Press, 1987)

Arnold-Foster, H.O., *The Citizen Reader* (London: Cassell, 14th edn, c. 1889)

Baker, H.W. (ed.) *Hymns Ancient and Modern*, Standard Edition (London: Printed for the Proprietors by William Clowes and Sons, 1916 [1861])

Barthes, Roland, 'The Death of the Author' in Stephen Heath (ed., trans.) *Image Music Text* (London: Fontana, 1987)

Beeton, Isabella, *Beeton's Book of Household Management, an Illustrated Facsimile of the First Edition* (London: Chancellor Press, 1994 [1861])

Black, Helen C., *Notable Women Authors of the Day* (London: Maclaren, 1906 [1893])

Blake, Andrew, *Reading Victorian Fiction* (Basingstoke: Macmillan, 1989)

Braddon, Mary Elizabeth, *Lady Audley's Secret* (London: Simpkin, Marshall, Hamilton, Kent, n.d. [1862])

Brewer's Dictionary of Phrase and Fable, 10th rev. edn (London: Cassell, 1967)

Bunyan, John, *The Pilgrim's Progress*, ed. George Offor (London: George Routledge and Sons, n.d. [Part 1, 1678; Part 2, 1684])

Burnett, John, *Plenty and Want* (London: Methuen, 1985)

Carey, R.N., *A Passage Perilous* (London: Macmillan, 1906 [1903])

—, *At The Moorings* (London: Macmillan, 1914 [1904])

—, *Aunt Diana* (London: Office of 'The Girl's Own Paper', n.d. [1885])

—, *Averil* (London: Office of 'The Girl's Own Paper', n.d. [1890–91])

—, *Barbara Heathcote's Trial* (London: Macmillan, 1915 [1871])

—, *Basil Lyndhurst* (London: Macmillan, 1904 [1889]) pp. 5–6.

—, *But Men Must Work* (London: Richard Bentley and Son, 1892)

—, *Cousin Mona* (London: Religious Tract Society, 1897 [1895])
—, *Dr Luttrell's First Patient,* serialised in *Girl's Own Paper*, 3 October 1896 – 20 March 1897
—, *Esther Cameron's Story* (London: Office of 'The Girl's Own Paper', 1914 [1883–84])
—, *For Lilias* (London: Macmillan, 1902 [1885])
—, *Herb of Grace* (London: Macmillan, 1903 [1901])
—, *Heriot's Choice* (London: Macmillan, 1899 [1877–79])
—, *Life's Trivial Round,* 2nd edn (London: Hutchinson, n.d. [1899–1900])
—, *Little Miss Muffet* (London: Religious Tract Society, n.d.[1892–93])
—, *Lover or Friend?* (London: Macmillan, 1915 [1890])
—, *Mary St John* (London: Macmillan, 1909 [1882])
—, *Merle's Crusade* (London: Religious Tract Society, n.d. [1886–87])
—, *Mollie's Prince* (London: Hutchinson , n.d. [1898])
—, *Mrs Romney* and *But Men Must Work* (London: Macmillan, 1899)
—, *My Lady Frivol* (London: Hutchinson, n.d. [1899])
—, *Nellie's Memories* (London: Richard Bentley and Son, 1892 [1868])
—, *No Friend Like A Sister* (London: Macmillan, 1906)
—, *Not Like Other Girls* (London: Macmillan, 1905 [1884])
—, *Only the Governess* (London: Macmillan, 1917 [1888])
—, *Other People's Lives* (London: Hodder and Stoughton, 1897)
—, *Our Bessie* (London: Office of 'The Girl's Own Paper', 1914 [1888–89])
—, *Queenie's Whim* (London: Macmillan, 1898 [1881])
—, *Robert Ord's Atonement* (London: Richard Bentley and Son, 1898 [1873])
—, *Rue With a Difference* (London: Macmillan, 1914 [1900])
—, *Sir Godfrey's Grand-daughters* (London: Macmillan, 1899 [1892])
—, *The Angel of Forgiveness* (London: Macmillan, 1911 [1907])
—, *The Highway of Fate* (London: Macmillan, 1902)
—, *The Household of Peter* (London: Macmillan, 1905)
—, *The Key of the Unknown* (London: Macmillan, 1909)
—, *The Mistress of Brae Farm* (London: Hodder and Stoughton, 1920 [1896])
—, *The Old, Old Story* (London: Macmillan, 1900 [1894])
—, *The Sunny Side of the Hill* (London: Macmillan, 1908)
—, *Uncle Max* (London: Macmillan, 1912 [1887])
—, *Wee Wifie* (London: Richard Bentley and Son, 1894 [1869])
—, *Wooed and Married* (London: Macmillan, 1902)
Carlyle, Thomas, *Past and Present*, ed. A.M.D. Hughes (Oxford: Clarendon Press, 1927 [1843])
Chodorow, Nancy, *The Reproduction of Mothering* (Berkeley: University of California Press, 1978)
Corelli, Marie, *The Sorrows of Satan* (London: Methuen, 1899 [1895])
Cowell, Raymond (ed.), *Critics on Wordsworth* (London: George Allen and Unwin, 1973)
Craik, Dinah Mulock, *A Woman's Thoughts About Women* [1858], entire text published in Elaine Showalter (ed.), *Christina Rossetti: 'Maude', Dinah Mulock Craik: 'On Sisterhoods' and 'A Woman's Thoughts About Women'* (London: Pickering Women's Classics, Pickering and Chatto, 1993)
Crisp, Jane, *Rosa Nouchette Carey (1840–1909) A Bibliography*, Victorian Fiction Research Guides 16 (Brisbane: University of Queensland, 1989)
Cunningham, Gail, 'Society, History and the Reader: the Nineteenth-century Novel' in Andrew Michael Roberts (ed.), *Bloomsbury Guides to English Literature: The Novel* (London: Bloomsbury, 1993)
Davidson, H.C. (ed.), *The Book of the Home* (London: Gresham, 1901)

Dickens, Charles, *The Christmas Books* (London: Cassell, 1910 [1846])

Edmond, Rod, *Affairs of the Hearth* (London: Routledge, 1988)

Enquire Within Upon Everything, To Which Is Added Enquire Within Upon Fancy Work, 42nd edn (London: Houlston and Sons, 1871)

Enquire Within Upon Everything, 96th edn (London: Houlston and Sons, 1899)

Ewing, Mrs J.H., *Jackanapes* [1879] in *Jackanapes and Other Tales* (London: J.M. Dent and Sons, 1931)

Flint, Kate, *The Woman Reader 1837–1914* (Oxford: Clarendon Press, 1993)

Forrester, Wendy, *Great Grandmama's Weekly* (Guildford: Lutterworth, 1980)

Foucault, Michel, 'What is an Author?' in Paul Rabinow (ed.), *The Foucault Reader* (London: Penguin, Peregrine Books, 1986)

—, *The Archaeology of Knowledge*, ed. A.M. Sheridan Smith (New York: Pantheon, 1972)

Fowler, R. (ed.), *A Dictionary of Critical Terms* (London: Routledge, 1991)

Freud, Sigmund, *On Metapsychology: The Theory of Psycho-analysis*, The Pelican Freud Library Volume 11 (Harmondsworth: Penguin, 1987)

Gardiner, Alan, *The Poetry of William Wordsworth* (London: Penguin, 1990)

Giberne, Agnes, *Floss Silverthorne or The Master's Little Handmaid* (London: John J. Shaw, n.d. [c. 1905–10])

Gilbert, S.M. and Gubar, S., *The Madwoman in the Attic* (New Haven: Yale University Press, 1984 [1979])

Girouard, M., *The Return to Camelot* (New Haven: Yale University Press, 1981)

Greenblatt, Stephen, *Learning to Curse* (London: Routledge, 1992)

—, *Renaissance Self-Fashioning* (Chicago: The Chicago Press, 1984)

Gregory, R.L. (ed.), *The Oxford Companion to the Mind* (Oxford: Oxford University Press, 1987)

Griest, Guinivere, *Mudie's Circulating Library* (Newton Abbot: David and Charles, 1970)

Hamilton, Paul, *Historicism*, The New Critical Idiom (London: Routledge, 1996)

Hawkes, David, *Ideology*, The New Critical Idiom (London: Routledge, 1996)

Hemans, Felicia Dorothea, *The Poetical Works of Felicia Dorothea Hemans* (London: Humphrey Milford, Oxford University Press, 1914)

Hodgson, J.A., *Wordsworth's Philosophical Poetry 1797–1814* (Lincoln,London: University of Nebraska Press, 1980)

Hollis, Patricia, *Women in Public: The Women's Movement 1850–1900* (London: George Allen and Unwin, 1979)

Honey, J.R. de Symons, *Tom Brown's Universe* (London: Millington, 1977)

Hughes, Molly, *A London Girl of the 1880s* (Oxford: Oxford University Press, 1985 [1946])

Jalland, Pat, *Death in the Victorian Family* (Oxford: Oxford University Press, 1996)

—, *Women, Marriage and Politics 1860–1914* (Oxford: Clarendon Press, 1986)

James, John Angell, *The Young Man From Home* (London: Religious Tract Society, n.d., [c. 1890])

Jeffreys, Sheila, *The Spinster and Her Enemies* (London: Pandora, 1985)

Johnson, Joseph, *Noble Women of Our Time* (London: T. Nelson and Sons, 1886)

Keating, Peter, *The Haunted Study* (London: Secker and Warburg, 1989)

Kennedy, E. and Mendus, S. (eds), *Women in Western Political Philosophy* (Brighton: Wheatsheaf/John Spiers, 1987)

Kingsley, Charles, 'Heroism' (1880) in Charles Kingsley, *Sanitary and Social Lectures and Essays* (London: Macmillan, 1892 [1880]) pp. 25–254

—, 'Woman's Work in a Country Parish', in Charles Kingsley, *Sanitary and Social Lectures and Essays* (London: Macmillan, 1892 [1880]) pp. 3–18

Kingsley, F.E., *Charles Kingsley: His Letters and Memories of His Life* (London: Macmillan, 1890 [1883])
Kirton, J.W., *Happy Homes and How to Make Them* (Birmingham: The Educational Trading Co., n.d. [c. 1871])
'Le Voleur', *By Order of the Brotherhood: A Story of Russian Intrigue* (London: Jarrold, 1895)
—, *For Love of a Bedouin Maid* (London: Hutchinson, 1897)
—, *In the Tsar's Dominions* (London: Hutchinson, 1899)
—, *The Champington Mystery* (London: Digby, Long, 1900)
Lechte, John, *Fifty Key Contemporary Thinkers* (London: Routledge, 1995)
Ledger, Sally, *The New Woman: Fiction and Feminism at the Fin de Siècle* (Manchester: Manchester University Press, 1997)
Lees, Harrington C., *The Divine Master in Home Life* (London: Religious Tract Society, 1915)
Longfellow, Henry Wadsworth, *The Poetical Works of Longfellow* (London: Ward Locke, 1882)
Lovell, Terry, *Gender and Englishness in 'Villette'*, in S. Ledger, J. McDonagh and J. Spencer (eds), *Political Gender: Texts and Contexts* (New York: Harvester Wheatsheaf, 1994)
Lucy, Mary Elizabeth (ed. Alice Fairfax-Lucy) *Mistress of Charlecote, The Memoirs of Mary Elizabeth Lucy* (London: Victor Gollancz, 1983)
Lyall, David, [Mrs Burnett Smith, *aka* Annie S. Swan], *The House Not Made With Hands* (London: Hodder and Stoughton, n.d. [1912])
Lyotard, J.-F., *The Inhuman* (Cambridge: Polity, 1993)
—, *The Postmodern Condition, A Report on Knowledge*, trans. Geoff Bennington and Brian Massumi, foreword by Fredric Jameson, Theory and History of Literature, Volume 10 (Manchester: Manchester University Press, 1987)
—, *The Differend: Phrases in Dispute*, trans. George Van Den Abbeele (Manchester: Manchester University Press, 1988 [1983])
M'Gregor-Robertson, J., *The Household Physician, A Family Guide to the Preservation of Health and to the Domestic Treatment of Ailments and Disease, with Chapters on Food and Drugs, and First Aid in Accidents and Injuries* (London: Blackie and Son, n.d. [c.1888])
Macdonell, Diane, *Theories of Discourse: An Introduction* (Oxford: Basil Blackwell, 1987)
Mackay, Alexander, *Manual of Modern Geography* (Edinburgh: William Blackwood and Sons, 1861)
MacKenzie, Charlotte, *Psychiatry for the Rich: A History of Ticehurst Private Asylum* (London: Routledge, 1992)
Maudsley, Henry, *Body and Mind* (London: Macmillan, 1873)
—, *Responsibility in Mental Disease,* The International Scientific Series Vol. 8 (London: Henry S. King, 1874)
Mayo, Isabel F., 'Leaving Home,' *The Sunday At Home*, no. 1726, 28 May 1887, pp. 341–5
Meiklejohn, J.M.D., *The English Language: Its Grammar, History and Literature*, 28th edn, enlarged (London: Meiklejohn and Holden, 1907)
Mills, Sara (ed.), *Gendering the Reader* (Hemel Hempstead: Harvester Wheatsheaf, 1994)
Newsome, David, *Godliness and Good Learning* (London: John Murray, 1961)
Palgrave, F.T., *The Golden Treasury* (London: Macmillan, 1890)
Patmore, Coventry, *The Angel in the House* (London: George Bell and Son 1896 [1854])
Paull, Mrs H.B., *The Two Neighbours: A Tale of Every-day Life* (London: Frederick Warne and Co., 1887)
Poovey, Mary, *Uneven Developments* (London: Virago, 1989)
Preminger, Alex, Golden, Leon, et al. (eds), *Classical Literary Criticism: Translations and Interpretations* (New York: Frederick Ungar, 1974)

Prichard, J.C., *On the Different Forms of Insanity in Relation to Jurisprudence* (London: Hippolyte Baillière, 1847)
Pykett, Lyn, *Engendering Fictions: The English Novel of the Early Twentieth Century* (London: Edward Arnold, 1995)
—, *The 'Improper' Feminine* (London: Routledge, 1992)
Quiller-Couch, A.T. (ed.), *The Oxford Book of English Verse* (St Albans: Granada, 1980)
Radway, Janice, *Reading the Romance* (London: Verso, 1987)
Readings, Bill, *Introducing Lyotard: Art and Politics* (London: Routledge, 1992)
Robertson, J. Logie, *A History of English Literature*, 3rd edn, revised (Edinburgh: William Blackwood, 1900)
Rousseau, Jean Jacques, *Emile*, trans. Barbara Foxley (London: J. M. Dent and Sons, 1963)
Rowbotham, Judith, *Good Girls Make Good Wives* (Oxford: Basil Blackwell, 1989)
Ruskin, J., *Sesame and Lilies* (London: George Allen, 1906 [1865])
Schooling, J. Holt, 'Which is the Maddest Part of the Kingdom?', *Pearson's Magazine*, Vol. 3, January–June 1897, pp. 183–8.
Sedgwick, Eve Kosofsky, *Between Men: Literature and Male Homosocial Desire* (New York: Columbia University Press, 1985)
Seidler, Victor, *Rediscovering Masculinity* (London: Routledge, 1989)
Selden, Raman, *A Reader's Guide To Literary Criticism*, 2nd edn (Hemel Hempstead: Harvester Wheatsheaf, 1989)
Shorter Oxford English Dictionary, The, 2 vols (Oxford: Clarendon Press, 1991)
Showalter, Elaine, *A Literature of Their Own* (London: Virago, 1988)
—, *The Female Malady* (London: Virago, 1991)
Skultans, Vieda, *Madness and Morals: Ideas on Insanity in the Nineteenth Century* (London: Routledge and Kegan Paul, 1975)
Smart, Ninian, *The Religious Experience of Mankind* (Glasgow: Collins, 1979)
Smiles, Samuel, *Character* (London: John Murray, 1897 [1878])
—, *Self Help* (London: John Murray, 1902 [1859])
—, *Thrift* (London: John Murray, 1876)
Spender, Dale, *Man Made Language* (London: Routledge and Kegan Paul, 1987)
Stoker, Bram, *Dracula* (Oxford: Oxford University Press, 1983 [1897])
Swedenborg, Emanuel, *A Compendium of the Theological Writings*, ed. Rev. S.M. Warren (London: The Swedenborg Society, 1909)
Tennyson, Alfred, *The Poetical Works of Alfred, Lord Tennyson* (London: Ward, Lock, n.d.)
The Nuttall's Pronouncing English Dictionary (London: George Routledge and Sons, 1879)
Thomson S. and Steele, J. C., *A Dictionary of Domestic Medicine and Surgery*, 34th edn, thoroughly revised and enlarged by A. Westland, G. Reid and J. Cantlie (London: Charles Griffin, 1899 [1882])
Veith, Ilza, *Hysteria: The History of a Disease* (Chicago: Phoenix, University of Chicago Press, 1965)
Vicars-Harris, Rosalie, and Fordham, David (eds), *Dearest Beatie My Darling Jack, A Victorian Couple's Love-Letters* (London: Collins, 1983)
Vicinus, Martha, *Independent Women: Work and Community for Single Women 1850–1920* (London: Virago, 1985)
Watt, Ian, *The Rise of the Novel* (Harmondsworth: Penguin, 1968)
Williams, Raymond, *Marxism and Literature* (Oxford: Oxford University Press, 1977)
Winter, John Strange [Mrs Arthur Stannard], *A Magnificent Young Man* (London: F.V. White, 1896)
—, *A Blameless Woman*, 3rd edn (London: F.V. White, 1896)

Wood, Mrs Henry, *Lady Adelaide* (London: Richard Bentley and Son, 1896 [pre-1887])

Wordsworth, William, *Selected Prose*, ed. John O. Hayden (Harmondsworth: Penguin, 1988)

—, *The Essential Wordsworth*, selected and with an introduction by Seamus Heaney (New York: Ecco, 1988)

—, *The Works of William Wordsworth* (Ware: Wordsworth, 1994)

Wynter, Andrew, *The Borderlands of Insanity* (London: Robert Hardwicke, 1875)

Yonge, C.M., *Womankind*, 2nd edn (London: Mozley and Smith, 1877)

—, *The Clever Woman of the Family* (London: Virago, 1985 [1865])

—, *The Daisy Chain or Aspirations: A Family Chronicle* (London: Macmillan, 1920 [1856])

Index